PAGEANTRY OF THE LAW

PAGEANTRY OF THE LAW. The procession from Westminster Abbey to the House of Lords for the Lord Chancellor's Breakfast at the opening of the legal year. It is led by the Lord Chancellor himself, preceded by his mace-bearer and purse-bearer. Next comes the Lord Chief Justice, followed by the Master of the Rolls, and so on down the judicial hierarchy, every judge wearing his State robes for the occasion.

PAGEANTRY OF THE LAW

BY

JAMES DERRIMAN

OF LINCOLN'S INN, BARRISTER-AT-LAW

LONDON 1955

EYRE & SPOTTISWOODE

TO MY WIFE

This book, first published in 1955, *is printed in Great
Britain for Eyre & Spottiswoode (Publishers) Ltd.,
15 Bedford Street, London W.C.*2, *by C. Tinling &
Co. Ltd., Liverpool, London and Prescot.*

CONTENTS

	Preface	9
1	The Inns of Court and the Bar	11
2	Reading for the Bar	19
3	Call to the Bar – and beyond	31
4	Dinner-Time	48
5	Counsel of the Crown	57
6	Solicitors	70
7	My Lords the Queen's Justices	78
8	The Sheriff and His Men	102
9	Her Majesty's Judge of Assize	121
10	The Old Bailey	143
11	The Circuit Mess	150
12	The Greater Judges	154
13	The Lesser Judges	178
14	The Legal Year	191
	Appendix: the assize circuits of England and Wales	213
	Addenda	215
	Index	216

ILLUSTRATIONS

Facing page

Pageantry of the Law. The procession from Westminster
Abbey to the House of Lords for the Lord Chancellor's
Breakfast   *Frontispiece*
(Photo: P.A.-Reuter)

Call to the Bar. At Lincoln's Inn   32
(Photo: Illustrated)

Luncheon in Hall. At Lincoln's Inn   33
(Photo: Illustrated)

Judicial costume I. The Court of King's Bench in the
15th century, from an illumination now in the Inner
Temple library   144
(Picture Post Library)

Judicial costume II. Sir Edmund Anderson, Chief Justice
of the Common Pleas 1582-1605. (From a painting by
an unknown artist in the National Portrait Gallery)   160

Judicial costume III. Sir John Holt, Chief Justice of the
King's Bench 1689-1709. (From a painting by R. Van
Bleeck in the National Portrait Gallery)   160

Judicial costume IV. Sir Charles Abbott (afterwards Lord
Tenterden), Chief Justice of the King's Bench 1818-32.
(From a painting by J. Hollins after W. Owen in the
National Portrait Gallery)   161

Judicial costume V. Lord Goddard, Lord Chief Justice of
England 1946-   161
(Photo: Barratt)

An assize procession of the mid-19th century   192
(Picture Post Library)

Assize pageantry of today. Monmouth: 1938   193
(Photo: Fox)

7

Payment of the City of London quit-rents: early in
19th century. At the Court of Exchequer　　　　208
(Picture Post Library)

Payment of the City quit-rents today. In the "court" of
the Queen's Remembrancer　　　　209
(Photo: Kemsley)

PREFACE

THIS book is about the pomp and circumstance of the Law in England and Wales.

The procedure of the English courts has much custom and ceremonial of its own, linked with the development of the law itself: but that is a study for which there are many learned textbooks. This volume has a different scope: more superficial, in a sense; more recondite, perhaps; but certainly less thoroughly explored.

Where and how is a new judge sworn in? What is the official costume of a sheriff? Why is an assize judge given an old coin at Newcastle and a pair of gloves at Oxford? And who was the first Queen's Counsel? So far as I know, there has until now been no single book in which the answers to questions like these could be found easily and in non-technical language. And certain apparently simple points, I found, presented problems even to experienced law librarians. What, for instance, is the origin of the Lord Chancellor's gold-laced robe? When was the first Westminster Abbey service for the opening of the legal year? No one knew, and apparently no one had even tried to find out. As for the rules governing the wearing of robes of different colours by Queen's Bench Division judges, it seemed that the judges themselves gained their knowledge by word of mouth from their senior colleagues.

Pageantry, after all, is only an outward sign. So the difficulty in writing this book has been to explain enough of the historical and legal setting to enable the costume, customs and ceremonies of the Law to be seen in their true values—and yet avoid boring the ordinary reader with technicalities, or the lawyer with elementary "shop."

It is almost inevitable that there are gaps, and perhaps inconsistencies and errors, in the text because detailed information on each point is confined to so few sources—some of these sources being unwritten traditions surviving to holders of an office. For such defects I can only ask indulgence and emphasize that they are no fault of the many learned authorities who cheerfully helped me to dig out facts which must often have seemed tiresomely remote to them. There were so many who

9

gave me assistance and facilities that it would be impossible to name all of them here. My thanks are especially due to officers of the four Inns of Court; to Mr. Francis Cowper, the erudite historian of Gray's Inn, who kindly read this book in manuscript and made a number of useful suggestions; to Mr. J. F. Austin of Ede and Ravenscroft, Ltd.; and to the willing staff of Sydenham public library. I am grateful to the editors of the "News Chronicle" and the "Law Times" for permission to use small portions of this book which have appeared in their journals.

I am grateful also for permission to use brief extracts from the following works: Snell's Principles of Equity (Sweet and Maxwell); Carson, by H. Montgomery Hyde (Heinemann); and On Circuit, by the late Sir Frank MacKinnon (Cambridge University Press).

I have thought it necessary to quote many authorities in the text, because only a lifetime study of legal history would enable one to resolve some discrepancies and to discriminate among the finer points. For the sake of easier reading I have modernised the spelling of most of the older authors quoted.

The more I worked on this subject, the more fascinating by-ways opened up. In costume, it would have been interesting to look at such out-of-the-way examples as the robe of the Vice-Chancellor of the Duchy of Lancaster with its red roses. Among the historic offices of the Law, one could explore those of the Coroner, the Queen's Remembrancer, and the City Solicitor and Remembrancer of the City of London. Each of the many local courts has a history of its own. But a limit had to be set somewhere, and at least there is now a book where none has existed before.

Of what use is the pageantry of the Law? Is it perhaps time to do away with the wig, the robe and the black cap? These are questions on which no opinion is ventured in this book. It may be safely said, however, that pageantry without significance is mere superstition and rigmarole. If this book helps to make the significance and history of legal pageantry in this country more widely known, its existence will be justified.

1. The Inns of Court and the Bar

T HE man on the Clapham omnibus finds it easy to sum up his views on lawyers. In his opinion (and the words of Thackeray) they spend their time "a livin' at their ease, a sending of their writs about, and droring in the fees."

The law, it is true, does not do much to dispel this notion or to publicise itself at all. Any other profession or organisation with half the history and colour of our legal system would long ago have appointed a public relations officer, held an exhibition and arranged for illustrated brochures to be handed to every customer. Confident in its supremacy and knowing it is indispensable, the law can afford to be modest. Its unique and rich pageantry must accordingly be sought out. A passing glimpse of wigged barristers leaving a court is as near as most citizens get to legal pomp and circumstance. Perhaps, in fact, that is not a bad point from which to begin a journey behind the scenes. Watch those barristers, then, as they leave the grey Victorian-Gothic Law Courts in the Strand on their way to lunch.

Some cross and pass beneath an ancient archway into the seclusion of the Inner and Middle Temple. Others, leaving by the "back door" of the Law Courts, make for Lincoln's Inn or more distant Gray's Inn. It is in these four historic Inns of Court that we may find the pageantry of the law at home.

Every judge is chosen from the ranks of the Bar; solicitors have always been the less prominent branch of the profession, however important their place in the workaday world today. So the barrister is, historically and ceremonially speaking, the basic figure of the law. The Inn of Court is to the barrister at once a college, a club, a trade union and an office.

Pass through the great gate of one of the Inns—they are still closed each night against outsiders—and you are in another world. There is little traffic and many of the courts and squares, with their Georgian houses and shady trees, seem scarcely changed—despite war-time damage—since Dr. Johnson's day. Near the centre of the Inn you will find features resembling those of the medieval colleges of Oxford and Cambridge: a great hall, a chapel, a library containing many an ancient treasure. The few black-coated figures to be seen pacing the smooth lawns stroll with a scholarly lack of hurry. It is time we discovered what kind of men, alone even among those of the learned professions, can make the best of the leisurely past blend so successfully with the working conditions of the present.

The massive doors of the Hall in our Inn are open, for it is lunchtime. Come in and see. The hall is arranged inside much like those college halls which it resembles. We enter through a great carved wooden screen, over which is a minstrel gallery. The walls of the Hall, up to the lofty roof, are well-nigh covered with coats-of-arms of distinguished sons of the Inn, emblazoned in gold and rich heraldic colours. On the wall facing us some great portraits hang above the "high table," which is now gleaming with fine silver. The few elderly gentlemen beginning their lunch there have the subtle air of confidence, experience and distinction which marks the leaders of the profession. They are "benchers," members of the committee of elders—mostly judges and Queen's Counsel— who control the affairs of the Inn.

There may be another and smaller table below the high table, and like it running crosswise. This is occupied (if our Inn is one which has retained the custom) by senior barristers not yet benchers, termed "ancients." From there nearly to the screen, along the length of the vast Hall, is a series of long tables. Some nearest to us are filling with groups of students; at the further ones and occupying most of the body of the Hall are the barristers, some still with white "bands" in place of tie, most in professional black coat and striped trousers.

Who are the barristers, and what is the Bar to which they are said to belong? In most foreign countries you can employ any lawyer to do any legal business for you—whether it be a matter of drawing up a will or of representing you as advocate before the highest court in the land. But in Britain the legal profession is divided into two quite distinct branches: solicitors and barristers. Barristers—those who practise are often referred to as counsel—are primarily advocates, and frequently tend to be specialists in one branch of the law, while most solicitors are general practitioners. Most of the barrister's work concerns the final preparation of lawsuits or criminal trials and their actual presentation in court. A barrister is forbidden by custom to be employed by a layman directly; he must be instructed only through a solicitor. Of course, a layman may normally conduct his own case without the help of either if he wishes. There are only about 2,000 practising barristers (compared with over 18,000 solicitors), though there are many more who for one reason or another do not practise. A barrister, unlike a solicitor, may not go into partnership. However, a number of barristers normally shares an office, usually in one of the Inns of Court and still known as "a set of chambers" from the days when, as we shall see, the Inns were fully residential societies.

The notion of employing professional advocates in courts of law came about very gradually in the course of history. Roughly it may be said to have had its origin in the 12th and 13th centuries, as a result of developments in the law. The Assize of Clarendon (a statute or law, not to be confused with the later courts of assize) in 1166 is said to have been the foundation of trial by jury. At the same period Henry II organised for the first time a system of itinerant judges which covered the whole country. The law developed rapidly and as one authority (Cohen, "A History of the English Bar," 1929) says, "Magna Carta (1215) alone was enough to create a race of lawyers and a harvest of litigation." The writ (the document used to initiate an action at law and naming the wrong alleged and remedy claimed) "would account for a rise of a specialist class," for on its precise wording largely depended the fate of a lawsuit.

During the early Middle Ages, when learning was largely confined to ecclesiastics, many advocates and judges were clergy, at least in minor orders. A curious relic of ecclesiastical usage is the cross or loop with which counsel mark their briefs on completion of proceedings; it is said to represent the Sign of the Cross. Gradually during the 13th century, as the law became more technical and Church discipline was tightened, the clerical element disappeared. Typical of the rulings laid down by the Church authorities at this period is a constitution of Richard Poor, Bishop of Salisbury, in 1217, stating: *"Nec advocati sint Clerici, vel Sacerdotes in foro seculari, nisi vel proprias causas, vel miserabilium personarum prosequatur,"* i.e., clergy might not act as advocates in the civil courts except in their own causes or to help in cases of hardship.

Meanwhile, by about 1260 there had appeared the first of the Serjeants-at-Law, a great rank or order of advocates which held supreme place in the profession until its abolition at the end of the 19th century. The serjeants—spelt with a j, equivalent to an i, because their Latin title was *servientes regis ad legem* (servants of the King at law)—were primarily the King's own advocates and legal advisers, though they were always free to take cases other than those of the Crown or even to appear against the Crown. When pleading in court they enjoyed precedence over all other ranks of counsel until the time of James I, when their privilege began to be invaded by the Attorney-General and Solicitor-General; later the newer rank of Queen's Counsel also challenged their supremacy. As a result of the Judicature Act, 1875, no more serjeants were created in England after 1877. The last English serjeant-at-law was Lord Lindley, who died in 1921.

The ranks of the serjeants were recruited from *apprenticii* (apprentices), first mentioned at the end of the 13th century. The number of serjeants was never great, and before long the apprentices were allowed to appear in court on their own account. By 1381, says Cohen, the apprentices were recognised as "the junior Bar"—that is, as what we should call ordinary barristers. The actual name "barrister" came later. The records of Lincoln's Inn—the Black Books—mention under Trinity Term, 1455 *"duo de optimis barrer"* (two of the best barristers). Nine or ten years later the same records refer to "utter barresters," a more precise definition whose meaning we shall shortly see. The first surviving use of the title "barrister" outside the Inn records is in an Act of Parliament of 1531.

The expression "the Bar" is used nowadays to refer to this branch of the profession as a whole. In origin it refers to an actual bar or bench in the halls of the Inns of Court. It was natural for the medieval apprentices in the law to group together in the house of some great lawyer or judge, under whom they studied. Gradually these groups formed into permanent societies, each with its Inn or premises where members lived a more or less communal life. These Inns of Court are today four in number: Lincoln's Inn, Inner Temple, Middle Temple and Gray's Inn.

They have changed little in their organisation during the 600 years or so since they were founded. A report on the state of the Inns made to Henry VIII in 1545 gives a picture which is broadly true today.

"The whole company and fellowship of Learners" at the Inn was divided into three groups: Benchers, Utter (i.e., Outer) Barristers and Inner Barristers (i.e., what we today call Students).

To the Benchers was "committed the government and order of the house, as to men meetest, both for their age, degrees and wisdoms, and of these is one yearly chosen, which is called the Treasurer . . ." Utter-barristers were so called "for that they, when they argue . . . Moots (debates in the form of mock trials), they sit uttermost (outermost) on the forms, which they call the Bar, and this degree is the chiefest degree for learners in the house next the Benchers. . . ." The Inner-barristers were "the youngest men, who for lack of learning and continuance are not able to argue and reason in these Moots," though when moots were held two of these young students sat on the same form and were given a small part to play.

The benchers, barristers and students of each Inn form a self-governing body entitled "The Honourable Society of Lincoln's Inn" (or whichever is concerned). No one knows when this prefix "Honourable" was first used.

The history of the Inns of Court is a fascinating story in itself, but outside the scope of this book. The following notes give some dates and other facts relevant to our subject:

Lincoln's Inn lies between Chancery Lane and Lincoln's Inn Fields, at the back of the Royal Courts of Justice or "Law Courts." The exact origin of Lincoln's Inn, or indeed of the others, is by no means clear. The first home of this Inn was in Holborn. It may have gained its name from Henry de Lacy, Earl of Lincoln, a royal justice—around whom students might be expected to gather—and who lived between 1286 and 1311 in a house at the north-east corner of Shoe Lane. However, about 1350 the Society is found occupying premises known as

"Lyncolnesynne," which they rented from Thomas de Lincoln, King's Serjeant (a serjeant more particularly retained for royal business). Between 1412 and 1422 it moved to part of the present site in Chancery Lane, which it first occupied as tenant of the Bishop of Chichester and eventually—in 1580—bought outright.

Lincoln's Inn has a fine, but small Hall built in 1489-91 and skilfully reconstructed in 1926-28. It is known as the Old Hall to distinguish it from the New Hall built in 1845, which is larger and now used for meals.

The armorial bearings of Lincoln's Inn are: Azure, semé de molines or; on a dexter canton or, a lion rampant purpure. From 1515 to 1702 the Inn used simply the arms of Lacy, Earl of Lincoln—or, a lion rampant purpure. In 1702 the molines, or mill-rinds, were added to commemorate Richard Kingsmill, a 16th century bencher prominent in the purchase of the freehold of the Inn. The mill-rinds (supports for mill-stones, heraldically shown as cross with forked head and tail) figure on the punning coat-of-arms of the Kingsmill family.

Inner Temple. From about 1160 the crusading Order of Knights Templar had their English headquarters in the area south of Fleet Street which is still known as The Temple. When the Order was suppressed in 1312, after charges of heresy had been made against its members, its possessions were granted to the Knights Hospitaller of St. John (though in fact much of them never reached the new owners). Edward II had already seized the English property of the Templars in 1309. The part of the Temple lying outside the City boundaries (i.e., west of Temple Bar) was granted to the Bishop of Exeter; this became known as the Outer Temple, and has now lost its identity. The remainder, either at once or after a period, was passed by the Crown to the Hospitallers. They in turn let the property to lawyers at some time during the 14th century—authorities disagree about the probable date.

This property was at some stage divided into two sections: the Inner Temple, being the consecrated part, and the Middle Temple, the part which was not consecrated. Two separate societies of lawyers held these sections, which became the two Inns of Court we know by the same titles today. The earliest mention of the Inner Temple as a separate organisation is in

1440. Cohen ("A History of the English Bar," 1929) says the severance of the two Inns is traditionally assigned to the early years of Henry VI (1422-). But Kent ("Encyclopedia of London," 1937 edition) says it is "now generally held" that the two societies have always been distinct. The Temple Church (consecrated in 1185) is shared between them.

The Inner Temple succeeded to the ancient Hall of the Templars, but this was demolished in 1866 and its successor was in turn destroyed by bombing in the second world war. A third Hall has just (1954) been built. The practice of emblazoning the arms of distinguished members on the walls of the halls of the different Inns has been seen as a survival of the custom of knights to hang their shields round halls in which they ate. The practice is maintained at all four Inns, however, and not only at those which succeeded to Templar property.

The arms of the Inner Temple are described heraldically as: Azure, pegasus with the wings expanded, argent. The pegasus, or winged horse, is said to be derived from the Templar badge of a horse carrying two men—which is interpreted either as a sign of the Order's poverty, or a representation of aid given to wounded pilgrims. By a curious and ancient custom, said to be derived from an old alliance in the revels held in Elizabethan times, the Inner Temple and Gray's Inn also display each other's arms.

Middle Temple. See Inner Temple, above. The earliest record of this Inn is in 1404, though its own existing records go back only to 1501. Middle Temple Hall, a particularly fine one, was opened by Queen Elizabeth I in 1576; although damaged in the second world war it has been restored to its former magnificence. In the Hall, below the dais, is a serving-table—known as "The Cupboard"—said to have been made from a hatchcover of Drake's ship *Golden Hind*. At this "cupboard" all important domestic ceremonies are carried out.

B

The arms of the Middle Temple are: Argent, upon a cross gules an Agnus Dei or. The Agnus Dei, or "Lamb and Flag," was used as a badge by the Templars at least as early as 1241.

Gray's Inn is on the north side of Holborn. The manor of Portpoole on this site was during the Middle Ages owned by a legal family named de Grey. A Walter de Grey was Chancellor 1206-14, and his nephew a judge. Reginald de Grey, a son of this nephew, became a judge and first Lord de Grey of Wilton. He died in 1308, and it has been suggested that the Society of Gray's Inn took possession of the Portpoole manor house from this date or at least during the same century. The more widely held opinion, however, is that (though it had existed for at least a hundred years) the society did not come into exclusive possession until the early 16th century. The de Greys sold the manor, in which they may never have lived, in 1505 or 1506. It passed in 1513 to the monks of Sheen, from whom the Society of Gray's Inn rented it. The earliest record of the Society still existing dates from 1569.

The fine Hall was built in 1556-60. Badly damaged in the second world war, it has now been restored.

The arms of Gray's Inn are: Sable, a griffin or. This coat-of-arms seems to have been adopted in the second half of the 16th century, for some reason unknown. Until that time the Society used the de Grey arms, differenced with a bordure quarterly or and azure, or argent and azure.

In addition to the four Inns of Court, there were once several subsidiary "Inns of Chancery," now remembered only by their names which sometimes survive on their sites—Thavies Inn, Staple Inn and so on. The serjeants had two Inns of their own, one in Chancery Lane and the other on the south side of Fleet Street.

2. Reading for the Bar

THE process of becoming a barrister is inseparably, and at first sight mysteriously, connected with "eating dinners." In one way the phrase is revealing, because it emphasizes how the idea of a collegiate life, with meals taken in common, is still an essential part of the Inns of Court system. In another way it is only a half-truth which dates from the period of the Inns' decadence, when the perfunctory eating of a number of meals in Hall was allowed to serve in place of the stiff academic course which once accompanied them.

To qualify for call to the Bar it is necessary today, just as it was 500 years ago, to spend a probationary period as a student of one of the Inns of Court. Basically there is little difference between the four Inns. Those who intend to practise in the Chancery courts often join Lincoln's Inn, which has had an Equity tradition since Chancery courts sat in and near the Old Hall during the 18th and 19th centuries. Gray's Inn suffered a low ebb in its fortunes a century or so ago, but is now as flourishing as the others. Often family associations are the deciding factor in a student's choice of Inn; it is possible to join a second Inn after call, on a fairly heavy payment.

The would-be student must apply to the Under-Treasurer (equivalent to secretary) of the Inn he selects, and must satisfy its benchers that he has complied with certain conditions. He must have been educated to a fixed standard, and must at once submit to professional discipline by promising not to engage in various specified occupations—that of solicitor is an obvious example—deemed to conflict with membership of an Inn of Court. References must be supplied and financial undertakings for payment of fees entered into. If all is satisfactory, the benchers will admit the applicant to be a student member of the Honourable Society of their Inn.

The chief conditions under which a student may be called to the Bar today are the passing of a law examination in two parts set by the Council of Legal Education (an organisation sponsored by the four Inns jointly); and the "keeping" of 12 terms by dining six times in the hall of the Inn during each "dining term," of which there are four in the year. (See Chapter 14). (Three dinners each term suffice for university undergraduates, and there are dispensations from some of the examinations for those with other qualifications).Thus between admission and call the ordinary student must eat at least 72 dinners in Hall, and at least three years must elapse. Nor can anyone be called to the Bar under the age of 21. There is, however, no restriction on the time at which the examinations are taken, except that the first part must be passed before the second is attempted. The examinations are held three times a year.

The student's introduction to the pageantry of the law will be on his first visit to the hall of his Inn for lunch or dinner. (For dining customs of the Inns, see Chapter 4). At dinner he must wear a student's gown, a plain, sleeveless garment of black stuff with a square-cut flap (the remnant of a hood) resting on the shoulders at the back. In the 17th century not only was the gown worn in Hall and in church—at least by students of the Inner Temple—but in term time a round cap was worn in addition. This cap was doubtless of the type, rather like a beret, commonly worn by apprentices and students in the second half of the 16th century. The modern student is bare-headed in Hall. His general clothing may be what he wills, though the law student tends to sobriety of suit and tie more than his contemporaries in other fields of study. Though this is now by inclination and custom, once it was enforced by the Inns: the student, in common with other members, was subject to strict rules of dress—treated more fully in this book in Chapter 3.

The freshman student of an Inn of Court today will be interviewed by the Director of the Council of Legal Education, and advised on his course of study. The Council provides a full programme of lectures by practising barristers, as well as a number of tutorial classes. But no student is obliged to take advantage of any or all of them, any more than he is obliged to attempt an examination or submit himself for call. The late Hilaire Belloc who joined Gray's Inn in his youth remained a student until his death at the age of 83. In the library of his Inn the student will find an ample collection of law books and reports, old and new, and many study and pass their examinations with little formal instruction at all.

Though not much is known for certain about the early days of the Inns of Court, it is clear that before long they developed their own system of legal education which became accepted in the profession and the courts. This system was at its height, with a resulting elaborate hierarchy among the members of the Inns, from the 15th to the 17th centuries.

The great 15th century judge Fortescue is tantalisingly vague: "of the details of their study, I need only say that it is pleasant in itself and effective for its object."

In the next century at least, the student had a stiff course in front of him. "Continuing by the space of seven years or thereabouts," says John Stow in his "Survey of London" (1598), "they frequent Readings, mootings, boltings (apparently similar to moots) and other learned exercises, whereby, growing ripe in the knowledge of the laws and approved withal to be of honest conversation, they are either by the general consent of the Benchers or Readers, being the most grave and judicial men in every Inn of Court, or by the special privilege of the present Reader there, elected and called to the degree of utter-barrister."

During these seven years the student must live within the Inn and submit to a rigid discipline. In the mornings, no doubt, many of the students went to Westminster Hall, to learn in the most practical way by sitting in court. The courts rose before mid-day, and after that there would be time to read and to take part in the very full educational programme of the Inn. The instruction of students in these halcyon days of the Inns of Court fell broadly into lectures, known as Readings, and moots or mock trials.

Each Inn appointed a Reader to lecture to its students during each of the two "learning-vacations" of Lent and Summer. During these vacations, while the courts were not sitting, the students could give all day to their studies. At Lincoln's Inn there was a Reader in 1464, and probably that is about the date when the office began in all the Inns. Each of the two "readings" lasted three or four weeks; one began on the first

Monday in Lent, and the other on the first Monday after the feast of St. Lawrence (Lammas, August 1 Old Style). One Reader was appointed for each of these periods, and—by the judges' regulations of 1596—they had to read at least thrice a week.

The Readers were chosen from among the senior utter-barristers of the Inn, and Readership qualified them to be made benchers more or less automatically when their term of office was over. The Reader had wide educational and even moral authority over the students, and also had ceremonial duties. At least in some Inns it was the Readers who called to the Bar those who were qualified, until this practice was stopped late in the 16th century (see Chapter 3).

Readers and benchers wore a black gown adorned with velvet and tufts of silk. This gown is of some interest in the story of legal costume, since it was for 200 years the recognised dress of those senior members of the Bar who were not serjeants: until, in fact, it was displaced at the end of the 17th century by the silk gown now worn by Queen's Counsel. It was worn even by Recorders, unless they happened to be serjeants. The serjeants used it only on certain occasions at the royal Court, having already their own ancient costume.

It is worn today by judges and the Attorney-General at the royal Court in specified circumstances, and by the Common Serjeant of London (who, despite his title, has never been a member of the Order of the Coif—see Chapter 13)—alone among the legal profession proper. It is used also by town clerks, whether or not legally qualified, by vergers of the Temple Church—perhaps by descent from members of the Inns —and possibly by others.

Gowns with adornments of velvet or other materials arranged in strips—known as guards, perhaps because the strips were originally binding to prevent fraying—became fashionable early in the 16th century. They came to be worn particularly by men of the rising middle class, and especially by those of learning. In sections of society where clothes indicated rank, such gowns were forbidden to the lower members. For instance Burleigh's orders of 1585 as Chancellor of Cambridge University prohibited students from wearing gowns with "guard, welt, lace, cut or silk." By 1572 it was the costume chosen for the portrait of a typical citizen of London in Braun and Hogenberg's "Civitates Orbis Terrarum." Still later it became synonymous with a kind of genteelness. When Shakespeare wrote "King Henry IV, Part I" in 1597-8, he made Hotspur say (Act III, Sc. 1) to his wife:

"Swear me, Kate, like a lady as thou art,
"A good mouth-filling oath; and leave 'in sooth,'
"And such protest of pepper-gingerbread,
"To velvet-guards and Sunday citizens."

The legal version of this gown was probably of cloth, faced with black velvet, with tufts of silk down the facings and on the fronts of the sleeves (according to Hawkins' Notes to "Ignoramus," 1788). In the legal profession as elsewhere the "velvet-guards" were respected citizens of the middle rank. Students and utter-barristers did not wear this gown. At a Temple Parliament (meeting of benchers) in 1584 it was agreed that "no velvet facings be worn except by Masters of the Bench." And the judges' orders for the Inns of Court made in 1627 laid down that "No Reader shall practise at the Bar at Westminster, but in his Reader's Gown, with the Velvet welt on the back; and that none but Readers in Court shall at all wear or use any such gowns." Since Readers customarily became benchers, and since benchers had all been Readers, it may be assumed that the two terms are here used fairly indiscriminately. The highest rank of the profession, the serjeants and judges, did not wear the velvet-faced gown since their costume was that of their own Order of the Coif. Barristers created serjeants at once left their own Inn to join one of the serjeants' Inns.

Readers were given half a year's notice to prepare their reading. By the early 17th century it was customary to invite past Readers to lecture again after a period. The great Chief Justice Coke tells us that in his time the Summer Reader was chosen as we have said above, but the Lent Reading was given by one who had previously carried out this duty. He was called a Double Reader, "it being commonly between his first and second reading about 9 or 10 years." From among these Double Readers the Attorney-General, Solicitor-General and other Crown officers were appointed.

The procedure at Readings is set out in detail by Sir William

Dugdale, in his "Origines Juridiciales," first published in 1666. It had altered scarcely at all since the report on the Inns made to Henry VIII in 1545, quoted in the last chapter.

"Howbeit," says Dugdale, writing of the Middle Temple, "the Reader, having first absented himself out of Commons for the space of a week, in which time he seldom comes abroad, that his entrance may be with the more state, appears first as a Reader at the Church the Sunday afternoon, next before his Reading, accompanied by such Benchers as are in Town; whereof two are appointed for his Assistants (being, for the most part, the two next precedent Readers) and attended by twelve or fourteen Servants, at the least, in one livery; and the same night, at Supper, he takes his place in the Hall, in a chair, at the upper end of the Bench-Table.

"The next morning, he makes choice for his sub-Lecturer, of a puisne Gentleman of the House, to whom he delivers his bag of books and papers; and then repairs unto the Parliament (benchers') House to Breakfast. Which ended, he goes into the Hall, where the whole Society expects his coming; and resting at the Cupboard (a central table in Middle Temple Hall), doth there take the Oaths of Supremacy and Allegiance. Then he takes his place towards the lower end of the Bench Table, where the Sub-Lecturer doth first, with an audible voice, read over the Statute, or at least that branch of it, that he hath chosen to read on.

"This ended, the Reader begins with a grave speech, excusing his own weakness, with desire of their favourable censures; and concluding with the Reasons, wherefore he made choice of that Statute. Then he delivers unto them his divisions made upon the Statute, which are more or fewer, as he pleaseth; and then puts ten or twelve Cases upon his first division; of the which, the puisne Cupboard-man (a senior barrister), before spoken of, makes choice of one to argue; and in his Argument, endeavours what in him lies, to oppose the Reader's conclusion. After him follow the rest of the Cupboard-men, standing at the Cupboard; then the Benchers, who are placed on a form opposite to the Reader, argue in their turns, and last of all, the Reader himself who maintains his own conclusion, and often times such Judges or Serjeants at the Law, as are of this Society, come to argue the Reader's Case; who at such time, come always in their purple Robes, and Scarlet Hoods, and are placed on a form, opposite to the Benchers, with their backs to the Reader.

"All Arguments, being ended, Dinner is served in, where he entertains the Company with a great Feast, at his own Table, with addition of one Dish extraordinary unto every Mess throughout the Hall."

In early times the students used to wait upon the Reader at the Bench table during Reading time, and in the late 17th century they still did duty as waiters at the Reader's Feast (see below) as well as on the Grand Days of All Saints and Candlemas. After dinner another case was argued. The same procedure was followed each Monday, Wednesday and Friday of the reading period, and on the other days members occupied themselves with feasting and entertaining notables.

In course of time the custom for the Reader to provide extra food during his office developed into the elaborate Reader's Feast, so expensive that the position was sometimes declined, although Readership was the qualification for becoming a bencher. Dugdale says that some Readers spent over £600—a huge sum by modern values—in twelve days.

Perhaps the greatest of all Reader's Feasts was that given by Sir Heneage Finch, then Solicitor-General, in 1661. It was attended by the King, Charles II, who arrived at the Inner Temple by water. When he landed, he was met by the Reader and the Chief Justice of the Common Pleas. His route to the hall was lined by the Reader's servants in scarlet cloaks and white doublets. Above them on each side were the benchers, barristers and students, in their gowns. Music was provided by an orchestra, with twenty violins. Fifty members of the Inn, wearing gowns, served dinner in Hall. The King and Duke of York sat under a canopy of state at the upper end of the hall, on a dais. The Lord Chancellor and noble guests occupied one long table, and the Reader and members of the Inn sat at another. (In the following year, incidentally, the Duke of York —afterwards James II—was made a barrister and bencher of the Inner Temple).

Readings in their ancient form finally disappeared a few years later. Printed books were by this time freely available to students. The Civil War and the Commonwealth had created an irreparable break in the continuity of the system. "Too long uprooted, they withered and it was useless to try to replant them," as Francis Cowper puts it ("A Prospect of Gray's Inn," 1951). At Gray's the last reading was in 1667, and at Lincoln's Inn ten years later. Occasionally in later years, towards the end of the 18th century, there were attempted revivals, with little success.

In recent years the office of Reader has been created anew, but a pale shadow of what it once was. The official instruction of Bar students has since 1852 been in the hands of the Council of Legal Education and the educational duties of the Readers under the old system would now be superfluous. Where Readers are appointed today, they are chosen from among the benchers—a reversal of the early practice by which Readership qualified for membership of the Bench. Their duties consist of delivering a lecture which may be of historical and domestic interest rather than instructional. The tufted, velvet-faced gown of the old Readers is seen no longer; modern Readers deliver their "readings" in the stuff or silk gown to which their rank at the Bar entitles them. In November, 1950, there was held the first Reader's Feast in Middle Temple Hall for many years.

Lincoln's Inn and Gray's Inn do not now appoint a Reader. At the Inner Temple a single Reader is appointed for the year, i.e., both the two customary readings of Lent and Summer. The Middle Temple as of old appoints two, one for each of the two readings. Quite separate from the revived Readerships of the Inns are the several appointments made by the Council of Legal Education of "readers" in this or that branch of the law. These appointments are, perhaps, more akin in a way to the ancient system and to that of the universities, for the Council's readers instruct the Bar students of today by means of lectures.

Side by side with the Readings of long ago went the Moots—mock trials of cases put by students and judged by benchers. The report on the Inns of Court to Henry VIII in 1545 tells us how moots which took place during the reading periods were conducted at the Middle Temple. After supper the Reader and two benchers would come into Hall to the "cupboard," the central table in which all important business is done at this Inn. One of the barristers propounded some difficult case, which was argued first among the benchers, and then by the barrister who had presented it. After this began a mock trial proper.

"The Readers and Bench sit down on the bench in the end of the Hall whereof they take their name and on a form toward the middle of the Hall sitteth down two inner-barristers (students) and of the other side of them on the same form two utter-barristers. And the inner-barristers do in French openly declare unto the Benchers (even as the serjeants do at the bar of the King's Courts to the judges) some kind of action, the one being as it were retained with the plaintiff in the action and the other with the defendant, after which things done, the utter-barristers argue such questions as be disputable within the case (as there must be always one at the least) and this ended, the Benchers do likewise declare their opinions how they think the law to be in the same questions, and this manner of exercise of mooting is daily used during the said vacations."

Procedure was modelled on that of the old Court of Common Pleas, in which the serjeants had exclusive right of audience. In that court, as in other courts up to this day (in theory if not always in practice) a wooden "bar" or barrier separated the judges from the body of the court. The "Bar" to which students were and are called is the bar of the Inn of Court, the "imitation" bar which separated off the benchers taking the part of judges in the moots which took place in Hall, and not the bar of the actual court. The rank of barrister is in origin a domestic one relating solely to the educational system of the Inns. Apparently a form or bench served as the bar in Hall, and those pleading at the moots sat on this form, the utter-barristers "uttermost" or outermost—which must presumably have been close to the benchers; and the inner-barristers or students innermost, looking from the benchers' table towards the lower end of the hall.

Moots such as these took place during the Reading Vacations of Lent and Summer, when the students were also expected to attend further exercises in the subsidiary "Inns of Chancery." There was a further period called the "Mean Vacation," but even then the poor student could not relax from his work. Cases were argued after dinner—says the report of 1545—and there were moots argued before barristers instead of before the benchers, who were enjoying their holiday. Apparently the

barristers and students never had a holiday in the modern sense
at all, though perhaps they made up for it at the feastings on
holy-days. As for term-time proper, "the only exercises of
learning is arguing and debating of cases after dinner, and the
Mooting after supper, used and kept in like form, as is hereto-
fore prescribed in the Vacation time": This, of course, in
addition to attending the courts at Westminster.

The system of moots declined or disappeared about the end
of the 17th century, just as the Readings did. In 1804, less than
150 years after Dugdale found education at the Inns virtually
unchanged since 1545, we read in Herbert's "Antiquities of the
Inns of Courts": "These mootings and disputations in the Inns
of Court and Chancery have been long since disused. Danby
Pickering, Esq., of Gray's Inn, was the last who voluntarily
resumed them (he was a barrister who gave a series of lectures
1753-69); but they were of no continuance, and at the present
day, so much has the course of legal education changed, that
scarcely any of the ancient customs mentioned by Stow and
the preceding authors, are known, except as matters of
curiosity. . . ." Cowper ("A Prospect of Gray's Inn," 1951)
thinks the system of moots did not completely lapse. At least
it was used as a qualification for call, he believes.

The moot exists today, but no longer as an official part of
legal education, and not at all at Lincoln's Inn. Moots today are
organised by a committee of which the Reader—where there
is one—is chairman, and there is a Master of the Moots
appointed from among the benchers as of old. The moots take
place either before or after dinner; in the latter case, those
taking part continue to wear their gowns in which they dined.
One bencher acts as judge, and a case—often modelled on some
recent controversial case of real life—is put by four students,
or by two students and two barristers. Procedure is no longer
restricted to that of any one court, and the moot may as well
be modelled on an appeal case as on one heard by a court of
first instance. After argument has been heard, judgment is
given by the presiding bencher.

Today the average student is called to the Bar after a period
of about three years—the minimum—from his admission to the
Inn. Both period and qualification have changed a good deal
through the ages.

Some sort of examination for call, no doubt held at the moots, existed as early as 1558, according to Sir William Ball ("Lincoln's Inn," 1947). In 1596 the judges' orders for the Inns of Court laid down that the student must before call be of "at least seven years continuance and have kept his exercises within the House and abroad in the Inns of Chancery." A further order of the judges in 1631 raised the period to eight years, but by the time Dugdale wrote later in the century it may have been back to seven. In 1762 this was reduced to five (three for university graduates); twelve terms must be kept by dining in Hall. The period was further cut in 1835 to the present three years.

By that date there had been no organised system of legal education for a century and a half. At the end of the 18th century "exercises" were still formally "kept," but they had become a farce. E. B. V. Christian (writing of barristers, *obiter*, in his "A Short History of Solicitors," 1896) quotes an account of the fantastic state of affairs, given by Bagehot—presumably Walter Bagehot, the classic writer on the English Constitution, who was called to the Bar in 1852.

"A slip of paper was delivered to you," he says, "written in a legible law-stationer's hand which you were to take up to the upper table, where the Benchers sat, and read before them. The contents were generally not intelligible; the slip often began in the middle of a sentence, and by long copying and by no revision the text had become quite corrupt. The topic was 'Whether C. should have the Widow's estate,' and it was said that if you pieced all the slips together you might make a connected argument for and against the Widow. . . . But in 1850 the trial case had dwindled down to the everlasting question 'Whether C. should have the Widow's estate?'. . . If you kept a grave countenance after you had read some six words, the senior Bencher would say 'Sir, that will do,' and then the exercise was kept. But this favour was only given to those who showed due gravity. If you laughed you had to read the 'slip' all through."

Apart from this the "eating of dinners" was the only preparation needed for call, and sometimes it was not even necessary to eat a whole dinner! In the latter part of the 18th century students of Lincoln's Inn were held to have dined if they merely ate oysters which were served before the meal, or even if they just entered the hall and then left to dine elsewhere.

Not until 1846 was any real attempt made to change this lackadaisical outlook on legal education. In that year the four Inns began to provide courses of lectures, followed by examinations—though it would appear from the account given by Bagehot that the old pretence at "exercises" was not at once dropped. The examinations were not compulsory, but students had to produce certificates that two out of the four courses of lectures had been completed. In 1852 the Council of Legal Education was formed, and in 1865 compulsory examinations were instituted.

3. Call to the Bar—and beyond

OUR student has passed his final examinations, is 21 years of age or more. and has eaten his 72 dinners in Hall. Now there approaches the decisive moment in his career, the event which opens for him at the most the opportunity to gain the highest judicial honours in the land: or at the least to enjoy for life the unique fellowship of the English Bar. Before taking his examination the student will have applied provisionally for call to the Bar, for he is officially requested to do so with an implicit optimism which he may not share. He must arrange with one of the benchers of his Inn to sponsor his call. Meanwhile his name and parentage, together with those of all other applicants for call—perhaps 20 or 30 from each Inn—are listed on the screen in the hall of his own Inn and similarly in the others. The lists remain for the eight days preceding Call Day so that (rather as with marriage banns) anything known to a candidate's discredit may be disclosed to the benchers.

At last the day arrives. It might be thought that calling to the Bar, the most significant step in the professional life of a barrister, would by now be surrounded with elaborate ceremonial. In fact it is one of the most simple occurrences in the pageantry of the law. This becomes less surprising when one recalls its origin as a purely domestic promotion of the law student within the educational system of his Inn.

Like other events in the communal life of the Inns of Court, call to the Bar takes place in Hall at dinner: to be precise, shortly before the meal is served. There is one call night in each term, which is the same for all four Inns—the 21st day of term, or if that falls at a week-end then the following Monday. At the Middle Temple and Gray's Inn students who are to be called, don for the first time the gown of a barrister (at Middle Temple, wig also) over full evening dress (in the case of women, dark morning dress). At the other Inns they wear the students' gowns to which they have been accustomed since first joining the Society. Others present wear gowns according to their degree, as always when dining in Hall.

The procedure, though basically similar, varies slightly in the different Inns. At Lincoln's Inn the candidates are lined up in order of seniority, i.e., priority of admission. As their names are called by the Under-Treasurer they go one by one to a position below the high table where the benchers are assembled in a semi-circle, the Treasurer in the middle. The candidate pauses before the Treasurer, who pronounces the brief operative words: "By the authority and on behalf of the Masters of the Bench, I publish you a barrister of this Honourable Society." A hand-shake, and a smile from whichever of the benchers has formally sponsored the student's call, and the ceremony is over. The new barrister goes to his place for dinner and another candidate moves up in turn. After dinner those who have just been called take wine with the benchers, and three toasts are drunk: "Her Majesty the Queen"; "This Honourable Society"; and "Ladies and Gentlemen called to the Bar this day."

Inner Temple candidates for call line up facing the high table, where the benchers are seated. The Treasurer then calls all the candidates simultaneously by telling them that "at a Parliament (benchers' meeting) holden at 6.45 p.m. you were duly called to the Bar." (The benchers having met shortly before—as in other Inns—to move the calls amongst themselves). After a few words on the tradition of the profession, the Treasurer calls on the benchers to rise and drink the health of the new barristers. The senior among those just called replies to the speech and asks his fellow-neophytes to drink the health of the benchers. They then take their places at the Bar tables and dinner is served. Benchers usually join the new members of the Bar at the meal.

The wigged and gowned candidates at the Middle Temple are called at the "Cupboard," a piece of furniture already mentioned (in Chapter 1) which has an important place in the tradition of this Inn. The Treasurer and Reader, with the other benchers, take up positions on the dais before the high table. The Reader then declares: "Master Treasurer, it is my duty and privilege as Master Reader to present to you those Students

CALL TO THE BAR. At Lincoln's Inn. The Treasurer has just pronounced the words which mark the beginning of a career which could end on the Woolsack: "I publish you a barrister of this Honourable Society." He shakes hands with the new member of the Bar, watched by Benchers grouped in a semi-circle.

LUNCHEON IN HALL. At Lincoln's Inn. The formality of the
scene is accounted for by the occasion—a Call Day in 1947, when
the custom of dining in Hall had not been resumed since the
war. Nowadays formality, and the wearing of gowns, is once more
confined to dinner. Benchers, at their high table on the dais, may be
seen at the far end of the Hall. As it is a Call Day, the students sit
at the four tables below the dais, gowned; barristers, ungowned,
are at the tables in the foreground.

of this Honourable and Learned Society whose proposals for Call to the Degree of the Utter Bar have been authorised by Parliament. After they have been called by you they will after the ancient manner enter their names at the Cupboard in the Book containing the Roll of the Barristers of this Inn." The Reader next presents each student to the Treasurer, who proclaims: "Mr. So-and-So, In the name of the Bench I call you to the Degree of the Utter Bar." The student just called then enters his name in the Roll and resumes his place. When all have been called the Treasurer gives a short address to the new barristers.

At Gray's Inn on call night the benchers rise after dinner to drink the health of the new barristers. When the benchers have left Hall to take their port and dessert, and the cloth has been removed, the senior barrister in Hall again proposes the toast of the newly-called. This time each is expected to rise and make a speech in reply, but traditionally all are shouted down.

Originally call to the Bar was a purely administrative act without ceremony. Even when Dugdale wrote in 1666 (of the Middle Temple) he could say: "Note, that there is no ceremony used in the calling of any to the Bar, more than that their election is at the end of the Parliament, declared by the High Treasurer to the rest of the Barristers, who are then called to be informed what the Bench hath concluded on, in that meeting. Their names then entered by the Under Treasurer; the next day, immediately before Dinner, they are called to the Cupboard, where the Treasurer of the House, with some of the Benchers assisting him, cause the parties called, or elected, to take the Oath of Supremacy, the one after the other; which being done, all is ended, and they remain Utter Barristers."

No oath has been required since the Promissory Oaths Act, 1868.

At first calls were often made by the Reader, who because of his position in the educational system was able to judge of students' qualifications. The judges' regulations for the Inns made in 1596 stipulated that where the Reader called, two candidates were to be called by the Summer Reader and two by the Lent Reader. At Gray's Inn the number was in practice double these figures, and in 1629 the benchers there decided

c

that they and not the Reader should perform the call in future. The following year the judges extended this last rule to all the Inns. The restriction to four new barristers each year seems to have proved unrealistic and was not long adhered to.

The first woman called to the Bar was Miss Ivy Williams, called by the Inner Temple on May 10, 1922.

Today a barrister may practise as soon as he is called, and needs no further licence or permission to perform the same professional functions as the most senior member of the "junior" Bar (i.e., any barrister not a Queen's Counsel). In this he is more favoured than the solicitor, who has to apply and pay for a practising certificate afresh each year. Most barristers immediately after call spend six months or a year in the chambers of an experienced junior counsel as pupil, for which privilege they pay a fee. During this period the new barrister will gain practical experience not to be acquired in the lecture room.

In earlier times "post-graduate" training was compulsory, although the period of studentship before call was much longer than today. The reason is perhaps to be found in the lower age at which "higher" education began in medieval times. The judges' order for the Inns in 1574 forbade barristers to practise for a period of five years after call. In 1614 this was reduced to three years, and this still held good in the order of 1664. During this time the young barristers were expected to continue to take part in the moots and other "exercises" of their Inn. These post-call restrictions disappeared, doubtless when the educational system itself fell into decay at the end of the 17th and beginning of the 18th century.

The costume of the English barrister, as now fixed by custom, comprises a full-cut black gown, lawn "bands" worn in place of neck-tie, and curled wig. At royal Courts a velvet court suit is worn. The different items of this costume have no common history, so they will be treated here separately.

The Gown of black cloth or "stuff" is of full cut, with wide sleeves and two curious appendages of cloth attached to the left shoulder and hanging down the garment. One of these appendages is shaped rather like a violin sliced in two lengthwise, attached to the back of the gown along the straight edge, the smaller (upper) part being closed off from the lower one, which is open at the bottom end. The second appendage is a long strip of cloth hanging down the front of the gown.

The true explanation of these odd features seems to be that given by Blackham ("Wig and Gown," 1932)—namely that the fiddle-shaped appendage is a diminutive representation of the ancient hood, and the strip of cloth is the liripipium which was an important part of the hood, as it indicated by its length the rank of the wearer. The common, but fictional, explanation of the flap at the back of the gown is that it is a purse into which grateful clients could slip coins—literally behind the back of the wearer! Barristers even today do not (in theory) work for payment; they cannot sue for unpaid fees since these are held to be merely honoraria. This seems to be a relic of the days when lawyers were in the main clerics who placed their learning at the disposal of lay litigants. One writer ingeniously suggests that the reason why the pocket is behind is in order that the barrister should not see the amount of the fee and be influenced thereby in his conduct of the case! The more usual explanation of the position is that money could be placed in the pocket without being handed over openly and thus causing offence to the advocate. The flap of cloth is of a peculiar design if it were ever intended for this purpose. But Blackham points out that "as both hood and hanging sleeves were formerly used as pockets it is not impossible that the old barrister's hood provided him with a primitive pocket"—so that the "fee" explanation of the appendage to which the hood has now shrunk may not be entirely without foundation.

The history of the barrister's gown is still obscure. Cohen ("A History of the English Bar," 1929) goes so far as to say that since the toga, the ordinary civil dress of the Roman, was the pleader's uniform, the gown of today descends "from even pre-Ciceronian days." He adds, however, the important qualification that during the Middle Ages the toga was the common form of garment worn by most citizens, clerical as well as lay. "Thus the 'long robe' though, no doubt, it came into our courts on the backs of priests, came at the same time, on the backs of laymen who had business there. And hence, at any rate, in the case of the latter it was not always, perhaps not commonly, black."

A leading writer on costume, Planché ("A History of British Costume," 1900), says that about 1340 there was a reaction against the then prevalent long gown in favour of a short, tight tunic or surcoat. Thus lawyers—who still wore the longer garment—became distinguished from other laymen as wearing "the long robe," a phrase first used by the 15th century judge Fortescue in his "De laudibus legum Angliae," 1468-70. Cohen quotes and supports this statement.

The hood, like the gown itself, was a common medieval article of dress. Stow, the 16th century historian, says of the commons' rising in 1381 "they took in hand to behead all men of Law, as well Apprentices as Utter-barristers and old justices, with all the jurers of the country . . . they spared none whom they thought to be learned especially if they found any to have pen and ink, they pulled off his hood. . . ."

Planché wrote that he could not find that clergy or lawyers wore black gowns in the time of Edward II. The illumination showing the Court of Chancery in the time of Henry VI (now in the Inner Temple Library, see Chapter 7) depicts apprentices-at-law (barristers) in variegated robes, though of course it is impossible to tell whether these formed an official costume or —as is more probable—were just everyday dress. Suggesting that the Bar gown developed from that of the medieval guilds-men, Blackham thinks that it probably acquired its sombre colour when guilds broke up at the Reformation. Certainly during the 16th century the Inns were repeatedly ordering their members to sobriety of costume (see below).

All things considered, it is extremely likely that the stuff gown of the junior barrister had become settled as a professional garment by (and probably not before) the beginning of the 17th century. It will be remembered that those barristers who were Readers or benchers of their Inns had black gowns ornamented with velvet, and the serjeants had a colourful garb of their own.

Bands, two oblong strips of fine white lawn, held in place by strings tied round the collar, are worn in place of tie. They are similar to those worn by some clerics.

The origin of the bands is disputed. The most fantastic "explanation" is that given by Pearse ("Guide to the Inns of Court," 1855), who says they were copied from the clergy from

the Jewish rabbis, and represent the two Tables of the Law—
the Ten Commandments—carried from Sinai by Moses. He
adds that the bands were adopted by "the early lawyers" from
clerical costume. It has been claimed that the bands are relics
of the amice, and Cohen says it seems likely that they
"developed from the overlapping borders of the mitre, tied
under the chin." Blackham ("Wig and Gown," 1932) says the
bands are the ends of a soft white "jabot" or neckband worn
before starched collars came into use.

Surely the true origin of the bands is in the square linen
collars of the Commonwealth period. Portraits of the judges, at
least, indicate that they were first adopted in the mid-17th
century and have been retained ever since. This date is
supported by F. A. Inderwick, Q.C., in "The King's Peace,"
(1895).

On the death of the Sovereign barristers wear mourning
bands, which have a thin longitudinal stripe on the white lawn.

The Wig worn by barristers is of fine white horsehair, with 30
curls arranged for the most part in three horizontal rows, and
a double queue or tail.

Wigs first became fashionable in the France of Louis XIV,
and came generally into use in England at the Restoration.
Lord Campbell (the 19th century judge and author) tells us that
they came into use by barristers only very gradually, for the
judges at first thought them so "coxcombical" that they would
not allow young members of the Bar to plead before them so
attired. The long, curled periwig in fashion during the reigns of
Charles II and James II was discarded by barristers (if indeed
they had ever adopted it generally) in common with other
gentlemen in the first quarter of the 18th century, in favour of
a more convenient short, curled model. The long, full-bottomed
wig continued to be worn by judges, serjeants and Queen's
Counsel. The barrister's wig in its final form has been described
technically as a combination of the tye wig and the Ramillies
peruke. Up to the early 19th century it was rather fuller than
at present.

The retention of the wig as a part of the barrister's official
costume must be ascribed mainly to the traditional conservatism of the profession, though it undoubtedly has a
levelling effect—and a dignifying one—on the variety of faces

whose owners plead in our courts. Powdered wigs were worn on the Oxford circuit long after the custom had disappeared elsewhere, according to Foote ("Pie Powder," 1911). Mr. George Bancroft, Clerk of Assize on the Midland Circuit, who retired in 1946, was still wearing a powdered wig in 1939.

A rule made by the judges in March, 1922—just before the first woman was called to the Bar—lays down that women are to wear wigs "which shall completely cover and conceal the hair." It is recounted that at the meeting which drew up this rule two judges—Mr. Justice Darling and Mr. Justice Horridge —proposed that women barristers should wear the biretta instead. This proposal was rejected by the votes of the other nine judges present.

Gloves are used by barristers only as part of court dress. There seems no evidence that gloves were ever regularly worn by the Bar, and clearly there would be no point in wearing them either in Hall, or when appearing in court where their use would impede writing. In the legal profession generally gloves are worn only ceremonially today, and the position of the junior Bar does not normally involve ceremonial outside the Inns of Court.

Without gown and bands, the barrister is officially "invisible" to the judge in court. The wig is perhaps not so essential a part of Bar costume, for a Sikh barrister was not long ago permitted to appear in an English court wearing a turban in place of wig.

The official dress for members of the junior Bar at royal Court functions is "Court dress." This consists of a black velvet court suit: tailed coat with black silk rosette (a relic of the little bag used to keep in position the tail of the [not specifically legal] wig) hanging over the collar at the back of the neck; lace stock and cuffs; knee breeches; silk stockings, patent leather shoes; cocked hat; sword; white gloves.

Nowadays the everyday "uniform" of black jacket, striped trousers and black homburg or bowler which barristers share with other professional men is at most a custom. The black jacket and waistcoat worn beneath the gown have the force of etiquette, which in contrast curiously ignores the clothing of the barrister's nether limbs. But Lord Coleridge, the 19th century Lord Chief Justice (who in his later years was responsible for reintroducing historic usages in judicial robes) is said to have shocked a court in which he appeared when a barrister by his unorthodox garb. "I listen with little pleasure," Mr. Justice Byles is said to have told him, "to the argument of counsel whose legs are encased in light grey trousers."

In the 16th century the everyday costume of members of the Inns of Court was regulated as strictly as that worn in court or when dining in Hall. In the reign of Mary I we find the Middle Templars forbidding members to wear "great breeches in their hose, made after the Dutch, Spanish or Almain fashion, or lawn upon the caps, or cut doublets," under a penalty of 3s. 4d. and, for the second offence, expulsion. At about the same time the Inner Temple ruled that its members must not wear beards "above three weeks' growth." A mid-16th century rule by all four Inns laid down "that none except knights and benchers should wear in their doublets or hose any light colours, save scarlet and crimson, nor wear velvet shoes, double cuffs in their shirts, feathers or ribbons in their caps, and that none should wear their study gowns in the city any further than Fleet Bridge or Holborn Bridge. . . ." It may be there was no consistent rule about the wearing of gowns, for about 1574 we find Gray's Inn ruling that gowns must be worn "even in the suburbs and fields". In 1584 a Temple Parliament decided that none was to walk the streets in cloaks 'but gowns,' and the same ruling provided that "no hat nor long nor curled hair be worn."

As Cohen remarks in his "History of the English Bar" (1929), the junior Bar has always been well dressed; in Victorian times tail coat and silk hat were invariably worn.

Even the colour of the cloth bag, embroidered with his initials, in which the barrister carries his briefs and books has a significance in the pageantry of the law. The junior barrister, when he is called, buys a dark blue bag. If he wins the good opinion of a Queen's Counsel by whom he is led in some case, the senior man may present him with a red bag.

The details of the presentation of a red bag are fixed by custom. The Q.C. hands the bag to his own senior clerk, who sends it by a junior clerk to the junior barrister's chambers. There the clerk presents the bag with his master's compliments, and is given a guinea for his trouble. A pound of this is the perquisite of the senior clerk, however, and the junior clerk has to be content with the odd shilling!

On the Oxford Circuit it is, or was until recently, the rule that only the circuit leader—the Q.C. who is senior in date of appointment—may present an unlimited number of red bags; other "silks" on the circuit may, on becoming Queen's Counsel, give two red bags. Sir Frank MacKinnon ("On Circuit," 1940) says that on some circuits (or so he believed) a junior was allowed to carry a red bag only if it were given him by one of the circuit leaders, but not if he received it from a leader not a member of the same circuit.

The history of the brief- or book-bag and its various colours is obscure.

Lord Ellenborough (Chief Justice of the King's Bench 1802-13) was given a red bag by one of the leaders of the Northern Circuit on his first round of the circuit as a young barrister. Lord Campbell ("Lives of the Chief Justices" 1849-51) records this, and adds: "Nowadays any young barrister buys a bag and carries it as soon after he is called to the Bar as he likes; but when I was called to the Bar (in 1806), and long after, the privilege of carrying a bag was strictly confined to those who had received one from a King's Counsel. The King's Counsel, then few in number, were considered officers of the Crown, and they not only had a salary of £40 a year, but an annual allowance of paper, pens and purple bags. These they distributed among juniors who had made such progress as not to be able to carry their briefs conveniently in their hands. All these salaries and perquisites were ruthlessly swept away in 1830. . . ." (See below, Chapter 5). Of this MacKinnon comments: "This suggests that there was only a red, or purple, bag, and that 'nowadays' a junior bought one upon his call. But Lord Campbell is so frequently inaccurate that it may be, that then, as now, he bought a blue bag and waited to be presented with a red one."

Two modern authors seem to differ, but may be merely following Campbell. One, Blackham ("Wig and Gown," 1932) says the presentation of a crimson bag "is a reminder of olden times when no junior possessed a bag to carry home his papers." Payler ("Law Courts, Lawyers and Litigants," 1926) says: "At different periods it was a heinous offence for a junior to take a bag of any colour whatever into an Equity or a Common-law Court, unless it had been presented to him by a member of the 'inner' Bar with whom he had appeared in some case." Again, "At one time red, purple, or blue bags were the special privilege of the Queen's Counsel, the Chancery lawyers and the Leaders of the Common Law Bar," says Christian ("A Short History of Solicitors," 1896, quoting the Law Journal for 3 May 1872).

It is said that "in the days of Queen Caroline and Queen Anne" (Payler) a green bag was de rigueur at the Bar. Blackham says the green bags acquired such unpopularity at the House of Lords "trial" of Queen Caroline in 1820 that the colour was changed to blue. He does not explain further. Was incriminating evidence at the "trial" produced from such a green bag? Certainly the judges to this day use green bags. Christian says that "subsequently" to Elizabethan times the bags carried by attorneys were green "and were so universally known that 'a green bag' meant a lawyer of the inferior branch. . . ."

At the Inner and Middle Temple there is a position in the hierarchy of the Inn mid-way between the ranks of barrister and bencher. The title of Ancient is given to the barristers (four at the Inner, eight at the Middle) who are the highest in seniority below the bench. At Gray's Inn (last appointment 1709) and Lincoln's Inn the rank is no longer used. Up to the second World War at least the Middle Temple Ancients were served in Hall with extra food and drink, a relic of the "exceedings"—the additional luxuries served to the Reader's guests and intimates in bygone days.

In the 17th century the Ancients at the Middle Temple were also termed the "Cupboard Men," for their table stood—as now —close to the ancient sideboard in the hall of their Inn known as the Cupboard. They were elected by the Parliament (assembly of benchers) of the Inn, four in Hilary Term and four in Trinity Term. At Gray's a barrister might expect to be called to the Grand Company of Ancients about 10 years after his call to the Bar. As many as 30 Ancients were called at a time.

Customarily the Readers were chosen from among the Ancients; and at the end of his Reading a Reader was translated from the Ancients to the bench. It seems also that utter barristers called to read but excused for some reason became Ancients by virtue of that fact.

The governing body at each Inn is composed of senior members known as the Masters of the Bench, or colloquially as benchers. As well as ruling the domestic affairs of their Inn—and the Inns are enclaves largely exempt from local authority jurisdiction—the benchers are responsible for admission of students, call to the Bar, and for disciplinary action for offences against the etiquette of the profession extending from a reprimand to suspension from practice and the facilities of the Inn, or permanent disbarring. Appeal from their rulings may be made to the judges.

Clearly some sort of ruling body must have existed almost from the first. Sir William Ball ("Lincoln's Inn," 1947) says the name Bencher appears in the Minutes of that Inn for the first time in 1441. The name derives from the bench on which the members of the ruling body sat in Hall. As early as 1456, Sir William adds, a craftsman was allowed 11d. for repairing "the Bench." However, the New English Dictionary gives 1582 as the earliest example of the word bencher as meaning one of the rulers of the Inns. However this may be, it seems that "Governors" (Gubernatores) was the first title given to those whom we now call benchers. Pulling ("Order of the Coif," 1884) says the list of governors of Lincoln's Inn runs from Henry VI's reign to 1574-5, when the same names appear again as "benchers." At the Inner Temple the list of governors similarly runs from 1505-6 to 1566, when the title changes.

Benchers are elected—or rather co-opted—from members of the Inn (except "honorary" benchers, who need not even be lawyers) by the existing Masters of the Bench. In early days the customary preliminary or qualification was service as Reader. When, in 1596, the judges made rules for the conduct of the Inns of Court—as they did periodically in those days—they recognised that occasionally members who had not served as Reader were elected as benchers. Such calls, they warned, were to be made "very sparingly," and those chosen must be "fittest both for their learning, practice and good and honest conversation." During the Commonwealth period, according to Cowper ("A Prospect of Gray's Inn," 1951), benchers of Gray's were appointed with a mere promise to read if called upon; after the Restoration fines were imposed for failure to carry out this undertaking. Soon afterwards the custom of appointing Readers disappeared; but where the office has been revived Readers are now, contrary to the ancient practice, chosen from among existing benchers: perhaps a relic of the 17th century undertaking to read if called upon.

It is customary to elect to the bench members of the Inn who achieve high judicial office, if they are not already benchers; and a considerable proportion of Q.C.s sooner or later attain benchership. Pulling says that "the King's ordinary counsellors in the law" (in addition to the King's Serjeants) e.g. the Attorney-General and Solicitor-General, were probably from the first elected to the bench of their Inns. The position of Queen's (or King's) Counsel caused some difficulty on this point a century or so ago. At first the Q.C. was a Crown counsel in much the same way as a King's Serjeant (see Chapter 5). For this reason it became customary for new Q.C.s to be elected benchers automatically on appointment. When the first Queen's Counsel were appointed in the 17th century, and right through the 18th century, the number holding this rank was small, and the practice caused no difficulty. But when in Victorian times the number of Q.C.s grew to scores—the office having outlived its original purpose—the benches of the Inns became overloaded with members qualified only by having "taken silk." In 1845 a test case arose, and the judges decided there was no automatic claim to benchership on appointment as Queen's Counsel.

Each Inn confers honorary membership of its bench to eminent men, within or outside the profession, whom it wishes from time to time to honour. Royal benchers are treated as ordinary, not honorary members. The royal family have a long-standing association with the Inns of Court, and in recent years it has been unusual for any of the benches to be without at least one royal member. Although Queen Elizabeth I had close links with the Temple—where she saw the first performance of "Twelfth Night" in 1576—she was not a bencher: doubtless her sex made it unthinkable. The present tradition began with James II who, when Duke of York, was called to the Bar and made a bencher of the Inner Temple in 1661. Edward VII was a bencher of the Middle Temple, and the first royal Master of the Bench to dine in Hall with his colleagues; the Duke of Windsor and Queen Elizabeth the Queen Mother also belong to that Inn. King George VI was a bencher of the Inner Temple; the Duke of Gloucester is a bencher of Gray's Inn. The late Queen Mary became the first woman bencher of any Inn when she was called to the bench in 1943 by Lincoln's Inn, of which her husband, King George V, had been a bencher.

The numbers of ordinary Masters of the Bench at the four Inns at the time of writing (1954) are: Lincoln's Inn, 69; Inner Temple, 91; Middle Temple, 64; Gray's Inn, 36. Lincoln's Inn has in addition 10 honorary benchers, Inner Temple 14, Middle Temple 23 and Gray's Inn 10.

The procedure for election and call to the bench is no more elaborate than that for call to the Bar. The method of election at the Inner Temple, which so far as I know is typical of all the Inns, is as follows: The week after a vacancy has been announced, proposals are called for among the serving benchers. When a further week has elapsed, there is a ballot, again confined to the Masters of the Bench. A few days later the result is confirmed by the benchers at a meeting or "Parliament."

At Lincoln's Inn call or "publication" to the bench takes place in Hall at lunch-time. Two sponsors lead the candidate to the Treasurer, to whom they say: "Treasurer, we present to you ———— a Barrister of this Society (or one of Her Majesty's Counsel learned in the Law, if the candidate is a Q.C.) qualified to be a Bencher of this Society." At the Middle Temple those who are to be called (usually already Ancients) take up position by the senior Bar mess. After Grace the head porter presents to each in turn the compliments of the Treasurer and other benchers, with an invitation to join them at the high table.

On nights when a new Middle Temple bencher is dining in Hall for the first time a loving-cup is circulated; more likely, as Blackham ("Wig and Gown," 1932) suggests, to be a link with the life of the Guilds, since the loving-cup is so closely associated with the customs of the Livery Companies, than with that of the Knights Templar. After dinner, when the new bencher leaves the Hall with his colleagues in procession, he is cheered by members in the body of the Hall.

When Dugdale wrote in the late 17th century benchers were wholly or for the most part recruited from Readers on concluding their period of Readership. He gives an account of the call to the bench of a Reader at the Middle Temple; explaining that the immediate past Reader (the candidate for benchership) was excluded from the first Parliament—meeting of benchers —held in term after his Reading. When the meeting, at which presumably he was elected, was over, he was admitted. "After the Reader is thus entered and placed, his last and immediate predecessor welcomes him hither with an Oration; and according to his merit reports of him to the rest of the Masters of the Bench; unto whom the Reader replies in another Oration, and excuseth his imperfections and inabilities; but is rejoined unto by the high Treasurer in a third Oration, and in the name of all their masterships, welcom'd thither and pronounced a Bencher; who from that instant is as absolute as any of them."

Nobody could term the system of rule by benchers, co-opted by other benchers, democratic, although the majority of barristers are satisfied that the arrangement works well. It seems that in early times other members of the Inn were called into consultation. The return made to Henry VIII in 1545 says the Pension or Parliament then denoted "nothing else but a conference and Assembly of their Benchers and Utter-Barristers only, and in some other of the houses, it is an assembly of Benchers" with senior Utter-Barristers, picturesquely known as the "Sage Company," co-opted.

It is curious that there are no less than three terms in different Inns for the periodic meetings of benchers to transact domestic business. At the Temple the term is Parliament, conceivably derived from the Norman-French of the Knights Templar; at Lincoln's Inn it is "Council"; and at Gray's Inn "Pension," derived from the Latin word for expenditure, the main domestic concern of the benchers as managers of the affairs of their Inn.

At all the Inns the chairman and "head" of the bench—and therefore of the Inn—is the Treasurer, elected in Michaelmas Term for the ensuing year. In addition to the Treasurer there is a number of other specific offices held by benchers in rotation. The names vary in the different Inns. At Lincoln's Inn there is a Master of the Library, Dean of the Chapel, Keeper of the Black

Book (the record of business transacted by the benchers—not a "black list"!), and Master of the Walks, who sees to the grounds of the Inn. Gray's and the two Temples have each a Master of the Moots among their officers. The Inner and Middle Temple each have a Reader, a Master of the Garden and a Master of the House. The Middle Temple has a Master of the Kitchen, and Gray's has a Master of the Common Room.

At Lincoln's Inn it is customary for six benchers to dine in Hall on Call Day, and (at least) three benchers every other day except the first and last days of term, and Grand Day in each term. Those holding office keep term by dining at least thrice during term. The Inner Temple requires a candidate for Treasurership to have kept the two terms preceding his election, dining four times in each. At Middle Temple benchers must dine five times to keep term—a necessary preliminary to office as Reader or Treasurer.

Nowadays benchers wear, when dining in Hall, the gown of the degree—either barrister or Queen's Counsel—to which they were entitled at the time of their promotion to the bench. Those judges who are benchers follow the same rule, except that if they were made judges before being elected benchers, their gown as bencher is that which they wore when last members of the Bar. For this reason, in some cases a judge raised from the junior Bar has continued to wear the stuff gown of a "junior" barrister in the hall of his Inn.

In former days, and presumably until the silk gown was adopted at the end of the 17th century, benchers wore the tufted and "guarded" black gown which was also used by Readers, and described in Chapter 2 above. Benchers were allowed more freedom than junior members of the Inns in the days when non-professional clothing was subject to strict rules. In 1557, for instance, the four Inns decided that "none except knights and benchers should wear in their doublets or hose any light colours, save scarlet and crimson, nor wear any upper velvet cap, or any scarf or wings in their gowns, white jerkins, buskins, or velvet shoes, double cuffs in their shirts, feathers or ribbons in their caps. . . ."

Each of the Inns appoints a chaplain—who is not a bencher —though only at Lincoln's Inn does he actually bear that title. At Gray's Inn he is known as the Preacher, and the Inner and

Middle Temple share the services of a clergyman who bears the ancient title of Master of the Temple. This latter arrangement dates from 1608, when the Crown handed over the freehold of the Temple to the two societies of lawyers occupying it, on condition that they kept up the office of Master and the house within the precincts attached to it.

4. Dinner-Time

THE evening meal at the Inns of Court holds a unique place in the pageantry of the law. It is very much a domestic affair, and its every stage is regulated by historic custom. At dinner-time in Hall distinctions of rank which weigh in the world outside, even in the courts of justice, count for nothing. Between the two grace prayers, barrister and judge, master and pupil, professional antagonists at the Bar, are all brothers in the law. It is the remaining core of the ancient communal life of the Inns.

At the Middle Temple members are summoned to dinner by a blast upon a silver-mounted ox-horn sounded by the porter, wearing his gold-laced top hat. In medieval times bread for the Temple was baked at Charing Cross and brought by river. When the supply arrived for dinner, the "pannier" or bread-porter who brought it sounded a horn to summon the Knights Templar to their meal. Waiters at the Temple Inns are still Known as panniers. At Lincoln's Inn the rule is "A Horn to be blown or bell sounded within the precincts of the Inn a quarter of an hour before the hour for dinner."

Members dining wear gowns (but not wigs or bands) according to their degree. Dark clothes must be worn beneath the gown, and at Gray's Inn it is a firm rule that a black coat must be worn. The printed dining regulations of Lincoln's Inn retain the old injunction: "Cloaks, Hats, Spurs, Swords and Daggers and any disorderly conduct are forbidden in Hall." This and similar rules at the other Inns were made in Elizabethan times. In the oaken tables of Middle Temple Hall are marks where daggers or knives were stuck into the wood perhaps four centuries ago.

Members now dine bare-headed. Although hats were forbidden—apparently as too dashing and worldly for the lawyer—a round cap was customarily worn in Hall until the adoption of the wig for everyday wear. For a further reference to this cap, see Chapter 2. Dugdale ("Origines Juridiciales," 1666, etc.) quotes a Gray's Inn rule of 1610-11 "that all the Gentlemen of this Society, except the Master of Requests and the King's Solicitor, should henceforth wear Caps in the Hall, both in Term Time and Vacation, except in the xii days at Xmas." The judges' order for all the Inns in 1627 laid down that caps must be worn in both Hall and Church.

The arrangement of tables in Hall is much the same at all four Inns of Court. At the upper end of the Hall there is a dais, on which is a table placed crosswise. This is for the benchers—who today are almost the only members who sit on chairs instead of benches. Below the dais at the Middle Temple is a second table crosswise, also with chairs, for the Ancients of this Inn. At the Inner Temple, the four Ancients take the highest places among the barristers but have no table of their own. Placed across or along each hall are several long tables parallel to each other, with benches, for the barristers (nearest the dais) and students —as the reader will recall from Chapter 1.

All members except the benchers sit along the tables in "messes" of four, two each side of the table. Students (except at Gray's), barristers and benchers all sit in strict order of seniority as to admission or call to Bar or bench. This rule applies no matter what the rank of the individual member outside the little world of his Inn, even if he be the Lord Chancellor himself. Most judges and a number of the most senior Queen's Counsel are in fact benchers of their Inns, and so take precedence among their fellow-benchers who will all be of some considerable seniority in the profession.

The place of the chaplain inevitably forms an exception to the general rule. At Lincoln's Inn he normally sits in the third mess at the first bar table. When Dugdale wrote of the Inner Temple in the 17th century the Master of the Temple was given first place in Hall "though any Nobleman or Judge were there," except in Reading times when the Reader took precedence. Now at the same Inn the Master—when he dines—takes his place among the benchers by seniority of appointment. No special place or precedence is assigned to him at the Middle Temple. At Gray's Inn the Preacher sits eighth among the benchers when he dines on Grand Nights.

Within each mess, the senior of the four members is known

D

as the captain. The captain sits on the right of the side nearer to the bench table (in the case of the first Bar table, placed lengthwise) and on the right of the side furthest from the bench table (in the case of the second Bar table). At Gray's Inn, when fewer than four benchers are present, by a democratic custom barristers or students are invited to the bench table to complete a mess of four—except, however, on moot nights.

The entry of the benchers just before the meal is to be served is a ceremony of varying solemnity. To escort them, each Inn has its head porter in official costume, carrying a staff or mace. These costumes and insignia are: Lincoln's Inn, chocolate-coloured frock coat and trousers, with blue piping, top hat with gold band, staff surmounted by the arms of the Inn wrought in silver; Inner Temple: brown gown with yellow cape and tassels, a six-foot silver mace surmounted by the Pegasus crest in silver; Middle Temple: purple gown, silver-topped mace; Gray's Inn: purple gown, staff surmounted by silver griffin crest. At Lincoln's Inn and the Inner Temple the porter in his ceremonial garb officiates only on Grand Days (see pp. 54-6 below).

Middle Temple benchers enter in procession through the hall, led by their porter carrying his mace, which is knocked on the floor as a signal immediately before entering. Those in Hall rise at the entry of the benchers, and the porter with his mace waits below the dais while the benchers two by two go up to the high table, and stand facing the mace. Then with a mallet the head porter strikes thrice upon the table. This is done also at Lincoln's Inn. At all the Inns the benchers customarily exchange bows or handshakes with the senior barristers in Hall. At Gray's the butler knocks for silence as the benchers enter (here in single file) and at Lincoln's he announces dinner with a single stroke of his mallet—after which all questions of precedence in Hall are deemed to be settled. Although it has been suggested that certain of these procedural details have survived from Templar usage, subsequently passed on to the other Inns, the point is far from proved. The porters and their staffs or maces have much in common with Guild or Livery Company practice.

The two Temple Inns announce grace before meat by banging on a book—theoretically, at least, the grace-book.

The graces used at the four Inns differ considerably. For convenience, the forms before and after meat are here printed together:

Lincoln's Inn uses, before meat, the familiar form: "Bless, O Lord, we beseech Thee, these Thy creatures to our use, and ourselves to Thy service, through Jesus Christ Our Lord."

After dinner: "God be praised for all His blessings: God preserve the Queen, the Church and this Honorable (sic) Society, and grant us His peace evermore, through Jesus Christ our Lord."

The Inner Temple uses the terse Latin "Benedictus benedicat" —"May the Blessèd One bless," and "Benedictus benedicetur,"— "May the Blessèd One be blessed," unless the Master is present when he uses the fuller Latin form, as at

Gray's Inn. This is the old Catholic form: "Benedic, Domine, nos et haec tua dona quae de bonitate tua sumpturi sumus. Amen."—"Bless us, O Lord, and these Thy gifts which we are about to receive from Thy bounty. Amen." After dinner: "Agimus tibi gratias, Omnipotens Deus, pro donis tuis, per Jesum Christum Dominum nostrum. Amen."—"We give Thee thanks, Almighty God, for Thy gifts, through Jesus Christ, our Lord. Amen."

The Middle Temple graces are perhaps the most interesting of all. That before meat is described by Blackham as "a Lutheran tisch-bot, somewhat varied from the form in which it appears in a black-letter Elizabethan Prayer Book of 1581." It is, however, undoubtedly a translation of the prayer "Oculi omnium" which, together with "Benedic, Domine" (as above), forms part of the long monastic grace. Before meat: "The eyes of all things look up and put their trust in Thee, O Lord! Thou givest them their Meat in due season; Thou openest Thine hand, and fillest with Thy blessing every living thing. Good Lord, bless us and these Thy good gifts which we receive of Thy bounteous liberality, through Jesus Christ our Lord. Amen." After meat: "Glory, honour, and praise be given to Thee, O Lord, who dost feed us from our tender age, and givest sustenance to every living thing. Replenish our hearts with joy and gladness, that we, having sufficient, may be rich and plentiful in all good works, through Jesus Christ our Lord. God save his Church, the Queen, all the Royal Family, and this Realm; God send us peace and truth in Christ our Lord. Amen."

Grace is said by the Treasurer or his deputy, unless the chaplain is present.

Each mess of four diners has its separate provision of food and wine. The captain chooses the wine on behalf of the mess, At the Middle Temple, where the choice is by majority though the captain has a casting vote. The wine and food go first to the captain, then to other members by seniority. The wine passes anti-clockwise, except the port which goes clockwise—apart (in the case of Lincoln's Inn) from the Chaplain's mess when he is present "and then it is passed to him by ancient courtesy and proceeds anti-clockwise." The Ancients, in the Temple Inns, are entitled to extra food and wine, a privilege which originated in the old Readers' Feasts (see Chapter 2). At Gray's Inn the junior of each mess is customarily entitled to be served first with the cheese.

At all the Inns, except the Inner Temple where perhaps the custom once existed but has lapsed, the first toast drunk is always a three-fold one to the fellow-members of one's mess. The procedure varies slightly. At the Middle Temple after *each* grace those present raise their glasses, bowing to each other member of the mess in turn: opposite, diagonally, and to the side, in a silent toast. Indeed it is forbidden to speak to members of any other mess, or to drink wine, until this toast has been drunk. It has been suggested that this symbolises the Cross —another of the possible survivals from the days of the Templars. At Gray's Inn each member toasts the other members of his mess, naming all three but drinking to all collectively in a single toast; by custom, not always observed, this should take place when wine is brought at the beginning of dinner. At Lincoln's Inn the corresponding ceremony is picturesquely described in the regulations: "The first toast is drunk vis-a-vis, the second diagonally, and the third cheek by jowl."

At Gray's Inn later in the meal each mess drinks the health of the mess immediately below "the members raising their glasses simultaneously and saying 'Gentlemen of the lower mess,' naming them thus, e.g., 'Smith, Brown, Jones, Robinson,' but without further words." The lower mess returns the compliment, drinking to the 'Gentlemen of the upper mess.' In accordance with Bar custom, barristers toasting each other— and indeed in ordinary conversation—use surnames without prefix, irrespective of the seniority of the man addressed. In the case of students or others, "Mr." or the appropriate title is used. And the senior barrister (not being a bencher) in Hall is always "Mr. Senior" at Grays.

The Inner Temple drinks no toasts on ordinary occasions, and at Lincoln's Inn no toasts are drunk in the senior mess.

At the end of the meal, the moment when members may begin to smoke is regulated by varying custom. At the Inner Temple it is the duty of the junior bencher to ask the Treasurer "Have twenty minutes elapsed (since the port was passed)?" The question is a formality, and is the customary form of seeking permission to smoke. Irrespective of the actual lapse of time if the Treasurer's reply is "Yes," members may light up.

The other Inns do not permit members to smoke until the benchers have retired to take their dessert and cigars in private. The captain of the first mess at Lincoln's Inn signifies permission to smoke by "ordering the candle to be lighted" and placed on the table at his mess. At Gray's the unfortunate junior student has the task of asking permission of Mr. Senior. As Francis Cowper, himself a Grayan, puts it ("A Prospect of Gray's Inn," 1951): "Now pandemonium breaks out. 'Up, Junior!' 'Up, Junior!' The junior in Hall rises nervously if he is new. 'Down, Junior!' 'Down, Junior!' The game of baiting the junior never palls. Somehow through the din he must get across to the far end of the Hall the petition 'Mr. Senior, Sir, may we have your permission to smoke?' When the Senior decides to hear him permission is granted."

For those who prefer, snuff is available, contained in boxes which have histories of their own.

When the benchers have left Hall at Gray's, Mr. Senior is kept busy deciding real or imaginary points of order. These may be put up by an entire mess, through their head, or by individual members personally. From his place in Hall the member addresses the Senior. "If he thinks fit" that functionary hears any person whose conduct is questioned, and then gives his judgment. An appeal can be made to the benchers. Mr. Senior can impose fines for any breach of rule or custom—a bottle of wine is theoretically still the usual form of fine, but in practice a three-shilling cash payment is now substituted. The price of wine is now so high that the retention of the old fine might discourage the raising of points for judgment—and much good-humoured entertainment would be lost as a result. Francis Cowper tells us of the sort of point which may arise: "Someone has dined in a coat which is not black. Someone in toasting has addressed the next mess as 'Members of the Upper Mess' when he should have said 'Gentlemen,' or conversely someone has addressed another mess as 'Gentlemen' when, a lady being among them, the form of address should have been 'Members.' The junior in a mess is perhaps aggrieved because he has not been allowed, according to custom, to be the first to help himself to the cheese. The charges are pressed and defended . . . So the evening lengthens out in mock indictments, in discussion and exchange, perhaps in song. . . . The port circulates. . . ." Trivial as the actual points may be, underlying the fun and opportunity for laughing at one's own profession is a recognition of the need for preserving the details which together make up a great tradition.

Fines are imposed at the Middle Temple as well as Gray's, and—as the reader will see in Chapter 10—the system is extended to the "Grand Courts" of the various circuits.

Two or three times a year each Inn observes a Grand Day, when distinguished guests are entertained by the benchers and a special menu is provided worthy of the occasion. All the Inns have customs peculiar to these dignified banquets, which are all that remain to remind us of the Grand Weeks of revels which used to take place at Christmas, Candlemas and All Saints, with a celebration also at Ascension.

Christmas revels in Tudor times took a special form. Each Inn held a kind of mock royal Court, with members appointed to offices corresponding with those in the royal household, and a junior member taking the part of the Sovereign. The whole thing was a frolic which lasted over the entire holiday season, but behind it was a useful purpose in teaching courtly accomplishments to the younger generation. In time, however, it developed into a kind of "rag."

The Inns were renowned for their singing and dancing, masques and plays. "Twelfth Night" is said to have been performed in Middle Temple Hall on Candlemas Day, 1601, in the presence of Queen Elizabeth I, who danced with some of the revellers. In 1594 "The Comedy of Errors" was given its "first night" at Gray's Inn Hall. In recent years the Inns have been regaining their reputation in this regard, by balls, concerts and plays within their precincts.

The true revels were—like the Readings—interrupted by the Civil War, resumed for a brief and brilliant spell at the Restoration and finally allowed to lapse by the end of the 17th century.

Nowadays Grand Day festivities are restricted to a banquet.

At Gray's Inn the guests are each announced and conducted the length of the Hall to the dais by the purple-gowned head porter with his silver-topped staff. Before grace, the benchers and their guests go down to the body of the hall and sit down there with the barristers and students on their forms. A loving cup is circulated, with small pieces of bread, and rank and age are forgotten while all drink together.

Though the entry of the benchers today is solemn, in the heyday of the Inns dinner on Grand Days was heralded by an even more stately procession for the ceremonial arrival of the dishes. "Upon great Festival days," says Dugdale in the 17th century, "the Gentlemen of the Inner Bar (students) do serve up into the Hall, the first and second Course from the Dresser, being attended on, at the first Course, with Music; the Master of the Revels following next to the Music holding a white wand in his hand; and the Treasurer, with his predecessor or successor, holding white staves."

At Lincoln's Inn the toast of the Sovereign is drunk sitting, by virtue of a privilege conferred by Charles II. The junior bencher is charged with the duty of seeing that the supply of wine is replenished when necessary. He must call loudly "Treasurer, ring the bell." The Treasurer demands to know "What for?" and the junior bencher tells him "More wine." A story quoted by Sir William Ball ("Law Times," 214-97) recounts how when the Prince of Wales—the future King George V—was Treasurer, Lord Chief Justice Alverstone charged the junior strictly that he must not call on the Prince to ring the bell. The junior demurred, but before dinner was over the royal Treasurer had been told about the custom and insisted that it should be followed.

The Inner Temple on Grand Days drinks the only toast which figures in its dining customs—that of "This Ancient and Honourable Society." At the Middle Temple a loving cup is passed round, and there is also a traditional passing of the salt and snuff-taking, as well as ceremonial toasts. When the high table has been cleared after the meal, before grace, a rose-water bowl is handed round.

At Gray's Inn during dinner the loving cup, circulated before-hand in the manner we have seen, is again passed round, beginning with the Treasurer. As each member drinks, the two immediately senior (except in the case of the Treasurer, who takes precedence by his office) and junior to him also stand. With a bow to these two, the member drinks to "The pious, glorious and immortal memory of good Queen Bess."

When the tables have been cleared and clothes removed, the loyal toast is proposed by the senior-in-hall, and drunk standing. Then the senior proposes the health of other members of the royal family. At his behest, the barristers drink the health of the students; the junior student replies, and the senior student then proposes the health of the barristers, which is duly drunk by the students. The junior barrister replies, while all barristers stand. Then the senior-in-hall proposes the toast of "Domus"— the Inn, known thus familiarly to its members as "The House" or "Home." (These and other Gray's Inn customs were, until the bombing of 1941, set forth on panels hung on the wall of the Hall; they are now embodied in a pamphlet, from which these details are drawn).

The two Temple Inns, always closely associated, hold a joint dinner each year, with the respective Treasurers by turn host and chief guest. In 1949 King George VI was honorary Treasurer of the Inner Temple and his Queen held a similar position at the Middle Temple; thus it fell to husband and wife to propose each other's health, and that of the Inn to which each belonged.

5. Counsel of the Crown

QUEEN'S COUNSEL

As legal office-holders go, Queen's Counsel are mere upstarts. It is only 350 years since the first of that title (at least in the modern sense) was created; and not for a century after that did such appointments become a regular thing. Ousting his rival, the serjeant-at-law, the Q.C. gained prominence in the profession—but in the process largely lost sight of his origin. Today the barristers in silk gowns who, by virtue of their rank as Queen's Counsel, conduct their cases from the front row in court have little of the prestige or duty of royal servants which their title would imply. Nor have they (with a few exceptions) even the fame and income of their Victorian predecessors. But there remains a subtle cachet conferred by the letters Q.C. after a man's name : a pale reflection, perhaps, of the departed glory of the serjeants.

The serjeants-at-law, who traced their history far back into the Middle Ages, were the ancient legal advisers and counsel of the Crown. They were *servientes regis ad legem*, and their primary duty was the royal service. They enjoyed for this reason precedence at the Bar, and had a monopoly of audience at the Common Pleas. In addition there were, from quite early times, the Attorney-General and the Solicitor-General, known as the Law Officers of the Crown.

Sir Francis Bacon, later Lord Chancellor, was the first King's Counsel who was not a serjeant or a Law Officer, according to Pulling ("Order of the Coif," 1884). This may not be strictly true, but Bacon may safely be taken as the first of the present line of King's Counsel. As Pulling, a fierce supporter of the serjeants against their modern rivals, puts it: Bacon "succeeded, for special purposes, in 1604 in getting himself appointed King's Counsel extraordinary. . . ." Pulling adds bitterly that he "thus afforded a precedent for a system of Royal patronage and promotion at the Bar which is altogether opposed to its ancient traditions and the public interest—a system admitted to be properly described as an anomaly." Nevertheless, it is the serjeants who have lost the struggle, and it is today generally recognised that Queen's Counsel have a special and useful part to play in the machinery of the law.

Bacon, a nephew by marriage of the statesman Lord Burleigh, persuaded Queen Elizabeth I to confer this rank upon him, but merely as an honour. Then when James I succeeded Elizabeth, Bacon managed to get the King to give him a formal appointment by Letters Patent, with an annuity of £40—then a considerable sum. This Patent (the text of which is given by Pulling, quoting Rymer's "Foedera") named Bacon as *Consiliarium nostrum ad Legem, sive unum de Consilio nostro erudito in Lege*—". . . one of our Counsel Learned in the Law," the phrase still used in appointing Queen's Counsel. It also granted Bacon the right of preaudience in the courts which was enjoyed by other royal counsel.

When Bacon became Solicitor-General in 1607 his appointment as K.C. "seems to have been treated as altogether ceasing." And the next King's Counsel was not appointed until 1668. In that year a similar patent was granted by Charles II to Francis North, later Lord Keeper of the Great Seal as Lord Guilford. Like Bacon, he was at the time neither a serjeant nor a Law Officer, and Pulling tells us that the leading members of the profession took a poor view of his elevation in this way. The benchers of the Middle Temple refused to elect him to their number. But North had influence, and the judges forced the benchers to relent by the simple expedient of refusing to hear any of them in court until North had been made a bencher! Also like Bacon, North became Solicitor-General three years after his appointment as K.C.

Both Bacon and North were King's Counsel Extraordinary, in the sense that the serjeants and Law Officers were still the customary representatives of the Crown. But from this time onwards the number of King's Counsel gradually increased, though it remained comparatively small up to the late 19th century, when the ancient order of serjeants was allowed to lapse.

Charles II appointed a total of 17 K.C.s, perhaps to secure a group of royalist counsel bound by oath not to accept briefs against the Crown—for King's Counsel were (and technically still are) so bound, though serjeants were always free to appear against the King. James II made 10 appointments, William and Mary 11, and Anne 10. George I seems not to have created any K.C.'s, but George II made 30, George III 93, George IV 26 and William IV 65. During the 18th century the number of King's Counsel was never more than a score at any one time. Pulling says that some of those appointed were barristers actually employed on Crown business, but some were "mere nominees of the Government of the day." "Not a third" of the 14 silks listed in the first Law list, for 1775, seem to have been in actual practice at Westminster Hall. In the same year there were 14 serjeants, including four King's Serjeants (those more particularly employed on Crown work) and 165 ordinary barristers.

Until the reign of William IV all King's Counsel received the £40 salary which had been paid to Bacon. They also got an allowance of stationery and of red bags in which to carry their papers (see Chapter 3). The appointment was regarded as an office of profit under the Crown, making it necessary for any M.P. so appointed to resign his seat. The emoluments were withdrawn in 1830, and this can probably be taken as the date from which the title of King's Counsel began to denote a mere rank rather than an actual Crown appointment.

About 1825 the number of K.C.s had risen to 30; but in 1850 there were only 28. In 1884, after the lapsing of the Order of the Coif whose members—the serjeants—had been bitter opponents of the precedence given to the upstart K.C.s, there were 44, and from this time the number increased rapidly to the 250-300 level maintained today. The call each year is about 15.

The first two women to be appointed King's Counsel at the English Bar received their patents in April, 1949. They are Mrs. Helena Normanton and Miss Rose Heilbron.

Since 1920 all Q.C.s have enjoyed open licence to appear in any case against the Crown, although they are still expected to give preference to Crown briefs when offered. By the fixed custom of the Bar, Queen's Counsel must, when they appear in court, be accompanied by a "junior" or ordinary barrister. They do not concern themselves with the preparatory work in a case, the drawing of the pleadings and so forth : all this is left to the junior. Nor do they take pupils.

The chief privileges now held by Queen's Counsel are the right to preaudience, and the right to sit in the front row of counsel's seats in court : that is, "within the bar." By way of exception they do not enjoy the latter privilege in the House of Lords or in some assize courts. Both these rights are held on the (now usually fictional) assumption that they are engaged on the Sovereign's business, and therefore entitled to pre-eminence in the royal courts.

The right of preaudience was enjoyed by the Law Officers and other counsel of the Crown, such as the King's Serjeants, before Queen's Counsel were thought of. They, with other serjeants and barristers who were benchers of their Inn, were allowed within the bar, at least in some courts, and the two privileges seem to have been linked.

Pulling ("Order of the Coif," 1884) tells us that the more advanced of the apprentices of the law—that is, junior barristers—were called in due form from the Outer Bar by special favour. And Dugdale, writing in the late 17th century, says : "The Benchers also do come within the Bar at the chapel of the Rolls (the Chancery court of the Master of the Rolls in those days) and sit there promiscuously amongst the Serjeants-at-law and the King's and Queen's Counsel (i.e., the Law Officers, etc.) learned. They are likewise heard by the Master of the Rolls, in course, and before all Utter Barristers, being called in by him from the Utter Bar, so soon as he first hath notice of their being called to the bench in their respective Societies." In the Common Pleas the serjeants had exclusive right of audience, so that no question of precedence, except among themselves by seniority, arose until this exclusive right was abolished in 1839; the serjeants practising there were always allowed to sit within the bar. Some time after 1839 the serjeants were allowed within the bar of the other Common Law courts—the King's Bench and Exchequer. They had always been given this privilege in the Chancery courts and at Nisi Prius, that is, the assize courts for civil actions.

The question of preaudience was once very important. Pulling says that prior to the time of Lord Mansfield (Chief Justice, King's Bench 1756-88) the practice at Westminster Hall was to begin with senior counsel within the bar, and to hear him for as long as he had cases. Only then would the court give audience to the next in seniority, and so on. Obviously this made for great unfairness, and Lord Mansfield allowed each counsel to move once only. Nowadays, generally speaking, all cases for hearing are listed in order, so that no question of privilege arises. As cases come in turn to the top of the list, so they are tried or otherwise disposed of.

Queen's Counsel—the title changes with the sex of the Sovereign—are appointed by letters patent on the nomination of the Lord Chancellor. Appointments are for life, but in special circumstances the letters patent may be revoked to enable the appointment to cease. There is no qualification laid down, but it is unusual for barristers of less than about 10 years standing to be granted patents. But by a recent custom, which has even more recently declined, Members of Parliament who were barristers could 'take silk' at any time if they applied for it, no matter how short their standing at the Bar.

Each spring the Lord Chancellor issues an invitation to barristers for those who wish to take silk to apply to him, giving details of their position at the Bar and reasons for the request. Those who apply must by custom write to all barristers senior to them (as regards call to the Bar) on the assize circuit or other section of the Bar in which they practise, notifying them of their application. Before the war—I think the custom has now lapsed—each barrister successful in his application left a special large visiting card, gilt-edged, at the town house of each of the judges, on the evening before his declaration to the Lord Chancellor. The new Q.C. presents his Chief Clerk with a new silk hat and morning clothes, or the equivalent in cash; his junior clerk receives a tip.

On the appointed day, the group of new Queen's Counsel don their velvet court suits, silk gowns and full-bottomed wigs for the first time and assemble at the House of Lords. There they pass one by one, in order of seniority, before the Lord Chancellor—who also robes, with full-bottomed wig—and make a formal declaration:

"I do declare that well and truly I will serve the Queen as one of Her Counsel learned in the Law and truly counsel the Queen in Her matters, when I shall be called, and duly and truly minister

the Queen's matters and sue the Queen's process after the course
of the Law, and after my cunning. For any matter against the
Queen where the Queen is a party save in so far as I may be
therein allowed or licensed I will take no wages or fee of any man.
I will duly in convenient time speed such matters as any person
shall have to do in the Law against the Queen as I may lawfully do,
without long delay, tracting or tarrying the Party of his lawful
process in that that to me belongeth. I will be attendant to the
Queen's matters when I be called thereto."

As each new Q.C. completes his declaration, his clerk—
resplendent in his new morning suit—is handed the letters
patent of appointment.

The next, and final, step in the debut of the new "silk" is his
formal "bowing-in" or admission within the bar of each court
at the Royal Courts of Justice in the Strand. The party of
wigged and gowned gentlemen who have made their declarations at the House of Lords go by car to the Law Courts, where
they form up in procession to visit each court in turn,
beginning with that of the Lord Chief Justice.

Whatever business is going on—no matter how important
the trial or appeal—is interrupted for a few minutes while this
ceremony is performed. Curiously it appears to date from not
earlier than the 19th century (according to Pulling), and
probably from the period when precedence began to be given
to Queen's Counsel irrespective of whether they were engaged
upon Crown business.

The little procession of new "silks" enters each court by one
of the swing doors at the back of the court, and halts just short
of the front row of counsel's seats. Once all the courts had little
gates separating this row "within the bar" from the seats for
junior counsel, solicitors and witnesses behind it. These gates
still exist in a few of the London courts.

As the court settles to a hush with the arrival of the
picturesquely-clad procession, the judge addresses the first in
line: "Mr. So-and-so, Her Majesty having been pleased to
appoint you one of her counsel learned in the law, will you
take your place within the bar?" The new Queen's Counsel
then moves into the front row, and bows first to the judge, then
to the other Q.C.s, and then to the junior barristers present.
Each returns the bow. Then the judge asks, in the ancient form,
"Mr. So-and-so, do you move?"—meaning, of course, have you

any motion to put to the court, since you now have precedence over the junior Bar to do so? Ordinarily such motions would be moved in the Divisional Court. On this occasion no reply is expected or given, though there is a classical story of a reply made, *sotto voce*, by Mr. John Harvey Murphy, a barrister of some bulk. To the question "Do you move, Mr. Murphy?" he murmured with literal accuracy "Not without difficulty, m'Lord." Normally the new Q.C. proceeds without more ado to bow himself out, as he came in, and his place is taken by the next in line. The procession of silks moves on to the other courts in turn, repeating the ceremony in each.

As there may be 15 or so new Q.C.s to be "bowed in," the business may take some minutes at each court. One judge, Lord Mersey, is said to have shortened things by asking "Do you, or any of you, move?" whereupon the entire line collectively bowed itself out. This, and the tale about Murphy, is told by C. P. Hawkes in his book "Chambers in the Temple."

The example of the late Lord Carson shows the importance attached to the performance of the ceremony, however. Carson, already a Queen's Counsel at the Irish Bar, moved his practice to England when he was elected to Parliament, and in 1894 applied to take silk in this country. (The patent of a Q.C. is applicable only to the country in whose courts he practises). His application was refused on the ground that he had only a year's standing at the English Bar—which at a later period would not have been a ground for refusal in the case of an M.P. Eventually Lord Herschell, the Lord Chancellor, yielded to persuasion and agreed to make Carson a Q.C., additionally to the group appointed when he had applied in the spring. So Carson went alone through the declaration ceremony and the bowing-in. Let Mr. Montgomery Hyde, in his biography of Carson (1953) take up the tale: "The last court which he visited was that of Mr. Justice Kekewich, a Chancery judge, whom he discovered had finished his work and risen for the day. Curiously enough the very first brief Carson had as an English Q.C. was in this very Court next morning. As Carson opened his case, the judge, who liked all the forms to be strictly observed, kept interrupting: "I can't hear you, Mr. Carson." Carson raised his voice, which eventually reached a shout. He said it had never been his experience in the past that his voice was not audible to the Bench. "Mr. Carson, you don't take my point," interposed the judge. "You have not been called within the Bar of my Court. But I don't propose to send you home to put on your knee-breeches, as perhaps I should." "I should hope *not*," said Carson. The judge sat up. "What's that? What's that you say?" he asked petulantly. "I warn you I shall tolerate no impertinence." Carson smiled. "I thought your Lordship could not hear me," he remarked pleasantly.

The costume of Queen's Counsel derives clearly from their connection with the Crown.

Their full dress, worn at the ceremony of declaration and admission to the inner bar and on other formal legal occasions, consists of a black velvet court suit—tail-coat and knee-breeches, lace stock and cuffs, black silk gown, full-bottomed wig and white gloves.

At royal Courts, State banquets and similar functions, Q.C.s appear simply in velvet court dress, with sword and court crush hat.

At levees, their dress is a black cloth court suit, lace stock and cuffs, black silk gown, full-bottomed wig.

When pleading in court the Queen's Counsel wears a court tail-coat of cloth, but trousers instead of knee-breeches, black silk gown, and bob-wig and bands similar to those of the junior Bar. By exception, Q.C.'s appearing in the House of Lords wear the full-bottomed wig. Frequently a "mourning" gown of stuff (see below) is worn in court, though strictly incorrect.

When the first two women were admitted to the inner bar in 1949, the court dress had to be altered for them, a skirt taking the place of knee-breeches and the coat being reshaped. One of the ladies lost no time in introducing a peculiarly feminine note. Only one set of lace stock and cuffs was available at the time, so Mrs. Helena Normanton, Q.C., made up her own from fine 17th century lace, worn at the court of Louis XVI. She unpicked it from a dress.

During Court mourning Queen's Counsel wear on ceremonial occasions a hemmed stock and cuffs with mourning bands (lawn, with a thin stripe down the middle) and (when not wearing gown) a crêpe band on the left arm. The gown worn at such periods is of a stuff material instead of silk. When pleading in court, white cuffs of muslin or linen known as "weepers" are worn over the sleeves of the coat and mourning bands.

The gown of Queen's Counsel differs considerably from that of the junior Bar. As well as being normally of silk, it is practically sleeveless, has a square-cut yoke or rudimentary hood at the back, and is without the traditional flaps of cloth attached to the junior barrister's gown.

The costume as a whole—court suit and gown—is said to date from the funeral of Queen Mary II in 1694, being reputedly the official Court mourning dress worn on that solemn occasion. (Some say the funeral of Queen Anne; there is a celebrated remark by the 19th century judge Sir Frederick Pollock that the Bench and Bar went into mourning at the death of Queen Anne and never came out again.) But in Michaelmas Term, 1697, Chief Justice Holt of the King's Bench told barristers he would hear them thenceforward only if they appeared "in their proper gowns and not in mourning ones." Before this period Queen's Counsel—what few there were—must undoubtedly have worn the gown adorned with velvet and tufts of silk used by all who had reached the degree of Reader of their Inn (see Chapter 2). It is curious that the gown which superseded this ancient costume should be one intended merely as a mourning garment, if indeed this is the case; and as a result actual mourning, such as at the death of the Sovereign, has to be shown nowadays in other ways. Perhaps the plain silk gown was simply found more convenient than the heavy tufted one; or perhaps the Q.C.s of this troubled period were specially anxious to leave no doubt about their connection with the royal Court. At any rate, from this time onwards the silk gown has been the distinctive costume of Queen's Counsel, who are now known to their colleagues as "silks," with the act of receiving such an appointment termed "taking silk."

THE ATTORNEY-GENERAL

By one of those curious paradoxes with which legal history abounds, "Mr. Attorney"—as he is addressed in court—is not an attorney (i.e., solicitor) at all, but a distinguished barrister. He is, in fact, the head of the Bar. He is the Government's chief legal adviser and appears for the Crown in cases of great importance.

E

The Attorney-General and his deputy, the Solicitor-General —known as the Law Officers of the Crown—are members of the Ministry though not (usually) of the Cabinet. Normally they are Members of Parliament; they are summoned to the House of Lords at the opening of each Parliament in an advisory capacity like that of the judges. They may also be summoned to the Lords at any other time to give their advice, though in practice this rarely occurs. One of the Law Officers must be present when any Standing Committee of the Commons is discussing the legal effect of a Bill. While in office they must not continue private practice.

The Attorney's official duties are many and varied. He is chief legal adviser to the Government. In cases of murder by poisoning it is customary for him to lead the prosecution personally : perhaps because of the difficulty of proof in such cases which was much greater before recent scientific advances. In a number of types of case his fiat (or permission) is needed before prosecutions can commence; and similar permission is needed for appeals from the Court of Criminal Appeal to go to the House of Lords. Only he can enter a "nolle prosequi"— "decline to prosecute"—after an indictment has been preferred. In civil cases his fiat is needed before certain actions may be brought; and he intervenes on behalf of the public in some matters including charity cases. In court the position of the Law Officers gives them a right to the "last word" or final reply.

As traditional head of the Bar the Attorney-General is the arbiter on points of etiquette concerning this branch of the profession.

The Attorney's title derives from a time when the "attornatus" was not a solicitor, or even a barrister, but simply anyone who represented another in an action at law. (Cf. the term "power of attorney" still used). At first the attorney was not a professional at all; gradually his duties develop until he has a clearly defined place in the legal world. Cohen ("A History of the English Bar," 1929) says : "Broadly it has been suggested that for an indefinite period the attornatus may do the whole of anyone's work in court and, of course, out of it, that in time he overlaps both the 'narrator' (pleader) and the 'serviens' (serjeant), sometimes doing their work and sometimes working with either of them and that finally he and the 'serviens' emerge as two parallel workers—the dual system, as we know it."

Long before the emergence of the dual system—solicitors and barristers—however, the Attorney-General's duties had become recognised. At first they must have been similar to those of the King's Serjeants, the serjeants particularly employed to act for the Crown. The first known mention of an "attornatus regis" is in 1280. About 1392-3, according to Cohen, the Government regularly retains and employs an attorney for the King.

Then in 1472 a certain William Husee was appointed Attorney-General of England, with power to appoint others to act for him in any of the main courts. From this time onwards there has been a single holder of the office known as the "general" attorney to distinguish him from the other royal attorneys then appointed for specific courts. The actual title "Attorney-General" in its present form grew up during the 16th century, the earliest example quoted in the Oxford English Dictionary being 1585. From 1673 the Attorneys have continuously sat in the House of Commons.

From the reign of James I until 1814 the Law Officers enjoyed precedence in court over all "except the two ancientest" of the King's Serjeants. Then in 1814 an Order in Council made Mr. Attorney head of the Bar (and incidentally marked another stage in the decline of the serjeants) by giving him and his deputy precedence over all the King's Serjeants. The Law Officers were "probably from the first," according to Pulling, made benchers of their Inns if they had not already attained that dignity.

The Attorney-General is appointed by letters patent, on the nomination of the Prime Minister. No qualification for the office is laid down by statute. He is customarily knighted, and if not already a Queen's Counsel he takes silk on his appointment.

His costume both in the courts and at State functions is that of Queen's Counsel, with a single exception. If, being a Cabinet minister (Sir Rufus Isaacs and Sir John Simon are probably the only examples) he "passes the royal presence" at palace courts, the Attorney-General wears on these occasions a black damask tufted gown and lace stock.

The tufted gown is a last survival of the old Reader's and

benchers' gown which was doubtless worn by the Law Officers until the adoption of the silk gown at the end of the 17th century (see above, under Queen's Counsel). A curious detail of dress is that—according to Norton-Kyshe, "The Law and Custom relating to Gloves" 1901—the Attorney-General wore gloves when in wig and gown, at any rate on State occasions such as Coronations, until "comparatively recent times."

The Attorney-General is one of the high officers who receives from the Corporation of London at each year's end a traditional $4\frac{1}{2}$ yards of "livery cloth." The "best black" cloth is selected by the General Purposes Committee of the Court of Aldermen in December. Recipients include, in addition to the Attorney-General, the Lord Chancellor, the Lord Chief Justice, the Master of the Rolls, the Lord Chamberlain and other officials of the royal household, the Solicitor-General, the Recorder, Chamberlain and Common Serjeant of London. The custom is of ancient, but uncertain, origin. It has been suggested that gifts of livery cloth were made in gratitude for an exception in favour of "guilds and fraternities and men of the mysteries of cities and boroughs" made in 14th and 15th century legislation directed against the number of liveried retainers of noblemen. This would scarcely explain the comprehensive list of recipients, nor the fact that such gifts are apparently confined to London. The true, and more general, explanation, is surely to be found in a statement in the City's "White Book" compiled in 1419 by the mayor, Richard Whittington, and the Common Clerk. The Book says "Seeing that it is quite impossible for the Barons and the body of citizens of London to do otherwise in Pleas of the Crown than pass through the hands of the King and his Justiciars, it is a matter of necessity that the Barons and all the citizens should court their favour and goodwill; by making ample presents to them, that is to say, and to their clerks. . . ."

Be this as it may, the recipients today find a ready use for their presents as material for black jackets.

THE SOLICITOR-GENERAL

The first Solicitor-General is said to be one Richard Fowler, appointed by letters patent of Edward IV in 1461 as "King's solicitor in all places within the Kingdom." His title derived from the fact that he dealt mainly with Chancery matters, in which solicitors were then especially employed.

Today he is invariably a barrister, not a solicitor, and his duties range outside purely Chancery business, being largely those of deputy to the Attorney-General. Since Elizabethan times the Solicitor-General has been a Member of the House of Commons (or in early days sometimes of the House of Lords). He is still appointed by letters patent, on the nomination of the Prime Minister, and is a member of the ministry. There is no statutory qualification for the position. He customarily receives a knighthood.

In dress the Solicitor-General conforms to the same rules as the Attorney-General, except that—never being a member of the Cabinet—he does not wear the tufted damask gown.

He is one of the high officers to whom the Corporation of London makes an annual present of "livery cloth." For this and some other details common to both the Law Officers, see under Attorney-General earlier in this chapter.

6. Solicitors

MANY people unconnected with the law may go through a lifetime without coming into contact with a barrister. Few do not at some time or another come across a solicitor. The solicitor draws up your will, sees to the legal side of your property transactions, prepares your case and instructs counsel if you become involved in litigation—and generally acts as adviser and confessor. The solicitor is so much a feature of local life, like the parson and the bank manager, that when most people speak of "a lawyer" it is to him that they refer. There are more than 18,000 solicitors, all over the country, compared with a mere handful of 2,000 practising barristers, almost all in London.

The two branches of the profession are entirely distinct, a system unknown outside Britain and the Commonwealth. This complete separation, enforced by Bar etiquette which frowns even upon "hob-nobbing" between individual solicitors and barristers, is not nowadays based on any "snob" system, though this may have been so in the past. It is simply considered best that barristers should not be thought in any way to tout for work, and that they should remain aloof and independent so as to be entirely impartial. There still remains an impression of "snob value" attaching to the Bar as a career compared with that of the solicitor, and this derives from the origin of the two branches.

The solicitor as we know him today does the work of two occupations of the past—those of the attorney and the solicitor —as well as a good deal of that once carried out by barristers.

At about the same period as professional advocacy came into being, in the 13th and 14th centuries, the right to be personally represented in an action by someone who was not himself involved, came to be recognised by the courts. At first the line of demarcation between counsel and attorney was indistinct, and the same lawyer might conduct the formal side of the case

—applying for writs and so on—as attorney and also plead in court. By about 1340 (according to Cohen, "A History of the English Bar," 1929) the two great branches were recognised as distinct. The attorney, unlike the serjeants and barristers, was (as the solicitor theoretically remains) regarded as an officer of the particular court to which he was attached.

"For a long time," said Lord Campbell in a celebrated case (Doe d. Bennett v. Hale, 1850), "the attorney only sued out process and did what was necessary in the offices of the Court for bringing the cause to trial and for having execution on the judgment." However, it has been remarked that even this was an important task because in the days when procedure was highly technical the slightest mistake might have disastrous effects on the client's case. As late as 1615 an order for the Inns of Court referred to "attorneys and solicitors which are but ministerial persons and of an inferior nature. . . ."

Solicitors, as distinct from attorneys, are first heard of in the 15th century. By the time they were mentioned in an Act of 1605, they were carrying out, in the Chancery court, the work which attorneys performed in the courts of Common Law. The interminable delays of Chancery proceedings, satirised at their ultimate height by Dickens in "Bleak House," offered plenty of scope for the hurrying along or "soliciting" from which solicitors are said to have derived their title. They were long considered inferior even to the attorneys, and they could not bind their clients as the attorneys could. There was not the same rigid control over the solicitors as there was over the attorneys. From the 18th century attorneys were often also solicitors.

Gradually the scope of the attorney's work increased, and with it no doubt his status and prosperity. The custom by which barristers may be instructed only by a solicitor, and not by a lay client direct, is of comparatively modern origin; it is still only a custom and not a rule of law, though invariably followed. Up to the early 1700's it was quite normal for counsel to be retained by the lay client, and for barristers to do all kinds of minor legal work.

"It was inevitable," says E. B. V. Christian ("A Short History of Solicitors," 1896) "that, when attorneys ceased to be ignorant of all but the nature of writs and the offices where they were issued, they should attain some share in giving advice, and that their opinion should often be followed without resorting to counsel at all. This had early been so in London; it must, one would think, have been even more the case in the country, where they alone were at hand to advise. The rules made under Elizabeth, James I and Charles I, probably ineffectual to restrain their growing importance, are undoubted evidence of the fact. By the time of the Stuarts their patronage was enough to give a young barrister opportunity to rise. Under the Georges they had come to advise and initiate as well as conduct legal proceedings, counsel merely drawing the pleadings and acting as advocates in court. . . . Before the middle of the eighteenth century the rule was so well established that the associated London attorneys felt able to protest against the acceptance by counsel of an irregular retainer, and obtained an apology." The question of counsel acting for a lay client has not been raised since 1850, when in the case mentioned earlier in this chapter, Doe d. Bennett v. Hale, Lord Campbell held that the practice still had not the force of law.

The Judicature Act, 1873, swept away the difference between attorneys and solicitors, just as it did in many ways that between the courts of Common Law and of Equity in which they had respectively practised. From this time all attorneys became known as solicitors, probably because solicitors had by this time come to enjoy a slightly greater prestige than their Common Law brethren.

Today the work of the solicitor includes a wide range of non-litigious matters such as conveyancing, the drawing up of wills and other documents, and giving legal advice on all kinds of matters at least in the first instance. In litigation, the solicitor not only engages counsel to plead the case in court, but himself takes all the preliminary formal steps, prepares the case, and may appear at interlocutory (preliminary) hearings in chambers. He may not himself appear as advocate except in a few courts in which solicitors specifically have a right of audience: notably the County Courts, magistrates' courts, and —if there is no barrister available—Quarter Sessions.

Other differences between the two branches of the profession today are that a solicitor unlike a barrister can sue for his fees, and may in turn be sued for negligence; he may enter a partnership, though a barrister may not; he is said to work in an office, not chambers.

The official title of solicitors is "Solicitor of the Supreme Court of Judicature in England," since they are still technically, as they once were in practice, officers of the court.

At first attorneys and solicitors shared membership of the Inns of Court with the barristers. But from the middle of the 16th century onwards the Inns waged a continual battle to keep them out. The barristers wanted to keep their privilege, and doubtless resented the growing importance of what they regarded as the inferior branch of the profession. The order of 1615 referred to above declared that "no common attorney or solicitor" should be admitted to any of the Inns "for that there ought always to be preserved a difference between a counsellor at law which is the principal person next unto Serjeants and Judges in the administration of Justice, and attorneys and Solicitors which are but ministerial persons and of an inferior nature."

The judges, in the second half of the 17th century, ordered that attorneys should be admitted to the Inns, because they realised the importance of the "ministerial persons" having fixed addresses within the responsible organisation of the Inns so that no dishonest member could disappear at the critical moment. However, the Inns won and to this day their rules lay down firmly that no solicitor may be admitted as a student or called to the Bar. It is, nevertheless, possible for a solicitor to leave his branch of the profession and enter the other, likewise a barrister may become a solicitor if he is first disbarred at his own request.

When solicitors and attorneys found themselves excluded from the ancient professional organisation of the Inns, they began to band together on their own. By 1739 there had arisen in London "The Society of Gentlemen Practisers in the Courts of Law and Equity"—the forerunner of the Law Society of today. Nowadays the majority of, but by no means all, solicitors are members of the Law Society, a body incorporated in 1848 by Royal Charter, for the protection of their own interests. And even those who are not members come to some extent under the influence of the Society, which is the instrument of the courts in registering solicitors and in disciplinary matters.

An entrant to this branch of the profession today must spend five years (three if a University graduate) as "articled clerk" to a practising solicitor. During this period, though termed a clerk, he is in fact an apprentice, and his articles of apprenticeship provide that his master must instruct him in the profession. In this respect his training more closely resembles the ancient system than does that of the barrister, for whom a term of pupillage is to some extent a work of supererogation. In addition the articled clerk—again unlike the Bar student of today—is required to attend a law school for a period. And before he can apply for "admission" as a solicitor he must pass examinations set by the Law Society.

In 1633 the Court of Common Pleas laid down six years as the period for which an applicant for admission as an attorney of the court must have served as attorney's clerk. But if the judges approved the candidate's education, that would do instead. In 1654, according to Christian (whose work is a chief source on this subject) a rule "of the Supreme Court at Westminster"—fixed the period as five years as clerk to a judge, serjeant, barrister, attorney or court official. A book published in 1676 gives a period of six or seven years, so probably no precise length of time was adhered to.

The rule of 1654 required the candidates to be examined by twelve "able and credible practisers." Christian says that some inquiry into the qualifications of would-be attorneys had in theory been required since 1292 (a statute of 1303-4 provided "that all the Attorneys shall be examined by the Justices"), but had not been enforced. Nor did the twelve-examiners system apparently last long. The modern rule of five-year articles entered into by contract was originated by an Act of 1729. This statute provided for judges to examine, but the examinations were not taken very seriously. The present scheme of examinations—again by an examining committee of twelve—began in 1836.

The candidate who has completed his articles and passed his examinations must apply to the Master of the Rolls, through the Law Society which acts as Registrar of Solicitors, for admission to the Roll of Solicitors. The Master of the Rolls' connection with this branch of the profession dates from the days when solicitors were officers of the Court of Chancery, in which he held (and still theoretically holds) a position second only to that of the Lord Chancellor (see Chapter 12).

The actual admission is signified in writing by the Master of the Rolls. The list of candidates to be admitted is screened in the Hall of the Law Society, in Chancery Lane, for three weeks before the month in which the admission is to take place, in the same way as with candidates for call to the Bar, so that any objections may be submitted. When the Master has formally admitted the candidate, the Law Society adds the name of the new solicitor to the Roll. (Notice that this has nothing to do with whether or not he becomes a member of the Society, which is entirely a matter of choice.)

Some sort of roll of attorneys was probably maintained from very early times by the courts to which they were attached. The Act of 1303-4 provided for a Roll to be kept. Compulsory enrolment was required by the Act of 1729, which at the same time permitted them to practise in courts other than that in which they had been sworn.

Nowadays there is even less ceremony attached to the admission of a solicitor than accompanies call to the Bar. In early times, however, attorneys were admitted in court, and could afterwards practise in that court. The admission was performed by the judges, and a law of 1322-3 forbade inferior officers of the court to carry out this function. In 1582 it was ordered that attorneys were to be admitted only once a year at a special meeting of the judges in Michaelmas term.

An oath had to be taken, and provision for one was made at least as early as the Act of 1303-4. That quoted in the "Book of Oaths" (1649—anonymous, but in fact compiled by a Jesuit, Fr. Richard Garnet) is a formidable document, and reads in part:

"You shall do no falsehood, nor consent to any to be done in the Court, and if you know of any to be done you shall give knowledge thereof unto my Lord Chief Justice, or other his Brethren, that it may be reformed; you shall delay no man for lucre or malice; you shall increase no Fees, but shall be contented with the old Fees accustomed; . . . ye shall not wittingly nor willingly sue, nor procure to be sued any false Suit, nor give aid nor consent to the same, in pain to be expulsed from the Court for ever; and furthermore you shall use yourself in the Office of an Attorney within the Court according to your Learning and discretion; so help you God. . . ."

The oath was administered by a protonotary (an official of the court).

The 1729 Act provided a short form of oath, virtually the same as the latter part of that quoted above : "I, ———, do swear that I will truly and honestly demean myself in the practice of an Attorney according to the best of my knowledge and ability. So help me God." This was abolished under the Promissory Oaths Act 1868.

Solicitors now wear a long black gown of "stuff" material, rather like that of the High Court ushers, with long hanging sleeves and a square rudimentary hood at the back. With the gown they wear bands (see Chapter 3)—but no wig. They robe only when appearing as advocates in courts where the judge is robed : the County Courts are the most usual case. As recently as 1950 the Law Society rejected by a large majority a proposal that solicitors should wear wigs in court, and full court dress for the Westminster Abbey service at the opening of the legal year. The gown and its usage seem to have been as at present for at least a century. The establishment of the County Court system in 1848, with its robed judges and its right of audience for solicitors as advocates, apparently caused a revival of a lapsed privilege among attorneys of wearing robes in court.

We know the dress of attorneys in the early 17th century from a portrait which forms the frontispiece of an edition, published in 1788, of a play performed before James I. The portrait shows a long gown, which appears to be made of dark cloth, with furred edges and sleeves. At the wrists are linen cuffs. The attorney wears a waistcoat, from which an inkhorn hangs, and breeches with stockings. His shoes are square-toed and adorned with rosettes. He has a big cloth cap with a wide brim and shaped, as Christian picturesquely puts it, like a sou'wester. A preface to the volume says that no trace of this costume—which Christian assumes to be accurately depicted in spite of the lapse of time— existed at that date, i.e., 1788.

Nowadays the brief-case might be said to be the solicitor's most characteristic luggage. But once, it seems, bags of black buckram were part of the attorney's equipment. These bags are mentioned in Elizabethan plays, and 'a buckram' was an accepted expression for these bags or even for a lawyer himself, according to Christian. The bags were used for the attorney's refreshments as well as his papers, it seems, and Christian gives the curious detail that, sandwiches not having been invented, sausages were the main portable food of the time! Later attorney's bags of green cloth were used, and "a green bag" accordingly became a synonym for an attorney." (Cf. bookbags used by barristers, Chapter 3).

Complaints of professional or other misbehaviour by solicitors come before the Law Society Disciplinary Committee, which holds an inquiry in public if necessary. The committee may recommend suspension or striking off the Roll, and in practice its decision is acted upon though in theory disciplinary power resides in the High Court and the Master of the Rolls. Appeal from the Disciplinary Committee lies to the Queen's Bench Divisional Court.

No doubt "striking off" was resorted to from the earliest times in which rolls were kept. In 1442 a judge of the Common Pleas fined an attorney for some professional offence, and ordered that his name should "be drawn from the roll of attornies." And in 1588 an attorney who forged a writ was ordered to be struck off the roll and "cast over the Barr"—i.e., the bar which marked off the court from the body of Westminster Hall—and also fined.

The present Law Society Disciplinary Committee was set up by statute in 1888; despite its name it is not strictly a committee of the Society. Before that disciplinary inquiries were held by one of the Masters of the court.

Although the solicitor has the right of audience only in a few, mostly lower, courts, he may nowadays practise otherwise in any court provided he is in possession of a valid practising certificate, to be obtained annually from the Law Society at a fee. This latter requirement is some 150 years old.

It should be added that the title Solicitor does not always imply a qualified member of this branch of the profession. The most important example is the Solicitor-General (see Chapter 5), who is invariably a barrister; but officials such as Solicitors to the Treasury need not necessarily be qualified, though in practice they almost always are.

7. My Lords the Queen's Justices

IT is no mean thing to be one of the judges of Her Majesty's High Court of Justice.

There is no other single post open to a commoner in which he receives the honours due to royalty; by virtue of which he is summoned to attend Coronations, the opening of Parliament and other State functions; from which he cannot be dismissed except by resolution of both Houses of Parliament, unless perhaps for serious misbehaviour; and in which the opportunity for serving the public long outlives him, for his decisions if they are wise may be quoted for centuries.

There is an old story which emphasizes in what a real sense a judge represents his Sovereign. At Liverpool late last century the two assize judges, Baron (this was the title given to judges of the old Court of Exchequer) Huddleston and Mr. Justice Manisty, were guests at an official banquet. When the Queen's health was proposed, Manisty stood up with the rest of the guests. His companion, it is said, did not rise, but tugged the other's sleeve, whispering "Sit down, Manisty, you ――― fool! We are the Queen."

At the same time so great a store is set by the independence of the judges that when National Insurance became compulsory on all a few years ago, it was decided that Judges should rank as self-employed persons! A judge, of course, does receive a salary and a pension from the State, and the salary had until lately remained unchanged for so long that a call to the Bench may involve considerable financial sacrifice to a barrister with a flourishing practice. These considerations are outside our scope, but it says a lot for the prestige of the High Court Bench that scarcely any member of the Bar would hesitate to accept a judgeship if it were offered him.

There have been judges in England almost as long as there have been kings to enforce justice. But the traditions of the Bench today may be said to go back to the early Middle Ages, when the various courts began to have an existence separate from the Curia Regis, or King's Council, which was the original medium for dispensing justice as well as for transacting State business of other kinds. Why are judges said to sit "on the Bench?" Because originally, in the days when the courts sat in Westminster Hall, part of the royal palace of Westminster, the judges did sit on benches. Nowadays chairs, first introduced by the Chancery judges, are used.

The High Court of Justice which we know today dates only from the late 19th century. Its structure was established by the Judicature Act, 1873, the climax of a series of piecemeal reforms of the entire judicial system, which had become rife with complications, delay and expensive procedures.

That Act set up a Supreme Court of Judicature, comprising a High Court of Justice and a Court of Appeal. The High Court was to consist of five Divisions: the Queen's Bench, Common Pleas, Exchequer, Chancery and Probate, Divorce and Admiralty Divisions. In 1881 the Common Pleas and Exchequer Divisions were merged in the Queen's (or King's) Bench Division.

To understand the historic pageantry of the High Court and its judges it is necessary to go back in history at least six centuries to notice the ancient courts whose mantle it has taken on.

The QUEEN'S BENCH DIVISION today deals mainly with Common Law cases—civil lawsuits based on the branches of law known as Contract and Tort. They include actions for breach of contract, for defamation, negligence, nuisance and many other wrongs. This Division is the successor of three historic Common Law courts. The first of these to take on an existence of its own was the

Court of Exchequer. Nowadays the Exchequer is associated for most of us exclusively with finance. As a financial department it became separated from the main King's Council as early as Henry I's reign (1100-35). Disputes naturally arose from time to time in the course of revenue collection, and by the mid-12th century a judicial side of the Exchequer had emerged for settling them. As time went on the court's jurisdiction extended to include a wide range of civil actions, originally through a fiction that a debt to the king was involved. The judges of the court were known as Barons of the Exchequer, and they were presided over by a Chief Baron.

Court of Common Pleas. Henry II appointed five judges to hear lawsuits between subject and subject, and in 1272 a separate Chief Justice was appointed for the Common Pleas. In this court the serjeants-at-law had exclusive right of audience, though ordinary barristers might plead in both the other Common Law courts. Although in theory the Common Pleas was the court by which all ordinary civil actions should have been tried, its jurisdiction was usurped by the other courts and it eventually declined because of its procedural disadvantages, and because of the necessity for briefing a serjeant in cases heard by it.

Court of King's Bench. This was the last of the Common Law courts to break away from the Council, at the end of the 14th century. Kings up to Henry IV actually sat as judges in this court; James I unsuccessfully claimed the right to do so. During the Middle Ages the court often followed the king in his travels. Probably because of its close association with the Crown, the King's Bench claimed for itself superiority over the other Common Law courts. Its jurisdiction, both civil and criminal (the latter has almost disappeared) originally comprised matters held to affect the rights of the king. In one way and another, the King's Bench gradually gained jurisdiction over civil cases which should have come before the Common Pleas judges. Its victory is now complete, in a sense, for its title survives when those of both its rivals are extinct.

The CHANCERY DIVISION is the successor of the old *Court of Chancery.* The medieval Lord Chancellors were both powerful officers of State and also, as Churchmen, "Keepers of the King's Conscience." The Common Law courts developed a rigid system, and hard cases arose in which justice could not be obtained from them. People who suffered in this way claimed relief from the King's Council, as the residual source of justice, and it fell to the Chancellor as the chief official to devise remedies to fit their cases (see Chapter 12). Gradually this judicial work became specialised. In 1474 the Chancellor is found for the first time making a decree apart from the Council, and before long the Chancery Court gained a separate existence. It developed its own system of law, known to us as Equity. It dealt, as its successor does today, with matters including trusts, mortgages, bankruptcy, partnership, and guardianship of infants.

After the Reformation the administration of estates passed gradually from the Church courts to Chancery.

The PROBATE, DIVORCE AND ADMIRALTY DIVISION seems to the layman to combine within its jurisdiction an odd miscellany of subjects. The key lies in the fact that Roman (or Civil) Law and Canon (or Church) Law, which have much in common, largely govern present law on these three diverse matters. Probate of wills and matrimonial law (divorce itself was unknown until the Reformation) came under special Church courts until well into the 19th century. Admiralty or nautical matters often depend on ancient laws based on the Roman system, which was known to most foreign sailors of the Middle Ages who would have been strangers to the Common Law system peculiar to England. A number of Admiralty courts sat to try this type of case.

Although the High Court is composed of three Divisions, each of which normally deals only with business of its own category, every High Court judge has power to deal with any case. This provision of the Judicature Act, 1873, ended the delays and complications which existed when there were many courts each with a separate restricted jurisdiction.

High Court judges are appointed by the Crown on the nomination of the Lord Chancellor. They must be barristers of ten years standing or more. The appointment is made by letters patent; apparently the form was once (in Henry III's time) by writ, a less formal method. The judges hold office—under the Act of Settlement, 1700—"during good behaviour," that is in practice until they wish to retire. Before 1700 their appointment was during the King's pleasure, sometimes an uncertain factor in times gone by. In most, if not all, circumstances a resolution of both Houses of Parliament would be necessary today to remove a judge from office.

Newly-appointed judges must, by the Promissory Oaths Acts, 1868 and 1871, take the oath of allegiance and the judicial oath in the presence of the Lord Chancellor. This is normally done at a private ceremony at the House of Lords. The oaths are as follows:

ALLEGIANCE: "I, ———, swear by Almighty God that I will be faithful and bear true allegiance to Her Majesty Queen Elizabeth II, her heirs and successors, according to law."

F

JUDICIAL: "I, ———— swear by Almighty God that I will well and truly serve our Sovereign Lady, Queen Elizabeth II, in the office of (Justice of Her Majesty's High Court of Justice), and I will do right to all manner of people after the laws and usages of this realm, without fear or favour, affection or ill-will."

Judges of the Queen's Bench Division are sworn in a second time before a Divisional Court, in which the Lord Chief Justice presides with two other Queen's Bench judges. (A Divisional Court is a survival of the custom for judges of the old Common Law courts to sit together "in banc" to try cases, instead of singly as is usual nowadays. It is empowered to deal with certain types of special and important cases). The senior of the two puisne (or ordinary) judges sits at the right of the Lord Chief Justice, and the junior on his left. Other judges who wish to attend to welcome their new "brother" stand on the bench dais in order of seniority.

Usually the ceremony takes place immediately after the new judge's first swearing-in before the Lord Chancellor. All present are robed. The new judge enters last, and stands beside the Lord Chief Justice. From a form handed him by the Master of the Crown Office—an official attached to the Queen's Bench Division —he reads the oaths, then appends his signature. The form is handed back to the Master, the new judge bows to the court and shakes hands with the Lord Chief Justice and other judges present.

It seems that it was once customary for the oath to be taken in the Court of Exchequer. Dugdale, the 17th century antiquary, says that in 1216-17 three special commissioners were sworn in the Exchequer, apparently before the Lord Treasurer. When the King's Bench judges were told to take their oaths there in 1307-8, "the record addeth, prout moris est" (for this is the custom).

In later times a new judge was sworn in and installed in his court at a combined ceremony. The students and barristers of his Inn accompanied him in procession to Westminster for the occasion. Dugdale gives details of the ceremonial with a reference to the 15th century judge Fortescue, but presumably as still observed in his own time. "The Lord Chancellor of England," he says, "shall enter into the Court, where the Justice is lacking, bringing with him the King's Letters Patents, and sitting in the midst of the Justices, causeth the Serjeant so elect to be brought in, to whom in the open Court he notifieth the King's pleasure touching the office of the Justice then void, and causeth the said Letters to be openly read, which done, the Master of the Rolls shall read before the same elect person the oath that he shall take; which when he hath sworn upon the Holy Gospel, the Lord Chancellor shall deliver unto him the King's Letters aforesaid, and the Lord Chief Justice of the Court shall assign unto him a place in the same, where he shall then place him, and that place shall he afterwards keep."

The oath was an elaborate affair. Its text is given in full in the anonymous "Book of Oaths" (1649), in which it is dated 1347. Part of it runs : "... and that ye shall do equal Law and Execution of Right, to all the King's Subjects Rich and Poor, without having regard to any person; And that ye shall not take by you, or by any other privily, ne appart any gift, or reward or Gold or of Silver, nor of any other thing, the which might turn you to profit. But if it be meat or drink, and that of little value, of any man, that shall have any Plea or Process hanging before you. . . . And that ye shall take no fees, as long as ye be Justice, nor Robe of any person, great or small in any case But of the king himself; And that ye shall not give any counsel or advice to any person great or small in any case, where the king is party. . . ." Barons of the Exchequer had a different oath proper to their office.

By the early 18th century the swearing-in had come to be carried out privately at the Lord Chancellor's house, and the Master of the Rolls no longer assisted. The custom of a public swearing-in before the Lord Chief Justice was apparently dropped and not revived until the appointment of Mr. Justice Kennedy in 1892. Nowadays the Lord Chancellor is not present at the public ceremony, so that to fulfil the statutory requirement that the oath be taken before him a separate swearing-in has to be held in private. The dual ceremonies apply only to Queen's Bench Division judges; others are sworn in privately only. The ancient form of oath was retained until 1868, when it was superseded under the Promissory Oaths Act, as were nearly all other old oaths applicable to judges and lawyers. All the old forms may be studied in full in the report of the Oaths Commission, 1867 (Parliamentary Papers 1867, XXXI).

Judges of the High Court are now invariably knighted on appointment. Dugdale finds instances of this honour as far back as the reign of Edward III (1327-77), when judges were made Knights Banneret, a rank which became extinct in the 17th century. While in office judges are entitled to the prefix "The Honourable," being formally referred to as "The Honourable Sir ——— ———, Knight, one of the Justices of Her Majesty's High Court of Justice." Since the 18th century they have been addressed in court as "My Lord" and "Your Lordship." In earlier times, from the 14th century, "Sir" was the customary form. High Court judges are informally addressed as "Mr. Justice So-and-so," and in law reports and other legal writings they are referred to as "So-and-so, J.," which is also the form of their official signature.

The judges of the High Court are summoned to assist at the opening of each Parliament, and may be called to the Lords at any time to advise—though in practice such occasions are rare. They were once required to sit on woolsacks during the session. Originally they may have sat and voted in the Upper House, and in any case some Knights Banneret were summoned as peers of Parliament. Since the 14th century the judges' summons has been "to treat and give counsel" only. Until 1345 they were sworn members of the King's Council.

There are now 39 judges of the High Court: 25 in the Queen's Bench Division; 7 in the Chancery Division; and 7 in the Probate, Divorce and Admiralty Division.

The number of judges of the three Common Law courts, now merged in the Queen's Bench Division, varied during the course of history, but for a long period up to the beginning of the 19th century each had a uniform three judges and a Chief Justice. The Lord Chancellor and the Master of the Rolls were the only Chancery judges until 1813, when the first Vice-Chancellor, predecessor of the present puisne judges of the Chancery Division, was appointed. The Probate, Divorce and Admiralty Division combines the jurisdiction of so many tribunals that no comparison of the number of judges can well be made.

During the early Middle Ages the Bench was recruited from the two classes which together held a monopoly of learning: the nobility and the Church. Although ecclesiastical authorities frowned on clerics acting as advocates in the civil courts (see Chapter 1), there was no similar restraint on their sitting as judges there. "Apparently mere noblemen disappear from the

Bench before the ecclesiastics," says Cohen ("A History of the English Bar," 1929). Gradually during the 13th century the clerical element also goes. "At first under Henry III there are many ... ecclesiastics, but before he dies the lay element among his judges 'is beginning to outweigh the ecclesiastical,' 'bishops no longer steadily sat in the law courts'; still, even under Edward I, 'not a few' judges were clerks. There is a sort of sensational transition. . . . By the end of Edward I's reign, perhaps, we may say that lay lawyers are solely left in possession of the lay courts."

By the time the great judge Fortescue wrote, about 1470, it was a firm rule (probably dating from considerably earlier) that the judges of the Common Pleas court were invariably chosen from among the serjeants-at-law who, it will be remembered, always had a monopoly of advocacy before this court. (Incidentally there is no known instance of a serjeant in Holy Orders). In time the practice was extended to both the other Common Law courts. However, when Coke wrote in the early 17th century some at least of the Barons of the Exchequer were not serjeants, though the Chief Baron was required to be. In later times all judges of the three courts were either chosen from among existing serjeants, or else made serjeants on appointment, on the nomination of the Lord Chief Justice and with the concurrence of the other judges. This rule lasted until 1877, when the Judicature Act of 1875 came into force—the death warrant of the serjeants' ancient order. A survival is the custom by which judges refer to each other as "my learned brother," for once all were brethren of the Order of the Coif.

Since the medieval Bench was recruited from the clergy and then from the serjeants-at-law, it is not surprising that judicial costume today has elements reminiscent of that worn by these two classes. In essentials the dress of the English judge has not changed since the 15th century.

The official wardrobe of the High Court judge comprises:

Robes. The judicial robe, of cloth, is not unlike a cassock in shape, with sleeves, a straight front fastening and a high neck without lapels. The deep cuffs are of white fur or of silk, and the front edges are trimmed with the same material for most of their length. Robes of this type were worn by the serjeants, and at the period when the Order of the Coif began there was little distinction between lay and clerical garments. Originally the robes were at least partly lined with fur, at first lambskin and later miniver (now called ermine). Early 16th century portraits show the lining barely visible at the end of the sleeve. The robe at this period and for some time after was much fuller than at present, more like a full-cut alb than a cassock. The lining gave place to a mere facing, with deep cuffs as if turned back to display the fur or silk, and a similar trimming at the front edges.

All High Court judges have a full dress or State robe of scarlet trimmed with ermine at cuffs and front edges, and also a gown— not robe, but of the pattern worn by Queen's Counsel (see Chapter 6)—of black silk, comparatively sleeveless. In addition, Queen's Bench Division judges have a black robe trimmed with ermine, one of scarlet trimmed with slate-coloured silk and one of violet trimmed with salmon-coloured silk. The two last are worn in summer to correspond with the scarlet-and-ermine and black-and-ermine worn in winter.

Scarlet was widely used as a judicial colour in medieval Europe. Inderwick ("The King's Peace," 1895) says the Venetian magistrates who formed the Council of Ten wore scarlet, and so apparently did the Florentine judges who tried Savonarola in 1495. The same writer adds that scarlet was a colour used by higher orders of clergy from whom judges would be drawn; but surely this is true only of Cardinals? Four illuminations (now in the Inner Temple library) of the time of Henry VI show the Court of Chancery and the three Common Law courts. The judges in all these courts are portrayed in scarlet robes lined with white fur. However, in early times there was considerable variation in colour. The violet robe now worn is said to date from the time of Edward I (1272-1307). During Richard II's reign, Common Law judges are seen receiving green cloth for their summer robes; and in Henry VI's reign the Chief Baron is found receiving violet cloth for a winter robe, and green for summer, while at the same time other Barons had violet for summer.

The Scarf or Stole of broad black silk is the next garment, in order of dressing. It hangs down like a preacher's scarf. One authority (Clinch, "English Costume," 1909) has suggested that like that garment it is derived from the ecclesiastical amice. This does not seem a very obvious derivation, for the amice is a rectangular piece of cloth; the judge's scarf is much more similar to the clerical stole and as such would be more likely to be adopted by laymen than would a purely eucharistic vestment such as the amice.

In Elizabethan times the scarf was "sometimes hung round the neck, stole fashion, when the mantle was dispensed with," according to Norris ("Costume and Fashion," Vol. 3, 1938). Certainly early portraits with mantle have no scarf, and the judges' Rules on dress made in 1635 (see below, p. 97) never refer to tippet, i.e., scarf, in the same costume as the mantle. Nowadays the scarf is always worn—surely an anomaly as the scarf would be unnecessary for warmth when the mantle was being worn.

The Casting-Hood. In its present form this garment is nothing like a hood, and is probably a mere relic of the strap by which the hood was attached. It is in fact a sash, a strip of scarlet cloth about five feet long and perhaps six inches wide at one end, tapering slightly towards the other. It is worn like the ribbon of an order of knighthood, from the right shoulder diagonally across to the waist at the left side. The judges' Rules on dress made in 1635 say that "by wearing the (Casting) Hood on the right side, and above the Tippet, was signified more temporal dignity; and by the Tippet on the left side only, the Judges did resemble Priests." The narrow end is worn to the front, the wider one behind.

A word must be said about the name of this garment. To those concerned with its day-to-day wear, such as judges' clerks, it is known colloquially as the "gun-case," a simple reference to its shape. Pressed for a more technical term, they will tell you it is the "tippet." Now there never was a more confusing word than this one, in this connection. "When I use a word," said Humpty Dumpty in "Alice Through the Looking-Glass," "it means just what I choose it to mean." And to different writers "tippet" means a hood, a scarf, or a sash (or casting-hood). Since judicial costume includes all three garments, obviously it is better not to employ the word at all. So we shall refer to the garment which is described above by its ancient and true identity of casting-hood.

There is a curious story that the casting-hood is an innovation of the late 19th century Lord Chief Justice, Lord Coleridge. However, it is clearly referred to in the 1635 Rules on judicial dress, and it seems certain that Coleridge's part in the matter was actually to enforce compliance with these Rules on the point. This was necessary because by the early 19th century a black silk gown had become customary for Nisi Prius (trial of civil actions). (The matter is discussed in Law Quarterly Review, 1946, 62/181, in an article by F. H. Newark from which this solution is taken).

The casting-hood is worn only when the hood proper is omitted—a rule (nowadays with one exception, the assize service, made for convenience) which becomes clear when the origin of the garment is considered.

The Girdle or Sash of broad black silk is worn over the ends of the scarf, and over the casting-hood when that is worn, and fastened with an imitation knot. It is said to correspond with the priest's girdle or cincture, and it is interesting that the ancient form of the judicial girdle does resemble much more nearly the cord-like ecclesiastical cincture. Portraits of Sir James Dyer, Chief Justice of the Common Pleas 1559-82 and of Sir John Popham, Chief Justice of the King's Bench 1592-1607, show what is apparently a narrow flat black girdle, knotted in front. Sir John Powell, a judge of the Common Pleas and later the King's Bench (1635-99), is shown in a portrait with a rounded and knotted girdle. And a statue of another King's Bench judge of the same name (d. 1713) in the Lady Chapel of Gloucester Cathedral, has a rounded girdle loosely knotted. (For an article on these girdles, see Law Quarterly Review, 1948, 64/205, by R. P. C-J).

On ceremonial occasions the black cap, when not being carried in the hand or worn, is tucked into the girdle.

The Hood is rather similar to an academic hood, and from the front view appears as a short shoulder-cape. In fact the garment does consist of such a cape, with a hood thrown back behind. A strip of cloth, about three feet long and four inches wide, hangs down from the hood itself, a relic of the strap by which it was fastened. A hood is not worn with a casting-hood, apart from the single exception mentioned above.

It may well be that Pulling ("The Order of the Coif," 1884) is right in saying that apparently the cape "like its Spanish original, was at first a short cloak worn quite separate from the robe, but in course of time made to form a part of the dress of the order." The same authority finds references to the "furred cape" in Piers Plowman, Chaucer and other 14th century writers.

All High Court judges have a scarlet and ermine hood as part of their full dress; in addition Queen's Bench Division judges have a hood of black and ermine, and corresponding summer hoods of scarlet and violet trimmed with silk instead of fur.

The Mantle, used only on State occasions, is worn over the cape portion of the hood, with the headpiece of the hood thrown back over it. It is a short cloak of scarlet cloth, partly lined with ermine (there is a corresponding silk-lined garment for summer wear). The lining is folded back so that to the observer the mantle appears to be reversed, i.e., with ermine outside.

In former days, when the courts sat in Westminster Hall, judges wore the mantle on the Bench, no doubt finding it a necessary protection against the cold. The judges' rules on dress of 1635 provide for that.

Cloaks shown in early portraits are much longer than the short cape-mantle at present in use. The corners of the mantle are fastened at the throat. Fortescue, the 15th century judge, wrote that after a serjeant was made a judge he "shall be habited with a cloak fastened upon his right shoulder." In many pictures and monuments down to the 17th century this right-hand fastening is shown, as the late Sir Frank MacKinnon noted in an article in Law Quarterly Review, 1945 (60/31). Of two portraits of Sir Edward Coke in the Inner Temple, he says, one shows the earlier method of fastening and the other the later one. A portrait of Sir James Dyer (Chief Justice of the Common Pleas, 1559-82) shows a centre fastening, however. It is hard to understand the reason for the different usages and, as MacKinnon says, the centre fastening is in accord with (what he presumes to be) the mantle's origin as a cope.

Bands of plain lawn, similar to those of the Bar. During Court mourning, special mourning bands are worn. For the origin and further description of the bands, the reader is referred to Chapter 3, where the subject is discussed under Barristers. In the earliest portraits of judges the robe fits closely round the neck, and there is no "neck-wear." During the Elizabethan and early Stuart periods the ruff was worn. A broad lace collar followed, and was succeeded by a plain version. Van Dyk's portrait of Lord Keeper Lyttelton (1641-3) shows an early example of the falling collar worn during the Commonwealth period. This was followed by bands, at first broad as they developed from the mid-17th century collar. They have been retained from that period to the present day.

Court suits of black velvet and of cloth. The ceremonial suit of velvet is worn by all judges as part of full dress, and also on certain royal Court occasions, with lace stock and cuffs. Judges of the Chancery and Probate, Divorce and Admiralty Divisions wear a cloth court coat with their black silk gown when sitting on the bench. During Court mourning judges of these two Divisions wear weepers—mourning cuffs of muslin—over the sleeves of their court coats.

Wigs. Judges, like Queen's Counsel, have a full-bottomed wig for State occasions. Until about 1850 this wig was always worn when trying crime. For day-to-day wear on the Bench judges wear a short tye-wig. This differs from the one worn by barristers in that it has only one curl—a vertical one just over the tail of the wig. On the crown is a small bare patch.

The judicial wig, like the barrister's wig, came into vogue in the late 17th and early 18th centuries. As late as the time of Sir John Powell, a Queen's Bench judge who died in 1713, it was not invariably worn for his statue in the Lady Chapel of Gloucester Cathedral shows him in skull-cap but no wig. During the second half of the 17th century the heavy, flowing periwig had been adopted by judges, who wore it over the coif, the close-fitting white cap which was the distinctive badge of the serjeants. One of the earliest examples, perhaps, is provided by Sir Cresswell Levinz, a Common Pleas judge until 1686. Soon after the accession of George II (1727) men began to tie their hair back into queues, and from this developed the tye-wig now worn on the Bench as well as the curled wig now worn by barristers. The judges and Queen's Counsel retained the full-bottomed wig—a white curled type replaced the periwig—for formal occasions. In this they were at first following fashion, for a full-bottomed wig was worn generally on important occasions considerably after it was given up for everyday wear.

When wigs were abandoned by the majority of men they were retained by Bench and Bar. The main change in legal wigs during the past century and a half has been a gradual reduction in size, particularly in the tye-wig and barrister's curled wig. Both of these were much fuller or more "bushy" in the early 1800's.

Lord Eldon (Chief Justice of the Common Pleas 1799-1801 and

Lord Chancellor 1801-6 and 1807-27) found it necessary to seek permission from the king to appear with his own hair when not sitting in court. He made this request to please Lady Eldon, according to Croake James ("Curiosities of Law and Lawyers," c.1880). Eldon pointed out to the Sovereign (which king is not stated) that "so lately as the reigns of James I and Charles I, judicial wigs were unknown." "True," replied the king, "I admit the correctness of your statement and am willing, if you like it that you should do as they did; for though they certainly had no wigs, yet they wore long beards."

The bare patch on the crown of the judicial wig is not a representation of a tonsure, but an ingenious idea devised to get over the problem of combining in a dignified way the wig fashion with the necessity for serjeants to wear their coif. In the patch was affixed a little circle of white lawn to represent the coif. In the case of judges at least, it was necessary also to indicate the black velvet skull cap which they still wore at the beginning of the wig period. This was done by superimposing a small black circle on the white one. Judges appointed after the Judicature Act, 1875, were no longer serjeants (apart from those who had become so previously) and the patch system was no longer needed, though the bare place on the wig has been retained.

The well-known story which illustrates this point concerns Mr. Baron Bramwell, an Exchequer judge, and Mr. Justice Hawkins. A prisoner wishing to distinguish between them referred to the Baron—a serjeant—as the "one with the sore 'ead." The last of the judges who "suffered" in this way was Lord Lindley, who died in 1921. He was also the last surviving English serjeant.

The Black Cap, a square cap of limp black cloth, is worn corner-wise. A flap of material similar to part of the headpiece of a 'mortar-board' (which the judicial cap rather resembles) resting at the back of the head. The black cap is part of the judges' full dress and is either worn or carried on all solemn occasions. The passing of the death sentence happens merely to be the most publicised of these occasions. It is not with any intention of creating a macabre effect that the cap is used at the climax of a murder trial; nor is the fact that it is black anything more than fortuitous!

At the death sentence the cap is not, strictly speaking, worn :

it is merely laid on top of the wig. It is actually worn on one occasion only—at the reception of the Lord Mayor of London in the Lord Chief Justice's Court when he comes to be sworn on November 9 (see Chapter 14). Judges carry the cap in their hand when attending the opening of Parliament, when going to and from court for trial of criminal cases, and when attending church. Sometimes the cap is tucked into the girdle.

The judges' Rules on dress made in 1635 give the following occasions on which the "cornered cap" shall be worn: when sitting at Westminster in term time; on circuit, when the judges are attending church on Sundays and at the reading of the commission; when attending St. Paul's Cathedral, during the sermon. No other occasion—not even the swearing-in of the Lord Mayor —is mentioned as one on which the cap must be worn.

The black cap dates from Tudor times, and was once customarily worn much more often than is now the case (cf. the Rules quoted above). Its use probably became restricted with the advent of the judicial wig. The cap, like the 'mortar-board', is a development of the biretta, the medieval academic cap. One of the earliest examples of its wear by a judge is shown in the portrait of Sir John More (d. 1530), the judge and father of Sir Thomas More, in the family group painting in the National Portrait Gallery.

Various suggestions have been made to explain the assumption of the black cap during the death sentence. Pulling ("Order of the Coif," 1884) refers to the cap as "the covering expressly assigned to veil the coif on the only occasion when the coif was required to be hidden," and says "the head of the administrator of justice was then covered or veiled as a token of sorrow by the black sentence cap." Quoting from the Bible (2 Sam. xv 30, xix 4; Jeremiah xiii 3-4; Esther vi 12), Pulling says that covering the head in token of mourning is a usage of great antiquity. This theory was supported by Lord Chief Justice Goddard when he gave evidence before the Royal Commission on Capital Punishment, 1949-53.

There is a simpler explanation, namely that the black cap is worn as official headgear by a representative of the Crown when performing a solemn duty with all the authority of his office. This view was upheld with regard to Scottish usage by the Lord Justice General in his evidence to the Royal Commission.

Perhaps the true answer lies in a combination of both theories.

During the period when the operation of the death penalty was suspended while the Criminal Justice Bill was before Parliament in 1948, the judges omitted to don the black cap although the death sentence was still pronounced. Its use was resumed when the Bill was passed without the clause which would have suspended the death penalty for a further five years. The use of the black cap when passing the death sentence was considered by the Royal Commission to be a matter which "may well be left to the discretion of individual judges."

The black cap has always been a formal headgear, its use being restricted in former times to those of academic standing such as judges and university graduates, in distinction to the round cap worn by mere students and apprentices. (See Chapter 2). On less formal occasions, and perhaps for day-to-day wear on the circuit Bench, the judges frequently wore a black velvet skull-cap. It was worn over the close-fitting coif, and was apparently retained even on occasions requiring the square black cap; which was then worn over both skull-cap and coif. The judges' Rules on dress made in 1635 say that when sitting at Westminster in term-time they are to wear "their Velvet Caps, and Coifs of Lawn, and cornered Caps."

The skull-cap was perhaps introduced during the 16th century; it lasted through the 17th, and is illustrated as late as the contemporary statue in Gloucester Cathedral of Sir John Powell, a Queen's Bench judge who died in 1713.

The adoption of the wig and tricorne hat were doubtless responsible for the use of the cornered cap becoming restricted, and the total disappearance of the skull-cap.

The Three-cornered Hat (tricorne) is worn by High Court judges today on only one occasion: the opening of an assize. During the reading of the assize commission, the judge bows when his name is mentioned, and covers his head with the three-cornered hat. Both the judge "in commission" (see Chapter 9) and his colleague carry the hat with their gloves in the opening procession, but the Nisi Prius (civil business) judge does not take his hat into court. Until recently the tricorne was carried (instead of the black cap) at the Westminster Abbey service for the opening of the legal year.

The tricorne hat was introduced from France at about the

same time as the wig: towards the end of the 17th century. It was generally worn in England during the whole of the 18th century. Its retention by the judges, like that of the wig, is doubtless due to a combination of factors—the tendency for a fashion to continue in use for formal occasions after it has been abandoned for everyday wear (the top hat is a modern example); the fact that judges are often elderly men whose habits of dress may have survived from their youth; and the natural conservatism of the legal profession.

In an 18th century picture of Westminster Hall on the first day of term, the judges are shown with tricorne hats over their full-bottomed wigs. It has been suggested that the tricorne was being worn in place of the black cap, to conform with the provision in the Rules of 1635 that the judges should wear the cornered cap when sitting at Westminster.

White kid gloves are carried on ceremonial occasions.

In Anglo-Saxon times judges were forbidden to wear gloves on the Bench—possibly because gloves, sometimes containing money, were a recognised form of bribe in the Middle Ages. Later gloves were customary court fees (see Chapter 9). In the engraving by Hollar of Charles II's Coronation procession, one of the judges is shown wearing gloves fringed at the cuffs. S. W. Beck ("Gloves, their annals and associations," 1885) notes this and also that portraits of the judges of the same reign in Guildhall, London, show them with fringed and embroidered gloves.

Now that we have looked at the separate items of His Lordship's wardrobe, we can notice the differing combinations of them prescribed by tradition.

For State and Court occasions the judges of the three Divisions of the High Court wear costume common to them all.

Their *State or full dress* consists of black velvet court suit, scarlet robe trimmed with ermine, ermine-lined scarlet mantle, scarlet hood trimmed with ermine, scarf, girdle, plain bands, full-bottomed wig, black cap, three-cornered hat, white gloves.

The occasions on which this costume is used include the opening of Parliament, services at St. Paul's Cathedral, the Lord Mayor's Day banquet at the Guildhall, London; and the Westminster Abbey service and Lord Chancellor's Breakfast at the opening of the legal year (first day of Michaelmas Term). Judges of the Queen's Bench Division also wear it upon certain other occasions peculiar to themselves, which will be noted later.

The costume is historically that of the Common Law judges, and it has come to be used by judges of the Chancery and Probate, Divorce and Admiralty Divisions only recently—perhaps as a result of the intention embodied in the Judicature Act, 1873, that all should share in circuit work. As late as the end of the 19th century judges of these Divisions attended the ceremonies at the opening of the legal year in black silk gowns.

At royal Courts, State banquets, Court balls and Mansion House dinners, High Court judges wear a velvet court suit, lace stock and cuffs, cocked hat (no wig) and sword. *At Levees* they wear a cloth court suit, lace stock and cuffs, black silk gown, full-bottomed wig, three-cornered hat and sword. *At Drawing-rooms and special Courts,* the prescribed costume is a court suit with tufted black damask gown and cocked hat (no wig).

On occasions other than those so far mentioned the judges' costume differs according to the Division of the High Court.

QUEEN'S BENCH DIVISION judges wear during Michaelmas and Hilary (the two winter) terms:

When trying criminal cases; when trying civil cases on Red Letter Days: Scarlet robe trimmed with ermine; scarf; casting-hood; girdle; bands; tye-wig. Gloves and black cap are carried when trying crime.

The Red Letter Days at present (1954) observed are: Jan. 25, Conversion of St. Paul; Feb. 2, Purification of the Blessed Virgin Mary; Feb. 6, Accession Day; Feb. 24, St. Matthias; (moveable) Ash Wednesday; Mar. 25, Annunciation of the B.V.M.; April 21, Queen's Birthday; April 25, St. Mark; May 1, St. Philip and St. James; (moveable) Ascension Day; (moveable) Holy Thursday; June (moveable) the Queen's Official Birthday; June 2, Coronation Day; June 10, Duke of Edinburgh's Birthday; June 11, St. Barnabas; June 24, St. John the Baptist; June 29, St. Peter and St. Paul; July 25, St. James; August 4, Queen Mother's Birthday; Oct. 18, St. Luke; Oct. 28, St. Simon and St. Jude; Nov. 1, All Saints; Nov. 9, Lord Mayor's Day; Nov. 14, Duke of Cornwall's Birthday; Nov. 30, St. Andrew; Dec. 21, St. Thomas.

When sitting in the Court of Criminal Appeal and the Courts-Martial Appeal Court: as last, but hood instead of casting-hood.

When attending assize service and opening assize commission: Full dress, with the following exceptions: The judge "in commission" (see Chapter 9) wears both hood and casting-hood —technically incorrect, but done for convenience because the hood is required as part of full dress and can be dispensed with when criminal trials begin immediately afterwards. The ermine-lined mantle is worn only when the assize service is held in a cathedral or in the University churches of Oxford and Cambridge.

At Nisi Prius (civil cases) except on Red Letter Days: Black robe trimmed with ermine, scarf; scarlet casting-hood; girdle, bands, tye-wig.

When sitting in a Queen's Bench Divisional Court: As last, but black hood trimmed with ermine instead of the casting-hood.

At the swearing-in of the Lord Mayor of London: Full dress.

At the nomination of county sheriffs: As at Nisi Prius.

During Easter and Trinity terms the order of dress for the various occasions (the last two mentioned, of course, occur only in Michaelmas term) is the same except that "summer" robes and mantle are substituted. The scarlet robe and hood are trimmed with slate-coloured silk instead of ermine. Lord Chief Justice Coleridge (1880-94) introduced trimmings of salmon-pink (as worn with the Nisi Prius robes, see below), but this seems to have been frowned upon and abandoned. The mantle is of silk. The Nisi Prius robe is of violet instead of black, and trimmed with salmon-coloured silk.

CHANCERY DIVISION and PROBATE, DIVORCE AND ADMIRALTY DIVISION judges wear, when sitting in court, a black silk gown similar to that of Queen's Counsel, over a cloth court coat and trousers, bands, and tye-wig.

During Court mourning judges of these two Divisions wear, in addition to mourning bands, "weepers"—muslin cuffs—over the sleeves of their court jackets.

The costume of the Common Law judges—represented today by those of the Queen's Bench Division—has remained unaltered in essentials since at least the 15th century. With minor differences, it is also that of the serjeants-at-law, from whose ranks the judges were long chosen. In some respects there is an apparent resemblance to clerical dress. But it must be remembered that in the days when clergy sat on the lay Bench there was not a great difference between their costume and that of laymen of a corresponding class.

Monumental brasses form the earliest source for knowledge of medieval judicial costume. The dress of 14th and 15th century judges as shown on brasses is described by Muriel Clayton ("Catalogue of Rubbings of Brasses, Victoria and Albert Museum," 1929): "They wear a long plain gown reaching to the ankles, a long mantle lined with minever, fastened on the right shoulder and caught up over the left arm, and a hood." This is illustrated in the brasses of Sir John Cassy, Chief Baron of the Exchequer, 1400 (Deerhurst, Glouc.) and Sir John Juyn, Chief Justice of the King's Bench, 1439 (St. Mary Redcliffe, Bristol). The brass of Sir William Laken, a King's Bench judge, 1475 (Bray, Berks.) shows him with a belted gown, rosary and dagger-sheath.

The next important source is a series of four illuminations now in the Inner Temple Library, believed to date from about 1450 and to represent the three Common Law courts and the Court of Chancery. In the King's Bench court are five judges, all wearing scarlet robes, trimmed and lined with white, probably white fur. All of them wear the coif. The seven judges of the Common Pleas court are similarly dressed. In the Exchequer court the presiding judge wears scarlet robes and a scarlet hat over the coif; on each side of him sit two others—presumably Barons, i.e., judges—wearing mustard-colour robes and hats. The Chancery court has two judges in scarlet robes trimmed with white fur; one is bare-headed and tonsured, the other has a brown cap. These are taken to be the Lord Chancellor and the Master of the Rolls.

The great medieval judge Sir John Fortescue (Chief Justice of the King's Bench 1442) described the robes regularly worn by judges and serjeants as the coif, the long robe, with a furred cape, and a hood. A serjeant made a judge must wear a cloak closed on the right shoulder instead of a hood; he must not wear parti-coloured robes (as the serjeants usually did in those days), and his fur must be minever instead of lamb.

A group of serjeants called to that degree in October, 1555, each subscribed for a robe of scarlet, one of violet, one of brown-blue, and a fourth of mustard and murrey.

Coke, who wrote early in the 17th century, pointed out that he had known Barons of the Exchequer who were not serjeants and who wore the dress of apprentices of the law, i.e., barristers.

In 1635 all the judges of the courts at Westminster—that is,

the King's Bench, Common Pleas and Exchequer—met and made
a series of rules on dress to be observed by them all in future.
These Rules are worth giving at length because they illustrate
how little change in judicial costume has occurred since that
date.

"The Judges in Term time are to sit at Westminster in the
Courts in their Black or Violet Gowns, whether they will, and a
Hood of the same colour put over their heads and their Mantles
above all; the end of the Hood hanging over behind; wearing
their Velvet Caps, and Coifs of Lawn, and cornered Caps.

"The facing of their Gowns, Hoods and Mantles, is with
changeable Taffeta; which they must begin to wear upon Ascension Day, being the last Thursday in Easter Term; and continue
those Robes until the Feast of St. Simon and St. Jude; And upon
Simon and Jude's day the Judges begin to wear their Robes faced
with white furs of Minever; and so continue that facing till
Ascension Day again.

"Upon all Holy days which fall in the Term, and are Hall days,
the Judges sit in Scarlet faced with Taffeta, when Taffeta facing
is to be worn; and with Furs of Minever, when Furs and Minever
are to be worn.

"Upon the day when the Lord Mayor of London comes to
Westminster to take his oath, that day the Judges come in
Scarlet. And upon the fifth of November (being Gunpowder Day)
unless it be Sunday the Judges go to Westminster Abbey in
Scarlet to hear the Sermon; and after go to sit in Court. . . .

"When the Judges go to Pauls to the Sermon, upon any Sunday
in the Term time, or to any other public Church, they ought to
go in Scarlet Gowns . . . and . . . in Taffeta Tippets; and then the
Scarlet Casting Hood is worn on the right side, above the Tippet,
and the [Casting?] Hood is to be pinned abroad towards the left
shoulder. . . .

"At all times, when the Judges go to the Council-Table, or to
any assembly of the Lords; in the Afternoons in Term time, they
ought to go in their Robes of Violet, or Black, faced with Taffeta,
according as the time of wearing them doth require: and with
Tippets and Scarlet Casting-Hoods, pinned near the left Shoulder
unless it be a Sunday, or Holy day, and then in Scarlet.

"In the Circuit the Judges go to the Church upon Sundays, in
the foreNoon in Scarlet Gowns, Hoods and Mantles, and sit in

their Caps. And in the afterNoons to the Church in Scarlet Gowns, Tippet and Scarlet Hood, and sit in their cornered Caps.

"And the first Morning at the reading of the Commissions, they sit in Scarlet Gowns, with Hoods and Mantles and in their Coifs and cornered Caps. And he that gives the charge, and delivers the Gaol, doth, or ought for the most part, to continue all that Assizes the same Robes, Scarlet Gown, Hood and Mantle. But the other Judge, who sits upon the Nisi prius, doth commonly (if he will) sit only in his Scarlet Robe, with Tippet and Casting-hood: or if it be cold he may sit in Gown, and Hood and Mantle.

"And where the Judges in Circuit go to dine with the Sheriff or to a public Feast, then in Scarlet Gowns, Tippets and Scarlet Hoods, or casting off their Mantle, they keep on their other Hood.

"The Scarlet Casting-Hood is to be put above the Tippet, on the right side; for Justice Walmesley, and Justice Warburton [two late 16th century judges], and all the Judges before, did wear them in that manner; and did declare that by wearing the Hood on the right side, and above the Tippet, was signified more temporal dignity; and by the Tippet on the left side only, the Judges did resemble Priests. Whensoever the Judges, or any of them are appointed to attend the King's majesty, they go in Scarlet Gowns, Tippets, and Scarlet Casting-Hoods; either to his own presence, or the Council Table. . . .

"Also the first Sunday of every Term and when the Judges and Serjeants dine at my Lord Mayor's, or the Sheriff's, they are to wear their Scarlets, and to sit at Pauls with their Caps at the Sermon.

"When the Judges go to any Reader's Feast, they go upon the Sunday or Holy Day in Scarlet; upon other days in Violet, with Scarlet Casting-Hoods, and the Serjeants go in Violet, with Scarlet Hoods.

"When the Judges sit upon Nisi Prius in Westminster, or in London, they go in Violet Gowns, and Scarlet Casting-Hoods and Tippets, upon Holy Days in Scarlet."

The main changes since 1635 appear to be these: The black and violet robes are now fixed as winter/summer alternatives, instead of being worn at choice. Mantles are not now worn in court, for a centrally-heated Law Courts building has replaced the chilly Westminster Hall of the 17th century. The skull-cap and the coif have disappeared, and the black cap is not now worn in court on ordinary occasions, nor in church. The casting-hood, which in 1635 was at least enough of a hood to be "pinned near the left shoulder," has become a mere symbol. The wig, the three-cornered hat, and the bands have become part of judicial costume; so has the court suit.

From at least the early 19th century until 1870 or later a black silk gown was used when sitting in Nisi Prius.

The black gown worn by Chancery Division judges may have been adopted for day-to-day wear by the Lord Chancellors when it came into use as a Court gown at the end of the 17th century (but see Chapter 12). In the case of the judges of the Probate, Divorce and Admiralty Division, it was no doubt adopted when the Division was formed because no more distinctive robe was available, the academic gowns of the ecclesiastical judges being no longer appropriate.

Judges use a green book- or robe-bag in distinction to the blue or red bags used by members of the Bar. It is said that green bags were once used by Bench and Bar alike, but that they became unpopular at the "trial" of Queen Caroline in 1820. Was it perhaps the case that important evidence against the Queen, who held much sympathy, was ostentatiously produced from such a bag?

The Admiralty Oar, a symbolic oar of silver, rests on brackets in front of the desk of the judge sitting in Admiralty, into whose court it is carried by the Admiralty Marshal. In the Law Courts procession at the opening of the legal year it is carried before the President of the Probate, Divorce and Admiralty Division. It used to be carried by the Admiralty Marshal when he led the procession at the execution of pirates.

The use of this emblem is of considerable antiquity, and its origin is unknown. The oar now in use is just under three feet long, with a foot-long paddle-shaped blade. One mark upon it may date from the reign of Edward III (1327-77). On the front of the blade in relief are the arms of Henry VII, and below them those of William IV, the last Lord High Admiral. On the lower end of the oar is a knob or button on which is engraved the Admiralty anchor, and the name "Jasper Swift Marshal of the Admiralty" (who held office about 1585). The date of the oar as it now exists is given by Jewitt and St. John Hope ("The Corporation Plate, etc., of England and Wales," 1895) as 1798-9. The blade, they consider, probably dates from 1660.

The oar was used in the old Court of Admiralty, which sat in Doctors' Commons, until the Judicature Act of 1873, which established the present High Court. Similar oars, used in former colonial "Vice-Admiralty" courts, are preserved in Bermuda, Boston (Mass.) and New York. There is also an oar in Jamaica.

8. *The Sheriff and His Men*

WHEN Queen Elizabeth II came to the throne one of her first official acts, appropriately enough, was to choose the High Sheriffs of her English and Welsh counties by marking a list with the most womanly of tools—a bodkin.

For everyone today who has distantly heard of this curious ceremony of "Pricking the Sheriffs," there are probably ten whose mental image of such an officer is connected with Robin Hood or (more likely) with the gentleman who guards law and order in the Wild West aided by a six-shooter and something called a "posse." At a recent assize, indeed, the sheriff who had turned out in all his glory to escort Her Majesty's judges heard this comment by a small onlooker "Garn, 'e ain't no sheriff— where's his gun!" The truth is that the sheriff, who bears perhaps the oldest official title in the kingdom and was once its most important official outside the central government, has been sadly eclipsed.

The title itself is derived from the Anglo-Saxon "shirereeve," meaning governor of the shire. And that is just what the sheriff was, from pre-Conquest times until well on in the Middle Ages. He was the King's representative in the county, executed court writs, collected royal rents and taxes, and was charged with maintaining the peace. Prisoners were in his care. He was judge in two courts of his own, one criminal and one civil.

Even before justices of the peace were first appointed in the 14th century the sheriff's criminal jurisdiction had begun to be transferred elsewhere, and it had lapsed altogether by the 17th century. His civil court sits occasionally even today for various special purposes, usually to assess damages in some action decided in the High Court. He still has supervision over capital punishment within his county and is responsible for executing certain writs for putting into effect judgments of the High Court. He is returning officer at elections.

Most of his old duties have not been abolished, but have

merely fallen into disuse. Up to 1938 he could take steps to have a man "outlawed," and thereafter summon his "posse"—that is, you and me and everyone else in the county—to chase the outlaw with a view to his punishment, as happened with Robin Hood until that gentleman turned the tables on the high sheriff of Nottinghamshire.

Among the chief duties of the sheriff are those connected with the assizes for his county. He is responsible for the summoning juries for the assize courts and providing of facilities for the assize business, and is also master of ceremonies and a chief participant in the pageantry which takes place during the judges' visit. The sheriff is personal host to the judges while they are within his territory. Within his county the high sheriff takes first place, having precedence over any nobleman there.

In all this we have been writing of the high sheriffs of the English and Welsh counties. Cambridge and Huntingdon share one sheriff, appointed in turn triennially from these two counties and the Isle of Ely. In Scotland the sheriff is a much more active functionary than his English opposite number has now become, and the two offices can hardly be compared.

Certain English and Welsh boroughs also have sheriffs of their own. One of the privileges coveted by every town of importance during the Middle Ages was exemption from the jurisdiction of the Crown-appointed county sheriff. A number of boroughs were successful in obtaining full county status, with the right to elect sheriffs. These places are known as counties corporate, or counties of cities (or towns, as the case may be): not to be confused with the modern local government creations known as county boroughs. The City of London has enjoyed this privilege since the 12th century, and Bristol since the 14th century. "By 1689," say Sidney and Beatrice Webb ("The Manor and the Borough," 1924) "they (the sheriffs) had come to have very varied functions in the different towns, but they were rapidly becoming merely ceremonial officers." The borough sheriff, unlike his county colleague, has to be content with second rank within his territory, yielding precedence to the mayor; for it is the Corporation, and not the sheriff personally, who is responsible to the Crown for the conduct of the borough shrievalty.

The list of counties corporate with the right to elect their own sheriffs is as follows: Berwick, Bristol, Canterbury, Carmarthen,

Chester, Exeter, Gloucester, Haverfordwest, Hull, Lichfield, Lincoln, London, Newcastle, Norwich, Nottingham, Oxford (*not a county, but has its own sheriff*), Poole, Southampton, Worcester and York. Until the Municipal Corporations Act, 1835, many boroughs appointed two sheriffs (namely Bristol, Carmarthen, Chester, Coventry, Gloucester, Lincoln, London, Nottingham and York). "The origin and significance of this divergence of practice is quite unknown to us," the Webbs comment (op. cit.); nor have I discovered any explanation. The dual shrievalty survives only in the City of London. Up to 1888 the City of London sheriffs also acted jointly, by a curious fiction, as the sheriff (sic) of Middlesex. When the counties of London and Middlesex were separated from the City by the Local Government Act, 1888, the City kept its two sheriffs. The Crown now appoints a sheriff for each of the two counties.

The prefix "high" in "high sheriff" dates, according to the Oxford English Dictionary, from about 1500. The O.E.D. adds that its use "in England and Wales and in some Irish counties" is to distinguish from a deputy or subordinate. In practice, with one or two exceptions, only true county sheriffs are described as "high sheriffs."

The method of appointment to the shrievalty differs considerably as between the counties and the boroughs.

Apart from a brief period in 1264-5 when the high sheriff was elected by the freeholders of the county, the appointment of county sheriffs has always been made by the Crown, though on local recommendations. From time to time the Sovereign has nominated a sheriff of his own choice (a so-called "pocket" sheriff), and theoretically may still do so if the nominations submitted prove ineffective. There were one or two hereditary shrievalties but the last one—Westmorland—was ended by an Act of 1850.

The high sheriff holds office for a year and is not eligible for a second term until after a further three years, unless no one else is available. This precaution was designed to stop a sheriff remaining too long in office and wielding too much power. His only qualification for office is that he must hold some land within the county, although there is no definition of how much land is necessary. M.P.'s, serving officers in the Forces, and some others are exempt; peers are not normally chosen.

Today's high sheriff is a wealthy man (the first woman high sheriff in recent times held office for Montgomeryshire in 1941) because of the incidental expenses of his office, in spite of official allowances. He is usually a member of the landed gentry into the bargain because of the social implications of his position.

By the 17th century the entertaining and pageantry of assize time were already proving expensive and burdensome to the sheriffs, as will be seen later in this chapter. In earlier centuries an astute sheriff could make a good deal from fees paid to his courts and sums sliced from the revenues which he collected for the Crown. These perquisites faded with changing conditions, and no allowance at first took their place. Nowadays the sheriff receives fees for his judicial work, and an expense allowance for his assize obligations. There is no escape from his duties once undertaken. They are laid down by the Sheriffs Act, 1887, and woe betide any sheriff who treats them lightly. Within living memory (it was at Winchester in 1892) a high sheriff was remiss enough to forget he happened to hold that office and went off on a winter cruise to Africa when he should have been in attendance on the judge of assize. He was fined 500 guineas for his lapse.

Those eligible for the county shrievalty are named in a list which the serving high sheriff or his under-sheriff hands to the senior judge at the summer assizes. The late Sir Frank MacKinnon in his book "On Circuit," 1940 (which gives invaluable details of assize customs as he observed them in the 1920's and 1930's, and to which we must refer often in this and the next chapter) says the Yorkshire list alone has always been termed the "Lites." He points out that the Oxford English Dictionary gives *Leet*, subst. 2, as "now chiefly Scottish." Two definitions are given, firstly "a list of persons designated and eligible for some office"; and secondly, plural, "the candidates forming a leet."

The next step is the official nomination. This takes place—except for the counties of Lancashire and Cornwall—on November 12 (if that day is a Sunday, then the following day) at the Law Courts in the Strand. The formal description of the day is "the morrow of Saint Martin." The Statute of Sheriffs, 1315, provided that the nomination should be made on "the morrow of All Souls," that is, November 3. The date was changed to November 12 by the Act 24 Geo. II, c.48, one of the regulating laws made necessary by the change to the Gregorian Calendar in 1752.

The sheriffs as revenue-collecting officers of the Crown were nominated by the old Court of Exchequer, which was naturally very much concerned with who was appointed. This court, abolished by the Judicature Act, 1873, may be regarded as a sort of official assembly for the reception of revenue payments, as well as a court of law for determining disputes related in any way (and latterly very remotely) to revenue matters. The sheriffs had to visit the Exchequer at the two half-yearly reckoning times of Easter and Michaelmas, to make their payments and account for their receipts. Why was November chosen as the time for nomination? Michaelmas was the most important accounting time, and the beginning of the financial year : though Lady Day, March 25, was long counted the beginning of the year for ordinary purposes. (The Budget was presented at Michaelmas until 1799, when the date was changed to January 5, Old Christmas Day; and only in 1854 was it altered to April, by Mr. Gladstone, as late as possible consistent with allowing two months for debate before the House of Commons rose in June). Was the intention that the new sheriffs might be appointed as soon as their predecessors had accounted for their year of office at Michaelmas? Only a "view of account" was taken at Easter, the other accounting time.

This seems a possible explanation, for Michael Dalton ("The Office and Authority of Sheriffs," 1700) says "And the King's Letters Patents whereby the new Sheriffs are made, do commonly bear date the sixth day of November"—only four days, that is, after the nomination. And the swearing-in was to be done as soon as the patents were made, Dalton adds, "for until he be sworn he may not intermeddle. . . ." How, then, does it come about that the appointments—no longer by patent—are now not made until about Lady Day, four *months* after the nomination? I have not discovered when the change occurred, but it may well have been in 1752 with the calendar changes. The reason for it has eluded all my inquiries. Nowadays the preparation of the roll of those nominated takes some time to prepare, and the Christmas vacation intervenes; but this would hardly seem a sufficient reason.

On November 12 the Chancellor of the Exchequer, the Lord

Chief Justice (both of whom are Privy Councillors) and two or more High Court judges who have travelled the assize circuits assemble on the bench in the Lord Chief Justice's court. The Lord Chancellor, Lord President of the Council and other Privy Councillors are entitled to take part but do not normally do so. The statutory quorum is two Privy Councillors and two judges. When I attended the nomination in 1952 the Chancellor of the Exchequer sat with the Lord Chief Justice and three other judges of the Queen's Bench Division.

Although the Lord Chief Justice is present in his own court, the Chancellor of the Exchequer presides. This is because the sitting is in effect one of the Court of Exchequer, and the Chancellor represents his department, taking the place of the Chief Baron of the Exchequer whose office is now extinct. (Once the Chancellor himself sat as a judge in the Exchequer Court when it tried Equity Cases). He wears a robe of black silk damask with heavy bars of gold lace and a train : a robe similar to that of the Lord Chancellor. In this case the robe is possibly that worn by the Chief Baron, though since that officer was invariably a serjeant-at-law at all times since the barred robe came into use it is hard to see how this oft-asserted explanation can be the right one. (See Chapters 7 and 12). The Chancellor does not wear a wig. The Lord Chief Justice and other judges robe as for Nisi Prius (see Chapter 7).

The Queen's Remembrancer, in full-bottomed wig and black gown, stands at the associate's (or clerk's) desk below the bench. The Remembrancer, who is nowadays the Senior Master of the Supreme Court, holds an office which was one of the most ancient in the Exchequer, being mentioned as early as 1254. His duties, laid down in 1323, were once chiefly concerned with the accounting of Crown revenue. Formerly at the nomination ceremony the Queen's Remembrancer administered to the judges and officials a Norman-French oath by which they swore impartiality.

Nowadays he reads out, county by county, in alphabetical order, the list of those who were nominated for office in the preceding year, three for each county. The name of the high sheriff at present serving is struck out. At this point it is open to other candidates to submit excuses for not wishing their names to go forward, such as lack of means. The excuse may be made in

open court by the candidate or his counsel, but is more often sent
to the Privy Council office beforehand, in which case it is stated
at this point by the Clerk to the Privy Council. (In 1952 for
example there were eight names withdrawn, all without discussion, and all through the Privy Council clerk. Causes were death
(2), ill-health (2), no property in county (2), exchange of nominee
(1), lack of means (1). MacKinnon in his book "On Circuit," 1940,
says "As I remember this function, as a spectator and youthful
barrister, the proceedings were longer and more contentious.
Gentlemen desiring exemption appeared by counsel, and their
claims were argued. . . .").

The court decides whether the excuse is valid or not. If it
decides in favour of exempting the candidate, then the name is
struck out and the Queen's Remembrancer says "Two new
names wanted." If no request for exemption has been submitted
for a county, then he asks only "One new name wanted"—to
take the place of the serving sheriff whose name has just been
struck from the list. One of the judges—in the case of the
counties of London and Middlesex it is always the Lord Chief
Justice—then reads out and nominates the necessary name or
names from the list given in at the summer assizes by the serving
sheriff. These are added to the name or names which still stand,
subject to the same procedure for objections, if any.

When the list for each county is completed in this fashion, the
Queen's Remembrancer reads it out and says "The names now
stand. . . ." All having been gone through, the brief ceremony—
it takes only some half-an-hour—is over.

The entire list of nominees, three for each county, is afterwards engrossed by one of the scriveners of the Royal Courts of
Justice. The names are set out, in a fine hand, on a parchment roll
comprising several skins and about 14 feet long, by a foot broad.
The Queen's Remembrancer signs the roll, which is then sent to
the Privy Council to be "pricked" by the Sovereign in due course.

A date in February or March is chosen for the "pricking" ceremony, which takes place at a meeting of the Privy Council held
in one of the royal palaces. The roll is handed to the Queen, who
signifies her choice for high sheriff of the various counties by
pricking or piercing a tiny hole, opposite or through the name
selected, with a bodkin. By custom the first of the three names
for each county is chosen.

The origin of the custom is uncertain. The first actual piercing seems to have been in the reign of Queen Elizabeth I, and the traditional explanation is that Queen Bess was at her needlework in the garden when the list was brought her, and she marked it with the instrument to hand. Before Elizabeth's reign the names were marked with a dot or tick, but the process was termed "pricking" nonetheless. The earliest known complete roll, of the reign of Henry VIII, was thus marked. So it does not seem that the reply given to King Edward VII on the subject by the late Sir Almeric Fitzroy, Clerk of the Privy Council, 1898-1923, was entirely correct. He told the monarch that the custom derived from a time "when your Majesty's ancestors were more expert with the sword than with the pen." MacKinnon says the method of marking by piercing is known elsewhere. At the universities, he adds, the attendance of men in chapel was so marked, and proctors thus record votes in Convocation.

The bodkin used at present is believed to have been made for Queen Victoria when she came to the throne in 1837. It has a silver gilt knob for handle, and the blade is round, with a sharp point. It is $4\frac{1}{2}$ inches long, and weighs nearly 8 ounces. On the flat top of the knob are engraved insignia like those used by the Privy Council, including a rose and a thistle between the lion and unicorn. At Windsor Castle there is an earlier bodkin, thought to date from about 1780.

The pricking ceremony over, the names of the new sheriffs are published in the London Gazette. The Clerk of the Privy Council sends warrants to the candidates chosen, with copies to the Clerks of the Peace for the counties concerned. Before taking office the sheriff must sign a declaration before a judge or justice of the peace. In this long document he promises to "well and truly serve the Queen's Majesty . . . and promote her Majesty's profit in all things that belong to my office as far as I legally can or may; . . . I will not respite or delay to levy the Queen's debts for any gift promise reward or favour where I may raise the same without great grievance to the debtors; I will do right to poor as to rich in all things belonging to my office; . . . I will truly return and truly serve all the Queen's writs according to the best of my skill and knowledge. . . ." and so on.

This declaration, whose form is now laid down in a schedule to the Sheriffs Act, 1887, is almost word for word the same as the oath for sheriffs given in the anonymous "Book of Oaths," 1649, and abolished in 1868. The few differences in the 17th century form include : "Ye shall truly acquit at the Exchequer all those to whom ye shall anything receive of the King's debts" and "Ye shall make to cease all manner of Heresy and Errors, commonly called Lollardies. . . ." This last clause had, in fact, disappeared before 1649 by a curious circumstance. Charles I was minded to keep certain political opponents, including the great lawyer Sir Edward Coke, out of the House of Commons. So he "pricked" them as sheriffs, since that office under the Crown would render them ineligible to become M.P.s. Coke, however, claimed to be excused on the ground that the shrieval oath, as it then stood, was illegal. Among other reasons, he pointed out that "Lollardies," under the respectable cloak of the Anglican Church, had become the established religion of the realm, against which no sheriff could be expected to swear! The clause, of course a survival from pre-Reformation times, had to be struck out, but Coke was required to take the amended oath and served as high sheriff of Buckinghamshire in 1626.

About the end of March or beginning of April—according to the date on the warrant—the new high sheriff takes over the duties of office from his predecessor.

The royal duchies of Lancaster and Cornwall are excepted from the elaborate arrangements for nominating and appointing the sheriffs of other counties. The high sheriff of Lancashire (corresponding to the Duchy of Lancaster) is chosen by the Sovereign as holder of the dukedom from a list provided by the Chancellor of the Duchy. Similarly the high sheriff of Cornwall is chosen by the Crown or the Duke of Cornwall, a title held by the eldest son of the Sovereign. Appropriate alterations are made in the wording of the declaration signed by sheriffs of these counties.

Sheriffs of counties corporate are chosen, in general, on November 9. Those of the City of London are chosen at Mid-summer, June 24.

The procedure for appointing sheriffs of counties corporate (excluding London) is laid down by the Municipal Corporations Act, 1882. The Act says that a "fit person" shall be appointed on November 9, at the quarterly meeting of the council immediately after the election of the mayor. He shall hold office until the appointment of his successor. Nowadays election is by the vote of the council. Before 1835, when local government began to be strictly controlled by Parliament, various procedures were customary in different towns. But the appointment was always by the Corporation of whom borough sheriffs are the agents. In some places the election was by votes of the liverymen or freemen instead of the councillors.

A woman, Mrs. Lucy Green Wells, was sheriff of Canterbury in 1923.

The sheriff of a county corporate makes the same declaration as his colleagues in the true counties.

London still differs in its practice. The election of the City's two sheriffs takes place in Guildhall on Midsummer Day, June 24. The electors are the liverymen of the City Companies, but their choice must be approved by the Sovereign. Candidates must be (a) aldermen who have not previously served as sheriff; or (b) freemen (up to three) nominated by the Lord Mayor between January 1 and March 1, and who remain nominated for five years; or (c) freemen nominated on the day of election by any two liverymen. In practice the shrievalty is often a step towards the mayoralty (an Act of the Common Council of London in the reign of Richard II laid down that the Lord Mayor must be chosen from among aldermen who have previously served as sheriff), and the City sheriffs sometimes receive knighthoods, just as the Lord Mayor customarily receives a baronetcy. Where there is a contest a poll may be demanded, and is taken on the third day after the demand. The returning officer for the poll is the Secondary (see below). The procedure is set out in the City of London Ballot Act, 1887. There is a fine for declining office when elected.

On Michaelmas Eve, September 28, the new sheriffs are sworn in at Guildhall. The Lord Mayor presides, seated on the herb-strewn "hustings" or dais. The new sheriffs robe, and receive the chains of office, placed on their shoulders by their predecessors. In addition to the statutory declaration taken by other sheriffs, they take oath, in 16th-century wording, peculiar to the City of London. This says in part: "Good customs I will none break nor evil customs arrere . . . And ready will I be at reasonable warning of the Mayor for keeping of the peace and maintaining the state of this City. . . ."

On some date before September 30 the Queen's Remembrancer delivers to the Secondary warrants under the Exchequer seal giving the Sovereign's approval of the choice of sheriffs. About a month after this the City Solicitor and the Secondary go to the Law Courts to account to the Queen's Remembrancer on behalf of the outgoing sheriffs. There follows the picturesque quit-rent ceremony, described in Chapter 14.

On official occasions the high sheriff's costume is court dress—the velvet knee-breeches suit, either old style with silk "wigbag" rosette, or new, without it—or uniform of the Services or as Deputy-Lieutenant if he is entitled to it. At first sight it seems odd that the county shrievalty should have no more distinctive official costume. The office of sheriff was as prominent during the 13th century, when the judiciary was evolving its impressive robes, as it has ever been. The sheriff had important judicial and representative duties, as well as his executive tasks as tax-collector. The reason must lie in the fact that the sheriff was never required to be a lawyer or even a man of learning; nor was he an ecclesiastic, or a peer, or connected in any way with the town guilds. Cut off from all these spheres in which ceremonial costume developed, he fulfilled all his duties in the everyday dress of his period.

Sheriffs of counties corporate wear the same official dress as their county brethren, with the addition of a robe and, in London and eleven other towns, chain and badge of office. The sheriff of a town or city is often an alderman and wears his aldermanic robe. In other cases he wears a shrieval robe whose colour varies. In some counties corporate it is black; in Exeter it is dark blue, edged with black velvet and fur, and with a fur collar. The City of London provides for its two sheriffs to wear violet or scarlet gowns (according to the occasion, as with Queen's Bench judges), and a plain chain of office with a badge which "should be a design appropriate to the ward, district or individual."

Referring to the 17th and 18th centuries, Jewitt and St. John Hope ("Corporation Plate and Insignia," 1895) say the shrieval robe was sometimes scarlet as at London and York, but purple at Chester, Lincoln and Norwich. An order made in 1568 prescribed the London sheriffs' robes as scarlet, violet and black.

At many places the sheriff customarily carries a wand. This symbol of his authority is of very ancient origin. In 1321, the itinerant judges are recorded as telling the London sheriffs they must come within the bar of the court and "deponere virgas suas albas"—"put down their white wands." Jewitt and St. John Hope consider the wand as an emblem of "straightness and integrity of rule." A "plain and slender rod," these authors add, "has from very ancient times been borne before the sovereign by high officers of state, and before dignified and important personages by attendants of lesser degree, and is still retained by the sheriffs and officers in courts of justice." A manuscript book of 1835 (in Newcastle-upon-Tyne public library), giving details of the form to be used in assize ceremonial, describes the high sheriff and under-sheriff as with a white rod each, in distinction to the jailer, who has a black rod. In 1929 MacKinnon ("On Circuit," 1940) observed that the sheriff of Hampshire was carrying a wand with a carved ivory top—"this appears to be the local practice." In the following year he noted the high sheriff of Gloucestershire carrying a wand.

A curious custom, apparently extinct only recently if indeed it does not survive, is that of fixing two ornate lamp-posts outside the door of the sheriff's private house. This was done in several counties corporate, including Newcastle-on-Tyne. The same purpose was served in some cities by posts, sometimes finely carved, erected outside the homes of the sheriffs (and of chief magistrates). Sidney and Beatrice Webb ("The Manor and the Borough," 1924) refer to this latter practice as "in 1689 not yet wholly abandoned." In a play of 1632 ("A Woman Never Vexed," by Rowley), a character says: "If e'er I live to see thee sheriff of London, I'll gild thy posts." An illustration of such posts erected outside the home of the Mayor of Norwich in 1592 is to be found in "Chambers' Book of Days," 1869, vol. i, p. 162. Those outside sheriffs' homes were used for "posting" royal proclamations. References to the custom are to be found in "The Widow," by Beaumont and Fletcher; Archaeologia, vol. xix, 1821, 383-5; "Chambers' Book of Days," as above; "Remnants of Antiquity in Norwich," 1843; and Norfolk and Norwich Notes and Queries, 1897, 195-6. In Scotland a relic of the practice could be seen (when the Webbs wrote in 1924) in the lamp-posts nearest to the home of the provost, decorated with the town-arms. Edinburgh and Linlithgow are examples.

The legal, as distinct from the ceremonial, duties of the sheriff are nowadays—except in the City of London—performed by the under-sheriff. The Sheriffs Act, 1887, provides that every sheriff must appoint an under-sheriff within a month of his own appointment being gazetted. The under-sheriff is usually a solicitor, and for convenience' sake usually continues to act from year to year. He is required to make a declaration similar to that of the sheriff, before a High Court judge or a justice of the peace.

As in so many other cases, the City of London has its own practice in this matter. There, the corresponding officer is known as the Secondary: a title first mentioned about 1327. He is elected by the Court of Common Council and holds office directly from the Corporation. The oath which he takes on assuming office dates from at least as early as Edward III's reign. His duties include attendance at the opening of each session of the Central Criminal Court (Old Bailey), and on the first day of the attendance there of a High Court judge. The City of London sheriffs appoint under-sheriffs just as do their colleagues else-where. But in this case the title is an empty one. They need not even be lawyers, they have no legal status in the City and their duties are purely ceremonial. They attend the sheriffs on all state occasions. When the City sheriffs also exercised authority over Middlesex and what is now the County of London, it will be realised that the legal work was sufficient for the Secondary and two under-sheriffs as well, one for Middlesex and one for London. Until 1871, there were even two Secondaries. With the sheriff-wick now restricted to the City of London, the need for three officials has passed.

The official dress of under-sheriffs is morning dress, court dress or uniform. It is customary for them, when taking part in assize ceremonial, to carry a wand. As mentioned earlier, a manuscript book of 1835 refers to the under-sheriff of Newcastle carrying a white rod like that of the sheriff, in distinction to the jailer with a black rod. MacKinnon noted that the under-sheriff of Warwick had "a fine malacca cane with a silver top, as long as an 18th century footman's stick, and very likely that is its origin."

The secondary of the City of London wears a cloth court suit or (at the Old Bailey) court coat and trousers, with a silk gown similar to that of Queen's Counsel, with cocked hat and no wig.

Each sheriff appoints a chaplain of his own, who takes part in

the assize ceremonial and usually preaches the sermon at the
special assize service. At both Oxford and Cambridge, however,
the sermon is preached by a clergyman provided by the respective Universities; and the high sheriff of Oxfordshire, at least,
does not appoint a chaplain.

The sheriff's chaplain is best known to the public for his
solemn response of "Amen" to the pious ending of the death
sentence: "May the Lord have mercy on your soul." He attends
the sheriff on the bench at the assize court so long as criminal
business continues. When a capital charge is being tried, the high
sheriff is required to remain in court during the whole proceedings. It will be remembered that the due execution of the death
sentence is one of the responsibilities of the sheriff. Sheriff,
chaplain and under-sheriff all stand while the judge pronounces
a death sentence.

The official dress of the sheriff's chaplain, as given by Mather
("Sheriff and Execution Law," 1935), comprises a black silk court
gown, long double-breasted black silk cassock and sash, scarf and
white lawn bands, the appropriate hood for his academic degree,
and black corded silk three-cornered hat and white gloves.
"Strictly speaking" he should also wear black breeches with
silver knee buckles, black silk stockings and shoes with silver
buckles. He does not wear a surplice when preaching the assize
sermon.

Since royal judges first travelled the circuits 800 years ago the
high sheriff's most important ceremonial duty, as representative
of the Sovereign in the shire, has been to receive them in state.
In days gone by he had also to guard them from harm in their
journey from one border of his county to the other. For safety
and due ceremony the high sheriff must have retainers—men-at-
arms with javelins, a form of short spear, and trumpeters.
Though a large armed escort for Her Majesty's judges was
perhaps originally needed, the number of retainers was later kept
up for display by individual wealthy sheriffs who no doubt vied
with each other over the magnificence of their entourage which
included, besides countless liveried servants, many of the gentlemen of the county. The poorer sheriff thus found the pomp of
his office a grievous burden to maintain. It is a far cry from the
hundreds of men turned out by, say, an early 17th century
sheriff to the handful of policemen and Army trumpeters who

take their place to maintain tradition today. Nowadays heavy taxation forces most sheriffs to keep even this miniature display of pageantry to the minimum.

In 1634 the father of John Evelyn was sheriff of Surrey and Sussex (then combined in one shrievalty). The diarist records that he had 116 servants "every one liveried in green satin doublets" as well as "divers gentlemen and persons of quality who waited on him and also wore livery." Evelyn adds, however, that 30 or 40 was a more usual number of retainers. Mather quotes, but does not name, another 17th century writer: "In all the counties of England the sheriff comes to the edge of the county and receives the Judge from the hand of the sheriff of the next county, and conducts him to the county town, attended with the gentry, and there is a large house in the town hired . . . for the Judge, and all the sheriff's officers attend him, and he in person. . . ."

Obviously this sort of thing was a heavy drain even on the wealthiest county gentlemen. The Civil War impoverished many families of the class from whom high sheriffs were drawn, and as a result of representations to Charles II an Act was passed in 1662 to keep the customary pageantry within bounds. It ordained, among other things, that no sheriff should give any present to a judge of assize "for his provision," nor any gratuity to his servants; nor have more than 40 or less than 20 menservants in livery in attendance at assize times. For Welsh counties the minimum was only 12. The penalty for disobeying this Act was a £200 fine.

However, even an establishment of 40—all to be fitted out with liveries—was a burdensome obligation to some. So in 1680 we find a group of Buckinghamshire gentlemen, potential candidates for the shrievalty, forming a sort of mutual insurance society. Their articles of association (preserved now in the county record office) make interesting reading. The gentlemen decided not to set too high a standard, agreeing that "no subscriber . . . shall have above twenty liveries for his attendance . . . and shall not exceed 8 other his private servants to attend his person."

The scheme enabled its members to defray some of the costs of shrievalty by instalments. The second article reads: "That so soon as it shall happen that any of the subscribers shall be chosen Sheriff he that is so first chosen shall receive by his certain messenger agent or appointment fifty shillings from each and every the other subscribers . . . and therewith he shall provide twenty seven livery coats and hats the livery shall be a plain grey cloth edged and lined through with Blue, and Javelins to twenty of them suitable, the hats to be black."

Since only 20 livery servants were to be provided, the contributions of the members (26 subscribed in fact) would provide a pool of seven spare sets of clothing for replacements; or perhaps the surplus clothing was intended for personal service apart from the javelin men. Any cash left over from the purchase of equipment was to be divided among the first five subscribers to be chosen sheriff, towards the pay of their "twenty able and sufficient men well horsed and wearing these liveries."

At the end of each assizes or other ceremonial occasion "each of the said five Sheriffs that shall in order next happen to be of these subscribers shall take care that the said liveries hats and Javelins be laid carefully up and preserved as fresh as may be till the next assizes or other public occasion." Apparently the subscribers thought it unnecessary to look beyond the first five of their number to be chosen. They did, however, provide for further subscribers to join the scheme. When any of the members was sheriff, half the other members (one half serving for winter, the other for summer) would attend him. The member who was sheriff agreed to dine at an ordinary (what we should call a set lunch, or table d'hote, probably at an inn) during the assizes, and not to invite guests. The other members would dine with him but each would pay for himself at the ordinary which "shall not exceed three shillings for meat beer ale, and all wine at that ordinary shall be paid by those that call for it before it be drunk."

It would be interesting to discover just how many members of this curious association were chosen sheriff in the event. The benefit of it passed to the heir at law of any deceased member. And when did the scheme finally come to an end?

Notwithstanding the 1662 Act and the frugality of such as the Buckinghamshire gentlemen, considerable expense was still lavished by sheriffs on the pomp of their office. "The Office of the Clerk of Assize," published in 1682, gives this account of procedure as it then was:

"When the Judges set forth for that County, the Sheriff sends his Bailiff to the edge of the County, to bring them the best way to that place where the Assize for that County is to be held; and before they come thither, the Sheriff attended with his Under-Sheriff, and Bailiffs, with their white Staves and his Livery-men with their Holberds in their hands, and accompanied with the chief of the Gentry of the County do wait upon the Judges at the usual place, and conduct them from thence to their Lodgings at the Town where the Assizes be appointed to be held."

One high sheriff in 1778—no doubt exceptionally—had a retinue of 250.

It was the duty of the javelin men to keep order within the court precincts as well as to provide an escort. Eventually the County and Borough Police Act, 1859, relieved the sheriff of his obligation to provide liveried retainers if the Quarter Sessions for his county ordered that sufficient police be provided for these duties. The Sheriffs Act, 1887, replaced this by a similar provision, but required that in the absence of such an order by Quarter Sessions (and the order was in recent years invariably made) the sheriff must have "a sufficient number of menservants in liveries" to keep order and to protect the assize judge. Mather (quoting a Treasury circular of 1920) says "application may be made to the police authority for the provision of an escort not exceeding twelve men...." not including the mounted police escort which may also be provided.

An economy measure introduced during the Second World War has removed the obligation for a sheriff to provide either javelin men or trumpeters, and this is still (1954) in force, though sheriffs who can afford to do so usually maintain the custom.

A large collection of javelins is to be seen in the civil court at Lancaster. They bear on the heads the crests of past sheriffs. At Swansea MacKinnon noted in 1932 that the heads of the javelins used there were inscribed with dates from about 1760 to about 1785. At Aylesbury the javelins are housed between assizes in the county hall.

There is no set costume for javelin men. It is customary for them to wear footmen's dress in the colours of the sheriff's livery. Where policemen provide the escort nowadays, they carry the javelins but wear their normal uniform dress. At Caernarvon up to the 1860's the javelin men wore top hats; at Chester at one time they wore a soft hat a brim turned up on one side—which one might irreverently compare with that worn by some Corporation dustmen.

The second kind of retainers provided by the sheriff are the trumpeters. There are normally two of them, and it is their duty to herald the comings and going of Her Majesty's judge at the assize courts, and on other ceremonial occasions during the assize period. At some places the trumpeters also sound a call outside the judges' lodgings each morning as their Lordships set out for the court, and then at one or two prominent points of the town. They may, according to Mather, be either mounted or on foot; I have heard of no recent use of mounted men, though this would perhaps add to the dignity of the procession.

When the sheriff employs civilian trumpeters they wear frock coat and trousers, with a velvet peaked "jockey cap" like those worn by trumpeters of the Household Cavalry. Their shoulder knots are in the sheriff's livery colours, and their trumpets have pendant banners embroidered with his coat-of-arms. A description of the uniform worn at Appleby in the 18th century differs little from the present practice. The trumpeters wore black velvet peaked caps, black skirted coats with silver buttons, red waistcoats with silver buttons, white buckskin breeches and buttoned gaiters, with black shoes or boots. (In this particular case, the colours would not vary from year to year, for Westmoreland was then a hereditary shrievalty in the hands of the Tufton family). Their silver trumpets, according to a local historian, bore banners with the royal arms. It is curious that the sheriffs, as direct representatives of the Crown in the counties, did not make more frequent use of the royal arms and cipher rather than their personal armorial bearings. In Lancashire the banner on one of the trumpets bears the arms of the sheriff, but the second carries the arms of the Duchy of Lancaster.

Nowadays the trumpeters are often drawn from any Service unit which happens to be handy. The practice probably began with the first World War—sometimes the sheriff might borrow men from a unit in which he was or had been an officer—and became more firmly established with the second war. Military trumpeters may wear either full dress or khaki. At Oxford the local regimental depot provided the trumpeters for some time before the second World War, though the trumpets were the property of the county; the men wore their regimental walking-out dress. Since the war the local cadet battalion provides the trumpeters—one of the most modern branches of the Services continuing a custom older than the oldest regiment. At Bedford the trumpeters often come from the Royal Air Force station at Cardington, close by. Aylesbury has the strangest innovation. There, trumpeters are provided by the band of a large local printing firm; they wear their normal works band uniform when appearing at assizes.

Sheriff's trumpeters normally get little opportunity to display musical talent, though they sometimes attend the sheriff on occasions other than the assizes. But in Lancashire MacKinnon found the trumpeters "the best in all the counties. They wear a picturesque uniform; the trumpets are keyed so that they can play all sorts of tunes as duets; and from attending four times a year at lengthy Assizes at Liverpool and Manchester they get so much practice that they play admirably . . . 'D'ye Ken John Peel' is a tune they play with obvious gusto, and on the last day of the Assize at Manchester they play 'Auld Lang Syne' with much feeling." Not many years ago at Manchester the judges were greeted with "Wish me luck as you wave me goodbye"—more appropriate, perhaps, to prisoners than to the Bench.

At Lincoln Assizes there was once an occasion when the accustomed dignity was not quite maintained. The trumpeters, having played the judge into court, fell asleep in the entrance-hall knowing they would have nothing more to do until the court rose. A practical joker found their trumpets on the seat beside them, and stuffed the instruments with newspaper.

"When the Court rose for the day," recounts Ward ("Stuff and Silk"), "the trumpeters took up their positions and, at the correct moment, tried to give the herald, but they blew out their cheeks without any sound coming from their instruments. The under-sheriff, not realising the joke, and believing the trumpeters were neglecting their duties, exclaimed: 'Blow, you b———s, blow!'"

9. Her Majesty's Judge of Assize

To Miss Isabel Steel, who lives in the tiny, ancient town of Appleby in Westmorland, the majesty of the law is a simple thing. It is summed up by an old clock, pewter inkpots and quill pens.

Three times a year an elderly gentleman from London arrives to don wig and robe for a day or two as Appleby's judge of assize —unless, as often happens, everyone has been so well-behaved that his visit is not needed. When Miss Steel knows he is due she goes along to the police station, unhooks a large clock and carries it carefully to the assize court. While she moves it, a stationer for whom she sometimes works gets out his stock of inkpots and quills for judge and counsel.

A slender but strong thread of history links Miss Steel with a Plantagenet King. It was Henry II who first sent judges to travel regularly round the kingdom to bring powerful justice to its remotest parts—as they have done ever since. Edward I provided that assizes should be held three times a year, and divided the English counties (except the Palatinates of Chester and Durham) into four circuits for the purpose.

No provision was made for London and Middlesex. Civil cases for this county were tried at Guildhall and at Westminster, where the central Law Courts were situated until 1883. Criminal cases were dealt with at Westminster, or in the case of those from the City of London at Guildhall or the Old Bailey. Today London and Middlesex civil cases are still tried at the Law Courts (now in the Strand). In 1834 the Old Bailey was reconstituted as the Central Criminal Court, which deals with criminal trials from an area comprising London and parts of the Home Counties (see Chapter 10).

Wales is a comparative newcomer to the assize system. Even after Henry VIII brought its legal system into line with that of England it had, from 1542 to 1830, a separate judicial administration of its own known as the Great Sessions of Wales.

At intervals during the centuries since Edward I counties have been added to or taken away from different circuits, as regrouping seemed expedient. Within the counties, the towns appointed for assize court sittings have changed as the importance and convenience of different centres altered with the times. (See Appendix.)

It is only within living memory that assizes have taken place simultaneously with the sittings of the courts in London, which is the present practice. The ancient system, when vacations were much longer than they are today, was for all the Common Law judges to "ride the circuits" after the end of term. The "three times a year" provided by the statute of Edward I was a maximum. Until the early 19th century towns in the distant north, such as Appleby, were visited only once a year, in the summer, on account of the difficulties of travelling over bad roads in severe winter weather. This often resulted in great hardship for prisoners, who might have to wait eleven months for trial. Even elsewhere assizes were customarily held only twice a year, in the spring and autumn vacations. From the 18th century a third assize was commonly held in the winter vacation (following Michaelmas term). Still more modern is the arrangement for a fourth assize in Easter term at Manchester, Liverpool and Leeds where work is heaviest.

Each assize is held under commission from the Queen, which is formally read as evidence of authority before trials begin. At assize towns which are "counties corporate" (see Chapter 8)— Bristol, Exeter, Lincoln, Newcastle, Norwich, Nottingham and York—there are separate commissions which must be read before city cases, as distinct from the general county business, are tried. In recent times another category of assize town has been added, comprising the industrial cities of Manchester, Liverpool, Leeds and (soon to be added) Sheffield, included in the circuits to cope with pressure of work which would otherwise overload the county assizes.

At each assize town the judge or judges—the number visiting each place, originally two, now varies from one to four or more —sets up what is in effect a branch of the High Court. Normally there are two courts sitting at the same time, one to try criminal cases (known as the Crown court), and the other to try civil cases which would otherwise be brought in the Queen's Bench or

Divorce Divisions in London. When there are two judges of assize, the one who tries crime is termed the judge "in commission," and takes precedence as regards ceremonial. The judges travelling a circuit take it in turns to be "in commission."

Nowadays only the judges of the Queen's Bench and the Probate, Divorce and Admiralty Divisions are concerned in all this as a rule. Once it was customary for the judges of all three Common Law courts (Queen's Bench, Common Pleas and Exchequer) to go on circuit. When these courts were abolished, and a single High Court created, it was felt by the Queen's Bench judges that their Chancery brothers should take a share in the burden and expense of assize work. Chancery judges accordingly rode the circuits for a time, but it is said that their erudite remoteness was found scarcely suitable. One of them had never heard the nickname "Robert" for a policeman! Whatever the reason, the experiment was dropped and the Common Law judges were given an allowance to meet entertainment expenses on circuit. Divorce judges at one time seldom went on circuit but nowadays take more part in assize work.

The various circuits are allocated by the judges among themselves at their annual meeting, held at the Law Courts (formerly at Serjeants' Inn) on the first day of Michaelmas Term each year. Not all Queen's Bench judges go on every assize, or travel an entire circuit. The pleasanter towns tend to fall to the senior judges, who have first choice; and the "new boys" who have been appointed to the Bench only recently may have nothing but a few weeks' hard work as third or fourth judge at a northern industrial city.

The preliminary business, such as the obtaining of the commissions and the dispatch of precepts, or notices, to the sheriffs of the places to be visited, is dealt with by the Clerk of Assize, a permanent official of the circuit appointed from among senior members of the Bar.

Each assize judge takes with him a staff comprising a cook and two menservants, one of whom acts as butler and the other as the marshal's man. The judge's marshal is his closest attendant and companion while on circuit. The judge may appoint anyone he pleases to be his marshal for the duration of the assize, but normally confers this pleasant office on some young barrister whom he wishes to favour. The marshal goes everywhere with the judge on circuit and sits on the bench beside him in court.

Nowadays his only duty is to be a companion and social aide to the judge. It is customary for the marshal of the judge in commission to say grace at dinner on circuit. The ancient official duties of the judge's marshal are now extinct. The last to disappear was his office of administering the oath to the Grand Jury, until grand juries were abolished in 1933. In the days when persons convicted of certain crimes could claim "benefit of clergy" the marshal had to go to the dock to inspect the brand inflicted (in lieu of capital punishment) on those whose claims were admitted. He was required to assure the judge that it had been properly executed, reporting "Good mark, my lord." In later years all that was demanded as proof of the prisoner's "clerical" status was ability to read a single verse of a Psalm (at Newgate it was Ps. 51, 1)—the "neck-verse"; benefit of clergy was abolished in 1827.

Once the term "riding the circuit" had a literal meaning, for the judges, Clerk of Assize and members of the Bar travelled from town to town on horseback. Later came the coach, and finally the railway-train or car. Perhaps the last judge to travel his circuit on horseback—from choice rather than necessity— was Mr. Justice Day, in the late 19th century.

The assize judges tour the kingdom as representatives of the Sovereign, and their stay in the shires has always been surrounded deliberately with impressive ceremonial.

In these comparatively austere times, however, the arrival of Her Majesty's judges is not very spectacular. As a rule they are met at the station by the sheriff or even the under-sheriff, and driven by car to the Judges' Lodgings: some large house set aside for their use during their stay. However, it is open to them to opt, if they wish, for a formal reception. If they do, there are intricate rules of precedence and ceremony to be followed (all set forth in Mather, "Sheriff and Execution Law," 1935).

There is, says Mather, a proper order of procession between the platform and the carriages (or cars): "criers and attendants; County and City under-sheriffs; Mayor; City Sheriff; High Sheriff's chaplain; High Sheriff; Judge or Judges." Procession it would certainly be—and one may doubt whether this ceremonial scene will ever again grace the stations of British Railways as a regular thing. Sometimes the high sheriff, in pre-war days, even brought with him his two trumpeters to sound a fanfare as the judge (who had donned full-bottomed wig and scarlet robe en route) paced his dignified way from train to waiting carriage.

For the procedure used in the more spacious days of the late 17th century, see Chapter 8.

Although nowadays the ceremonial reading of the commission which officially opens the assize customarily takes place on the day after the judge's arrival, the arrival day is still known as "Commission Day," and it is still this date which is specified in the precept (the order to the sheriff summoning him to attend the assize). With speedier travelling in modern times the judge and counsel can make the journey from one assize town to another within a matter of hours, and to observe the old practice of opening a new assize on the day of arrival might (if that day were also the last day of the assize at the previous town) leave insufficient interval for convenience.

Almost as soon as the judges have arrived at their Lodgings, there begins a round of semi-social, semi-ceremonial duties which fall to them as Crown representatives.

In York the Lord Mayor and City sheriff, with the town clerk and Chief Constable, mace-bearer and sword-bearer, call upon the judges and the Lord Mayor invites them to a traditional breakfast held on the opening day of each assize in the city.

At Oxford the judge receives a pair of white kid gloves from the University and a second pair from the city. This presentation is made on the Commission Day of each assize, and is quite distinct from the custom of presenting white gloves at a "maiden assize," which we shall notice later in this chapter.

MacKinnon ("On Circuit," 1940) says that the university delegation which called upon him when he visited Oxford as judge of assize included the Vice-Chancellor, proctors and heads of houses. The Vice-Chancellor presented "a pair of white kid gloves, with small gauntlets of gold lace, and white silk ribbons." The City delegation which arrived subsequently comprises the Mayor, the town clerk and some aldermen. The Mayor handed the judge a pair of gloves "only slightly less ornate" than the university pair, "with a fringe of gold wire round the tops." The Vice-Chancellor told MacKinnon that he believed his offering was in token of the fact that there was no member of the

University to be tried at the assize. MacKinnon doubted—with very good reason—the correctness of this explanation. He mentions that in former times gloves were often presented on ceremonial occasions, especially in Oxford where they were readily obtainable from Woodstock, an ancient centre for their manufacture.

Gloves were presented to Queen Elizabeth I when she visited Oxford in 1566. One pair of these is now in the Ashmolean Museum—"they have an elaborately worked gauntlet in gold, and a fringe of gold lace very much like that on the gloves given me by the Mayor of Oxford," MacKinnon noted. No similar custom exists at Cambridge today. However, Norton-Kyshe ("The Law and Custom relating to Gloves," 1901) quotes an "account of expenses relating to St. John's College" Cambridge for a probable reference to gloves presented to King James I, the judges and other distinguished persons present when the King visited the town in 1614, to hear the first performance of the comedy "Ignoramus." Hull ("History of the Glove Trade," 1834) gives a presentation by the University of Cambridge in 1622.

The Oxford Corporation Acts indicate that the presentation of gloves by the city to the assize judge dates at least as far back as 1681; but a 16th century origin seems more likely.

The whole subject of gloves in this connection is a little involved, because such presentations seem to fall into three distinct classes: (a) purely ceremonial gifts, such as those at Oxford; (b) gifts of gloves as customary court fees, to officials of the court as well as judges, particularly by prisoners pleading royal pardons—a practice now extinct; and (c) gifts to judges, partly as fees and partly as symbols, at a maiden assize, a custom which is still maintained in legal pageantry. The last two categories will be discussed later in this chapter in connection with the maiden assize.

At Cambridge the judges are visited by the Vice-Chancellor, proctors carrying big, chained volumes of the University statutes, and heads of houses. The mayor, town clerk and some of the aldermen also pay a formal call.

Where the high sheriff does not meet the judges on arrival, he also will be an early visitor.

On the day after Commission Day the assize proper begins, with considerable ceremonial.

The judges robe before leaving their Lodgings. They wear full dress, with slight exceptions (noted in the account of judicial costume in Chapter 7).

A kind of official reception committee waits upon the judges at the Lodgings, all remaining bareheaded as in the presence of royalty. The high sheriff and his chaplain arrive in limousine or coach to drive the judges to the customary church service or (when the service is held on the first Sunday of the assize) to the courts. The under-sheriff and marshals go ahead in another carriage. In towns where there are both city and county commissions and the city commission is to be opened first, the city sheriff and mayor, instead of the county sheriff, take charge of the judge. At Appleby, though there is no city commission, the mayor by ancient custom takes precedence of the assize judge— a rare thing, if not unique.

Among the towns where state coaches are, or have been in recent years, used for the assize procession are Bristol, Cardiff, Chester, Derby, Hereford, Newcastle and Norwich. At Bristol it is the Lord Mayor's state coach which is used, and the Lord Mayor and Swordbearer accompany the city sheriff and assize judge to the Mayor's Chapel for the service. In a committee-room at Bedford town hall is preserved a collection of armorial panels from the sheriff's coaches formerly used in that town.

The procession is headed by javelin-men, if any, and trumpeters and is escorted by police.

Before the senior assize judge leaves his lodgings on the first day of the assize at Exeter there is an important custom to be observed. Two officers of the garrison call to present the "parade state" of their troops, and formally ask the judge's permission for the troops to be allowed out of barracks. At Chester a similar ceremony is carried out. There, a written "state" is presented, and the senior judge is invited to give his "commands" for the garrison. He requests and receives an assurance that the troops are "in good health and in good heart." Both judges then inspect a guard of honour mounted by the Cheshire Regiment, drawn up in the courtyard of the Castle, which houses the courts and is also the headquarters of the garrison. (The inspection ceremony is an innovation, introduced in 1946 by the then Commander-in-Chief, Western Command, General Sir Brian Horrocks.)

The size of garrisons has changed through the years, and at one town where a ceremony of this kind took place it is said that the garrison was once reported as "Seven—but three of them absent without leave."

As we have seen, when trumpeters are needed at assize time, the Army can usually oblige. When the judge is to be escorted, a sort of vestigial army of javelin-men is mustered. It must, therefore, seem odd to young soldiers in these garrison towns today that they require the formal permission of Her Majesty's judge merely to leave barracks at assize time.

The principle behind these observances is nearly as old as the English standing army. When memories of Charles I's use of his troops were still fresh, it was felt to be an essential safeguard that during elections and assizes troops should be removed from the towns concerned. Probably it was the Protestant "Faction" led by the Earl of Shaftesbury which exercised the pressure in the case of assizes. At all events the first such order (according to Clode, "Military Forces of the Crown," 1869) is probably that given by Charles II on July 5, 1672, referring to the Chelmsford assizes then shortly to be held. It required the removal of dragoons, among them units commanded by Prince Rupert, to the neighbouring towns of Ingatestone and Brentwood. The soldiers were to be quartered in inns, victualling houses and ale houses for the duration of the assizes.

The corresponding practice at elections is dated by Clode to the Commonwealth, but it became statutory for the first time in 1735 when—according to a speaker in the Upper House—"it was thought proper not to leave that to the prudence of ministers which might in some future reign be made use of for the over-turning our Constitution." In the case of assizes the practice, though long rigidly observed, for some reason never came directly into the statute book. It gained Parliamentary recognition indirectly in 1798, when in an Act ordering militia to be assembled it was thought necessary to provide that militiamen might remain in assize towns even though their assembly should coincide with the assizes.

At one period in the 18th century some Sussex innkeepers were so annoyed at having soldiers billeted on them at assize time that they ripped down their signs and gave up their licences. In 1790 the first barracks were built. (The idea at first met considerable opposition in Parliament, as tending to set the soldier apart from the citizen and thus make him an easy tool of an autocratic régime). Others followed, some being in assize towns. The practice of moving troops out of town during assizes was very inconvenient, and the time was ripe for a change.

The Secretary at War, Mr. William Wyndham, wrote to the judges suggesting that confinement to barracks would be easier than, and just as effective as, removal. After a long correspondence (quoted in Clode) this plan was adopted, though the judges attached considerable importance to the principle. (A similar change with regard to elections did not take place until 1847).

It was provided—and herein originated the custom observed today—that judges of assize could release the troops from their confinement at their discretion. In later years the confinement was not enforced by a general order, but a letter was sent by the War Office to District General Officers Commanding on the occasion of each assize.

The coup de grâce to the whole proceeding as an effective operation came in the Crimean War. Lord Campbell, then Lord Chief Justice of the Queen's Bench, asked the Commander-in-Chief, Lord Raglan, in the House of Lords for the formal abolition of the confinement rule. This had for some time been a dead letter, as judges were accustomed to release the men as a matter of course.

Since 1855 the judge's permission for the men to leave barracks has been required only by tradition.

The procedure for the assize procession seems to have changed little in the past three centuries. "The Office of Clerk of Assize" (1682) gives this description: "When the Judges have reposed themselves at their Lodgings and the Gentry have paid their respects to them, and they have put on their Robes, then the Sheriff covered, with his white Staff in his hand, attended by his Under-Sheriff bare-headed, and his Bailiffs, uncovered, with their white Staves in their hands, and his Livery-men, uncovered, with their Halberds in their hands, two by two on foot, wait on the Judges from their Lodgings to church. . . ."

At York the judges go first to the official breakfast given by the Lord Mayor at the Mansion House. This is a considerable social function, attended by guests of both sexes, As at the Lord Mayor's Day banquet in London, the judges wear their full dress, which

I

compels them to attempt the difficult feat of eating a meal in a dignified fashion while adorned with a full-bottomed wig.

On their arrival at the York Mansion House they are each presented with a large bouquet. This custom, like similar ones in other assize towns, doubtless originated in the days when noisome smells and the dreaded jail fever—one was regarded as the cause of the other—abounded. At York, in addition to the bouquet the assize judges are each given a small silver casket containing powdered dried herbs. At Exeter the judge is given a bunch of flowers as he goes into court, and at Derby a big bowl of flowers is provided by the high sheriff for the judge's desk. Both nosegays and dried herbs are used at the Old Bailey (see Chapter 10).

Among notable instances of jail fever in assize towns are: Cambridge, 1521: "The justices, gentlemen, bailiffs and others resorting thither took such an infection that many of them died, and almost all that were present fell desperately sick, and narrowly escaped with their lives" (Wood's "History of Oxford"); Oxford, 1577—"The Black Assize": Jurors died of the fever, and later the Lord Chief Baron, the sheriff and—it is said 300 others, within 40 hours (Holinshed, Baker's Chronicle); Exeter 1586: Disease appeared among prisoners in the jail, and of the "audience" in court "more died than escaped"; Taunton, 1730: Lord Chief Baron, a serjeant, the sheriff and hundreds of others died of jail fever (Howard). All these examples are quoted in Griffiths "The Chronicles of Newgate," 1884. For London and the Old Bailey, see Chapter 10.

It is likely that leaves of aromatic herbs once formed part of the bouquets. Probably the sweet-smelling plants were welcome to counteract the odour of unwashed humanity from the unreformed prisons, even if they were useless to perform their imagined function of warding off fever germs.

A special church service is normally held at each assize, usually in the principal church of the town (at Oxford in the university church), attended by the judges in state. This takes place as a rule on the morning of the first working day of the assize, but in some places—among them York, Lincoln, Exeter and Liverpool—where assizes last for a number of days the service is held on a Sunday, known as Assize Sunday.

The judges are attended by their marshals, the high sheriff and

other officials connected with the assize. The mayor and corporation may also attend in state. The dean or the vicar receives the
judges at the door of the church, and a procession is formed of
choir, clergy, sheriff and other officials, including sheriff's
chaplain, mayor and judges. The judges, of course, take the
principal seats.

Usually the service chosen is a shortened Morning Prayer,
though on Sunday the full service is used. A special collect is
incorporated : "Give wisdom, O Lord, we pray Thee, to all those
who are concerned in the administration of Thy Laws of Truth
and Justice, especially Her Majesty's Justices of Assize, and the
Magistrates of this Borough and County. Enable them to be
diligent in investigation and impartial in judgment, that their
work may tend to the diminution of vice and the removal of the
principal occasions of evil; and grant that their responsibility for
others may lead them to sincere preparation for that sentence
which they shall themselves receive from Thee, the Judge of all,
and to a faithful acceptance of the means of Thy Grace; through
Jesus Christ our Lord. Amen."

The Bidding Prayer which precedes the sermon runs in part :
"Ye shall pray for . . . the King's Most Honourable Council, and
for all the Nobility and Magistrates, especially for the . . .
Honourable Sir . . . one of the Judges of Her Majesty's High Court
of Justice, for the High Sheriff of the County, the Worshipful the
Mayor, the Recorder, the Aldermen and Burgesses of this
Borough, and for the whole Commons of this Realm. . . ."

The sermon is normally preached by the sheriff's chaplain
(who incidentally does not wear a surplice). But at both Oxford
and Cambridge it is preached by a clergyman provided by the
university. The high sheriff, in the case of Oxfordshire, does not
therefore appoint a chaplain. At Cambridge the sermon is
preached by a pro-proctor, and the sheriff's chaplain has no duty
to perform.

The opportunities and pitfalls for a chaplain who wishes to
choose an apt text for his assize sermon are naturally many, and
stories of humorous incidents are plentiful.

When the late Dr. Lang, Archbishop of Canterbury, preached
an assize sermon in Oxford during his younger days, he chose a
text to illustrate the lessening of respect for authority. It was
". . . Go up thou bald head" (Kings 2, Ch. 2, v 23) part of the story

of the mocking of Eliseus. It was not Lang's fault that as the judge entered the church, when it was too late to alter the sermon, his lordship's wig caught on a projection over the doorway, remaining for a moment suspended to reveal that the judicial crown was bald as an egg!

Another tale is told of the 19th century Mr. Justice Groves, very much a Common Law man. The late Judge Bosanquet records that when Groves was at an evening service during an assize he heard the words of the Canticle: "With righteousness shall He judge the world and the people with equity." The conflict between the Common Lawyer and his Chancery brother who practises the system of law called Equity is traditional. So, in Bosanquet's words: "A sort of murmur was heard to come from the judge's seat, 'Poor people.'"

A very unhappy text said to have been chosen once in York is "God shall smite thee, thou whited wall; for sitteth thou there to judge me according to the law, and commandeth me to be smitten contrary to the law?" A cleric in Wales, thinking to be polite, took care to bow to the judge as he read the words of the Te Deum "We believe that Thou shalt come to be our judge."

After the service at Ruthin, North Wales, the assize judge is met by the head boy of Ruthin School bearing a Latin letter asking for a half-holiday for the school. Similar letters are addressed to the judge elsewhere by the boys of other public schools, including Winchester, Shrewsbury and Bedford.

The service over, the judge, sheriff and other dignitaries drive to the courts for the opening of the assize. When they arrive at the courts they are greeted by a fanfare from the trumpeters. The sheriff and his chaplain escort the judge in commission to the Crown (criminal) court, while his colleague—if he has one—is taken to his room by the under-sheriff to await the completion of the opening ceremony.

Both judges, if they have arrived straight from the assize service, will be in full dress. If there has not been a service immediately preceding the opening ceremony, the judge who is to take civil business will be in his robes for Nisi Prius (see Chapter 7), with tye-wig, and carrying his three-cornered hat. Unlike his colleague who is in commission he does not take the hat into court.

On entering the Crown court, the judge who is to open the

commission stands at his desk on the bench. His three-cornered hat is placed on the desk before him. When it is the county commission which is to be opened, the high sheriff's place on the bench is on the judge's right, with his chaplain and under-sheriff to his own right. For a city commission, the city sheriff takes position at the judge's right, with his under-sheriff to his own right, and the mayor on the judge's left; otherwise the mayor and corporation if present may occupy the jury box, their mace placed on the Bar table in the centre of the court, with its head towards the judge as representative of the Crown.

All those taking part in the ceremony remain standing.

As the judge entered his clerk (not the Clerk of Assize) had proclaimed: "All persons having anything to do before my Lords the Queen's Justices of Assize, Oyer and Terminer and General Jail Delivery for this County of ———, draw near and give your attendance."

A pause, and now: "My Lords the Queen's Justices do strictly charge and command all persons to keep silence while Her Majesty's Commission of Assize is produced and read."

The modern assize commission is a comparatively brief document, and reads:

"Elizabeth the Second by the grace of God—of The United Kingdom of Great Britain and Northern Ireland and of her other Realms and Territories, Queen, Head of the Commonwealth, Defender of the Faith, to the Right Honourable (name of judge), Knight Justice of the High Court of Justice.

"To Our Judges of our Supreme Court of Judicature.

"To such of our Counsel Learned in the Law who are authorised by our Royal Warrant or by the warrant of our Lord High Chancellor to be of the Commission.

"And to the Clerk of Assize and Circuit Officers of the ——— Circuit.

"Greeting. Know ye that we have assigned you to inquire more fully the truth of all offences and injuries whatsoever within our County of ——— and to deliver the jail thereof and to take all the assizes juries and certificates within our County of ———.

"And therefore we command you that you shall make diligent inquiries about the said offences and injuries and hear and determine the same and take all the assizes juries and certificates doing therein what to justice does appertain according to the laws and customs of England.

"In witness whereof we have caused these our Letters to be made Patent.

"Witness Ourself at Westminster on the ——— day of ——— in the ——— year of Our Reign.

"God Save the Queen."

Once there were as many as six different commissions authorising each assize, all of them in Latin. The multiplicity of commissions is probably due to the fact that in the early days of the circuits justices—not necessarily the permanent judges—were often commissioned for a particular and single occasion, and did not always transact all the types of business later dealt with by the assize judges. Even today when there is an unusual amount of business to be dealt with at one particular assize, or in a specific town, an experienced Queen's Counsel may be made a Commissioner of Assize for that occasion only; but today he acts under the same all-embracing commission and has the same status as, the ordinary assize judges.

In 1682, when "The Office of Clerk of Assize" was published, judges sat by virtue of separate commissions of Assize, Association, Oyer and Terminer and Jail Delivery, and writs of Admittance and Si Non Omnes. A proclamation announced four other ancient assize procedures: Novel Disseisin, Mort d'Ancestre, Juris Utrum and Attaint. To explain the fields covered by these extinct formulae would require a whole chapter of legal history. A number of them derive from the disputes over real property which provided most of the business of early assizes. By the mid-18th century—according to MacKinnon—the forms seem to have been altered and in 1749 five commissions were used. The property, or possessory, assizes were abolished in 1833, but the variety of ancient mandates, each of which used to bear the Great Seal of England, was not reduced to the present single document, sealed only with a wafer seal, until 1914. It combines the surviving commissions of Assize, Oyer and Terminer and Jail Delivery, by which—with the Commission of the Peace (see Chapter 13)—the judges of assize now sit.

An Order in Council in 1884 directed that "the commissions at all assizes be opened by producing in court the commission or commissions under which they are to be holden before the commencement of the business of the assizes on the first day of the assizes on which a judge shall sit in court at each place without reading them at length, and by the officer of the court shortly stating that the judges or judge present at the assizes are, or is, thereby with others appointed to hold the assizes."

Nevertheless the ceremony of reading the commission is still an impressive one, with the judge in his scarlet-and-ermine, the high sheriff in court dress and his chaplain in robes, and the Clerk of Assize in wig and gown proclaiming the royal authority in the sonorous, antique English of the Law.

When the Clerk reaches the name of the presiding judge he turns and bows to him. The judge in response dons his three-cornered hat, bows, then returns it to the desk before him.

At the end of the commission—or so much of it as is read—the judge's clerk makes the response "God Save the Queen." The assize is now formally begun.

The judge takes his seat, and a message is dispatched to tell the other judge (waiting in his room) that the commission has been opened, and he can accordingly take his seat in the civil or Nisi Prius court. The under-sheriff will attend him on the bench there, as the sheriff attends the judge who tries criminal cases.

In the Crown court there is still a further ceremony to be performed: the formal return of the sheriff's precept. Before leaving London the Clerk of Assize had dispatched to each sheriff on the circuit a "precept" instructing him to attend the assize and to return writs, produce his prisoners, and perform other duties which fall upon him. This long document, which the Clerk of Assize signs with his surname only, is couched in classical legal phraseology. It says in part:

". . . To THE SHERIFF of the said County of ——— GREETING on behalf of our said Lady the Queen we command you that you omit not for any Liberty of your Bailiwick but that you cause to come before Us at ——— on ——— the ——— day of ——— 19—. All Writs of Assize Juries and Certificates before whatsoever Justices arraigned . . . together with the Panels Attachments Reattachments Summons and Resummons and all other Muniments whatsover any ways concerning those Assize Juries and Certificates . . . And also that you cause to come before the said Honourable ——— one of Her Majesty's Justices of the High Court of Justice and others his Fellow Justices of our said Lady the Queen assigned to deliver her Jail of the County aforesaid of the Prisoners therein being at the day and place aforesaid all the Prisoners being in the said Jail with their Attachments Indictments and all other Muniments any ways concerning those prisoners and a competent number of good and lawful Persons of the body of your said

County qualified according to law to try all issues whether civil or criminal which may then and there come on for trial. . . . And that you yourself and your Under-Sheriff together with your Bailiffs and other your Ministers be then and there in your own Persons to do those things which to you and their offices in this behalf appertain to be done. . . . And have you there and then the names of the Jurors Justices of the Peace Mayors Coroners Escheators Stewards Bailiffs Chief Constables. . . . And that you shall then and there have this Precept. Dated at Westminster, etc. . . ."

It is the judge's clerk who formally says: "Mr. High Sheriff of this County, be pleased to return the several precepts and writs to you directed and delivered or returnable here this day that my Lords the Queen's Justices may proceed thereon." In reply the sheriff—sitting beside the judge—receives from his under-sheriff a roll of documents including such things as a list of jurors, which show his compliance with the precept. This he has endorsed and sealed, and now returns. The sheriff hands to the judge the bundle of papers, tied with legal coloured tape, usually green. With a bow the judge accepts it, and passes it to the Clerk of Assize sitting below him.

This completes the formal opening of the assize. The judge in the Crown court retires for a moment to change his full-bottomed wig for the more comfortable bench wig, then returns to commence the trial of prisoners.

Until 1933 it was customary at this point for the judge to address the Grand Jury. By custom the Bar was not present during the address. Although intended to concern the business in hand, some judges in the old days used the occasion to unburden themselves of reflections on the state of the country at large. Lord Campbell (Lord Chancellor 1859) said—in his "Lives of the Chancellors"—that he found himself obliged, while in the House of Commons, to censure some of these speeches.

The assize opening procedure, like that for the procession from the Judges' Lodgings, has changed little since the 17th century. In 1682 (our authority is again "The Office of Clerk of Assize" published in that year), after a triple proclamation and call for silence by a Cryer, the Clerk of Assize had to read the Commission of Assize and the Commission of Association : both, of course, in Latin. At the first county in the circuit he followed these with the Writ of Admittance and the Writ of Si non omnes.

The Cryer then made another proclamation covering the old forms of Novel Disseisin, Mort d'ancestre, Juris Utrum and Attaint, as well as Certificate of Assize, Oyer and Terminer and General Jail Delivery.

The commissions for the latter two forms were read, and the Cryer then called on the sheriff to deliver his returns. When the sheriff had handed these over "then the Judge takes notice of the Sheriff, and speaks to him to be covered, but till then the Sheriff may not be covered." Then was called the roll—still mentioned in the precept—of justices, mayors, coroners and so forth; and the Grand Jury was sworn and charged.

When the court adjourned, at the end of each day, then as now, the judges were ceremonially escorted back to their Lodgings. A fanfare is sounded at their departure, but nowadays the javelin-men and other attendants are usually dispensed with for the return journey.

The sheriff and his chaplain remain in attendance every day at least until the end of criminal business, and during capital trials the sheriff must be in court all day.

By custom the judges of assize do a good deal of entertaining during their stay, returning the hospitality offered to them by local dignitaries as well as inviting private guests including members of the Bar.

At Oxford the judges entertain at dinner the Vice-Chancellor of the University, the proctors, the heads of houses, and the preacher of the assize sermon. At Cambridge the Esquire Bedels and the Public Orator are also entertained, but only in Hilary and Trinity terms—because the autumn assize is of comparatively recent origin.

Newcastle-on-Tyne claims to be the only city which entertains Her Majesty's judges of assize and their staffs as guests throughout their stay. Before the judges leave they give a dinner by way of some return to the Lord Mayor, senior aldermen, town clerk, city and high sheriffs, the Bishop, the senior Service officers and the Clerk of Assize.

When the Lord Mayor of Newcastle proposes the health of the judges, he presents each of them with a unique leave-taking present: a golden coin, traditionally a "Jacobus" (James I) to the senior judge and a "Carolus" (Charles I) to the junior. (The reigns and denominations are not strictly adhered to, and rose nobles and even spade guineas have been used from time to time). These gifts are commonly known as "dagger money," and the generally accepted origin has been that the city Corporation once used to provide an armed guard for the judges on their "perilous" journey from Newcastle to Carlisle. Later, the tale goes, the judges provided their own protection at the Corporation's expense.

Recent research, however, indicates that the gift—though certainly historic—is simply a handsome present intended to show honour to distinguished visitors. The name "dagger-money" seems to date only from the mid-19th century, when the custom was revived after a lapse. The evidence of its origin has been summed up by C. H. Hunter Blair in an article on "Judges of Assize at Newcastle-upon-Tyne" in Archaeologia Aeliana (Vol. XXI, 4th series, 1943).

Hunter Blair says that coin gifts to the judges are recorded only twice from the high sheriff of Northumberland—who might be expected to be at least as much concerned as the city officials with the safe transport of the judge through any country infested with bandits or raiding Scots. These two occasions were in July, 1627, and in 1628, the last appearing in the expenses account of Sir Thomas Swinburne as "to the judges Sir Henry Yelverton and Sir James Whitelocke either of them a peece at our parting upon Benwell Hills."

But in 1676 the Northumberland county sheriff did give the assize judges an odd present which may have something to do with the "dagger" explanation of the coin gifts. Roger North (quoted by Hunter Blair) wrote: "The Northumberland sheriff gave us all arms that is a dagger, knife, penknife and fork altogether." Was this an ingenious composite implement, like the schoolboys' knives which contain a gadget for removing stones from horses' hooves? Or was it merely that the entire set of useful implements was contained in one case? We are not told. Hunter Blair points out that no mention is made of the Scots—the usual danger of the Border country—and it was a gift from the sheriff of the county, not from the mayor of the city. He adds: "These are the only entries I have found of gifts from the High Sheriff to the Judges. In the accounts of Bertram Mitford (1835) and Ralph Carr (1846) 'leave is taken' of the judges, but no gifts are given."

This authority traces the coin-gift custom as far back as the 16th century. It was, he says, customary before 1561 for the mayor of Newcastle, at leave taking, to give each of the judges of assize an ancient coin, one out of circulation *and not legal tender*, "in reward," that is out of respect or regard for them. He quotes these examples: 1561 . . .30s.; 1566 . . . two olde ryalls 30s.; 1595 . . . two olde spur riolls, 15s. & 6d. per peece 31s.; 1626 . . . a spur royal in gold; 1659 . . . two rose nobles 42/6. However, it should be mentioned that the ryal at face value was 15s. from Mary's reign onwards; when introduced in Edward IV's reign its value was 10s.

The custom seems to have dropped out of use after the middle of the 17th century. It is next noticed in 1852, when Lord Campbell while on circuit as Chief Justice records in his diary: "at our departure (from Newcastle) the mayor according to ancient usage presented to me a gold Jacobus to buy a dagger, with which I might defend myself from Scottish freebooters."

Judges were not the only distinguished visitors to whom presents were given—but only they received ancient coins. The revival of the custom in the mid-19th century seems likely to be due to the publication of the details of 16th and 17th century gifts quoted above, in a tract published in 1849. Why the name and nature of dagger money should suddenly have become attached to the gifts is uncertain. It is true, as Hunter Blair points out, that tenants formerly escorted the judge through their manors on his assize journeys in the north. The 17th century gift of the "all arms" dagger may have become associated in people's minds with the presentation of coins.

An assize at which there are no prisoners for trial—a completely blank calendar—is termed a maiden assize. Until as late as 1840 or 1850, the term had a more restricted meaning, indicating an assize at which no prisoner was convicted of a capital offence—a situation which was rare in the days before the number of capital offences was drastically reduced in the 19th century.

It is customary at a maiden assize for the sheriff to present the judge, and in some places other commissioners such as the Clerk of Assize, with a pair of white—normally kid—gloves. The custom is observed also in Scotland, Ireland and in the Colonies. It may have originated (or survived when lapsed elsewhere) in

the north of England, for Brand ("Popular Antiquities," Vol. ii
Ed. 1841) speaks of it as "still prevailing" in that area. In Yorkshire the occasions in former days were extremely rare, since one
assize at York had to deal with crime from the whole of the vast
county. On the other hand in the sparsely populated Welsh
counties, such as Anglesey, Monmouth and Montgomery, the
custom has always been fairly often observed. Bards of the 19th
century, indeed, were wont to describe Wales as "Gwlad y
Menyg Gwynion," the Land of the White Gloves. The phrase is
still in current use.

The presentation is made by the sheriff, since in former times
it was he who had charge of the county jail and he still has
responsibility for county representation at the assize.

The gloves presented nowadays are plain. But at the opening
of the Lincoln Lent Assizes for 1856, for instance, the city sheriff
gave Lord Campbell "an elegant pair of white gloves, beautifully
embroidered and ornamented with Brussels lace, and having the
city arms embroidered in frosted silver on the back of each
glove." MacKinnon quotes Mr. Arthur Denman's Digest (1912)
as follows: ". . . the Sheriff presents white gloves to the Commissioners of Assize. In the case of the judge these are ornamented
round the wrists with gold lace, those given to the Clerk of
Assize being plain." MacKinnon suggests this may have been the
practice on the South-Eastern Circuit, of which Mr. Denman was
Clerk of Assize, but adds "on the few occasions when I have
received white gloves, e.g., at Haverfordwest, Carmarthen and
Lincoln, they have not had any gold lace on them."

One factor which has reduced the number of maiden assizes in
recent years is the provision in the Administration of Justice
Act, 1938, that assizes may be cancelled when there is "no
substantial amount of business to be transacted." However, even
if there are no criminal cases to be tried in a given town, the
judge may still hold an assize if there is an appreciable amount
of civil business. The white gloves custom has been extended in
recent times to Quarter Sessions, Magistrates' Courts and even
Juvenile Courts. The custom was generally maintained even
during the second World War when clothing was rationed—
though on at least one occasion cotton gloves had to be
substituted for kid.

Some of the few authorities on this subject (if so they can be called) seem to suggest that the custom fell into desuetude for a time, and was later revived. Fuller (quoted in Hazlitt, "Faiths and Folklore," 1905, vol. 1) says: "It passeth for a general report of what was customary in former times that the sheriff . . . used to present" white gloves at assizes where there was no capital conviction. And Brand says "in the North of England a custom still prevails . . . etc." Hackwood ("Story of the Shire," c. 1900) writes of the custom in the past tense, and says that in some counties, including Yorkshire, the judge's attendants claimed glove money—i.e., the equivalent in cash—"till these fees were abolished some fifty or sixty years ago."

There seems no completely satisfactory explanation of the origin of the white gloves custom. Writers who trouble to go into the matter at all agree that, whatever the practical reason if any, there is a symbolic meaning. Norton-Kyshe ("The Law and Custom relating to Gloves," 1901) says: "the hand is in the Roman Law as well as in the early German Law, a symbol of power." After referring to the hand's part in bargains, espousals and freeing (manumission) of slaves, he adds "that this symbolism should sometimes be transferred from the hand to the glove . . . seems but natural, it is in this transfer that we find the origin of the white gloves in question. At a Maiden Assize no criminal has even been called to plead (hold up hand) and the judge gets white gloves." Hackwood says the custom is "a piece of symbolism of Teutonic origin."

Symbolism maybe; but, as we have seen, gloves were a customary present to distinguished people including judges, and were also a customary court fee—in the days when fees were (legitimately or not) the personal "takings" of judge and court officials.

The history of gloves in England goes back to the 8th century, but they seem not to have been in general use here before the 13th century. William Hull, junior ("History of the Glove Trade," 1834) says that according to the Speculum Saxonicum, Lib. iii, judges were prohibited from wearing gloves on the bench. The gift of gloves, says this writer, was sometimes abused, and he suggests that such abuse was the reason for the Saxon prohibition. Sir Thomas More, when Lord Chancellor, was given a New Year present of a pair of gloves containing £40 in gold by a suitor whose case he had decided favourably. The gloves were accepted, the gold refused : but such a gift was doubtless far from unique.

A case in the Year Book of Edward I, 1302 (the Year Books are the earliest existing Law Reports) lays down that prisoners acquitted of manslaughter must pay a fee in the form of a pair of gloves to the justice's clerk, besides fees to the marshal. It was long the custom for prisoners pleading royal pardon to present gloves to judges and court officers. Norton-Kyshe says the first mention of these pardon presentations is in the case of Humfrey Bohm in the reign of Henry VI (reported in the Year Books), in which a man convicted of manslaughter pleaded pardon. The last such mention, according to the same authority, is in the report of a King's Bench case in 1676, when a prisoner presented gloves to all the judges on his pardon. An Act of 1692 made it unnecessary for outlaws to attend in person to plead pardon, and apparently the pardon gifts of gloves ceased from this time.

An early 18th century Northumberland sheriff's account says that 72 pairs of gloves were provided on one occasion by the sheriffs—the judges getting six pairs each, the remainder being divided among officials and others. It is not clear whether or not these gifts were for a maiden assize, but in any case gifts on such a scale have long died out—doubtless mainly because of the expense.

At the end of each assize it was once customary for the judge's clerk symbolically to break a willow-wand. A tale goes that someone, with the idea of saving expense, invented a wand jointed like a fishing rod. No sooner was it "broken" than it was reassembled ready for use at the next circuit town!

10. The Old Bailey

No name is more famous in the annals of criminal justice than that of the Old Bailey. On or near the spot close to St. Paul's Cathedral where the present building stands, surmounted by its golden figure of Justice with her sword and scales, the chief criminal courts of London have been held for nearly 700 years. From the early days of the historic Newgate Prison which housed London's malefactors, an "assize" and quarter sessions court was situated close to it. Now known as the Central Criminal Court, reconstituted and rebuilt, the Old Bailey remains on its old site although Newgate Prison was demolished half a century ago. Its very name is so ancient that the origin has been forgotten. Possibly it has some connection with the fortifications of the City wall adjacent to Newgate.

During the Middle Ages the court was held either in Newgate Prison itself or in some convenient house hired for the occasion. A charter of Henry I gave the City of London the right to choose its own Justiciar to hear pleas of the Crown—roughly corresponding with the major criminal offences. A charter of Edward III in 1327 made the Mayor of London for the time being one of the Justices for the Jail Delivery of Newgate, and from 1462 the Lord Mayor of the day has also been one of the Commissioners of Oyer and Terminer for the City of London. These are the ancient commissions for the trial of criminal cases, Jail Delivery being applicable to the trial of accused persons detained in prison, and Oyer and Terminer (Hear and Determine) to the trial of other defendants. It is by these commissions that sessions of the Central Criminal Court are still held, and the Lord Mayor is still technically a judge of the Old Bailey, though when he takes his seat nowadays he does so merely as a token act.

As long ago as 1291 there were eight jail deliveries of Newgate (i.e., eight sessions of the Old Bailey) in a year, and in 1304 there were five. Since in those days the prison was actually in the gatehouse of Newgate the frequency of the "deliveries" may have been due to the shortage of accommodation. In 1539 the first permanent Sessions House was built. This was rebuilt in 1774. By the 18th century there were nine or ten sessions a year. The Commissioners were the Lord Mayor, the Lord Chancellor, the Secretaries of State and Ministers, the Judges of the Common Law courts at Westminster, the Law Officers of the Crown, the Aldermen, Recorder, Common Serjeant and Judges of the Sheriffs' Court (a local court for trial of some civil actions) of the City of London. Any two of these formed a quorum for a trial. In practice the Lord Mayor, Recorder, Aldermen—as Justices of the Peace for the City, the two Sheriffs, and Common Law judges dealt with the cases. The Commission of Oyer and Terminer covered the County of Middlesex as well as the City of London.

In 1834 the Old Bailey was reconstituted by the Central Criminal Court Act of that year, and renamed the Central Criminal Court. It now has jurisdiction to try all crimes within the City and County of London, the County of Middlesex and suburban parts of Surrey, Kent and Essex. It is still in effect the Quarter Sessions court for the City of London, though not for the remainder of the area. Under the Act of 1834 separate commissions of Oyer and Terminer and of Jail Delivery are issued at the beginning of each new Lord Mayor's year of office.

The Commissioners under the Act are the Lord Mayor, the Lord Chancellor, the Lord Chief Justice and judges of the High Court, the Dean of Arches (judge of the chief ecclesiastical court of the Province of Canterbury), Aldermen of the City of London, the Judge of the City of London (formerly called the Sheriff's) Court, the Recorder of London and the Common Serjeant. Although the Lord Mayor and Aldermen do not now sit to try prisoners at the Old Bailey, an Alderman is always on hand in the building when only one judge is sitting—because by law there must be a quorum of two Commissioners present, as in the system prior to the Act of 1834. The judges who normally sit are one judge of the Queen's Bench Division, the Recorder, the Common Serjeant and the Judge of the City of London Court.

Quarter Sessions for the County, as distinct from the City, of London are not held at the Old Bailey; nor are the separate sessions for Southwark.

JUDICIAL COSTUME I. The Court of King's Bench in the 15th century, from an illumination now in the Inner Temple library. The five judges wear scarlet lined with white, probably white fur: a robe, a hood (of which the cape-portion can be seen) and over all a long mantle fastened at the right shoulder. On their heads they wear the coif.

The Commission of Jail Delivery at the Central Criminal Court runs in part:

"ELIZABETH THE SECOND By the Grace of God of the United Kingdom of Great Britain and Northern Ireland and of her other Realms and Territories, Queen, Head of the Commonwealth, Defender of the Faith.

"To the Central Criminal Court and to Our trusty and well beloved Sir ——— ——— Knight Lord Mayor of Our City of London and the Lord Mayor of Our said City for the time being etc. etc. . . . Know ye that We by virtue and in pursuance of the Central Criminal Courts Acts 1834 and 1881 and of all other powers enabling Us in that behalf have constituted you or any two or more of you Our Justices to deliver the prisons of all the prisoners therein being who are triable at the Central Criminal Court And therefore We command you that at such times and places . . . as have been or shall be appointed . . . you or any two or more of you do meet to deliver the prison of such prisoners as aforesaid doing therein what to Justice appertains according to the Laws and Customs of England saving to Us the amerciaments and other things to Us from thence accruing For We command our Sheriffs of Our City of London and of Our Counties of London Middlesex Essex Kent and Surrey and all other our Ministers Officers Sheriffs and liege subjects soever and every of them that at certain days and places . . . they . . . cause and aid one another where necessary in causing all such prisoners as aforesaid and their attachements before you . . . there to come In Witness whereof We have caused these Our Letters to be made Patent. . . ."

The Commission of Oyer and Terminer, addressed as the other, states:

". . . .Know Ye that We by virtue and in pursuance of, etc. . . . have assigned you or any two or more of you Our Justices to enquire more fully the truth by the oath of good and lawful men of Our City of London and Counties of London and Middlesex and of those parts of the Counties of Essex Kent and Surrey within the Central Criminal Court District and by other ways means and methods by which you shall or may better know (as well within liberties as without) by whom the truth of the matter may be the better known and enquired into of all treasons murders felonies and misdemeanours and also the accessories of them within the jurisdiction of the said Central Criminal Court (as well within liberties as without) by whomsoever and in what manner soever done committed or perpetrated and by whom and to whom when how and after what manner and of all articles and circumstances concerning the premises and every of them or any of them in any manner whatsoever and the said treasons and other the premises to hear and determine according to the Laws and Customs of England. . . ."

K

Nowadays there are at least twelve sessions of the Central Criminal Court each year, each session continuing until the cases set down for hearing are disposed of. August is the only month in which no session is held.

The dates of the sessions are fixed at a brief ceremony, to which all the Commissioners are summoned, on the first day of the legal year—normally October 1. The Lord Mayor attends in his scarlet gown, with the City Swordbearer in his picturesque fur hat and carrying a sword, the Serjeant-at-arms or Common Cryer, and the City Marshal. The Lord Mayor presides on the bench while the sessions are fixed by four High Court judges who attend in full dress. The Recorder is also present, and the dates of the sessions are announced by the Clerk.

Each session at the Old Bailey is opened with some solemnity, though with much less pageantry than that attached to assizes. The Lord Mayor attends in state, wearing his scarlet gown; the City's "Handbook of Ceremonial" published in 1933 provides for him to arrive in a coach and four. The Aldermen, Recorder and Sheriffs also attend in their scarlet robes, which incidentally they also wear when present on any Red Letter days (see Chapter 7 for list).

The Lord Mayor is conducted to the bench in a procession comprising the Under-Sheriffs, Sheriffs, City Marshal, Swordbearer, Common Cryer, Lord Mayor, Aldermen and Secondary. The Lord Mayor takes the central seat on the bench while the usher reads a proclamation—similar to that used at assizes—calling "All persons who have anything to do before my Lords the Queen's Justices" to "draw near and give your attendance."

Unlike the assize opening ceremony, the commissions are not read, and on the Lord Mayor's departure the business of the session begins at once.

On the third and following days of each session a judge of the Queen's Bench Division—often termed the "Red Judge" because of his scarlet robes—attends to try murder and other serious cases. One of the City sheriffs drives to the Law Courts to escort the judge to the Old Bailey where he is received ceremonially. On the first attendance of a "red judge" in each legal year the Lord Mayor himself receives him. A procession is formed, in the same order as at the opening of each session, with the High Court judge walking behind the Lord Mayor. In the summer months the judge and others taking part carry the traditional posy, once intended to ward off unpleasant smells from the jail (see below for a further account of this custom). Arrived in court, the Lord Mayor takes the central position on the bench, beneath the City's Sword of Justice (which dates from 1563), with the judge on his right and other Commissioners on his left. The sheriffs also have seats on the bench, as at assizes. In each of the several courts at the Old Bailey the central seat is thus reserved for the Lord Mayor or aldermen, and left empty in their absence.

On each succeeding day of the judge's attendance a procession is formed to escort him into court. The procession comprises the under-sheriffs, sheriffs and/or aldermen; junior aldermen precede their seniors, but on leaving the bench the order is reversed so that the seniors lead.

The Lord Mayor and sheriffs provide luncheon at the Old Bailey every day for the Commissioners. Often some members of the Bar and others are also invited. A curious tradition is that the final course shall always consist of a slice of fruit cake and an apple; why these relatively commonplace items should have acquired the dignity of a custom, history does not relate.

The modern luncheon is a relic of the substantial dinners provided each day in an age when eating and drinking were taken more seriously. The Old Bailey dinners, at which the Lord Mayor took the chair, were noted by the early 19th century and probably originated much earlier. The antiquary Strype (writing in 1720) tells us that over the court-room in the Old Sessions House—originally built in 1539—there was "a stately dining-room, sustained by ten stone pillars."

A writer in the Quarterly Review in 1836 described the procedure in his time like this: "The first course was rather miscellaneous, and varied with the season, though marrow-puddings always formed a part of it; the second never varied, and consisted exclusively of beef-steaks. The custom was to serve two dinners (exact duplicates) a day, the first at three o'clock, the second at five. As the judges relieved each other it was impracticable for them to partake of both; but the aldermen often did so, and the chaplain, whose duty it was to preside at the lower end of the table, was never absent from his post. This invaluable public servant persevered from a sheer sense of duty, till he had acquired the habit of eating two dinners a day, and practised it

for nearly ten years without any perceptible injury to his health
... We are sorry to be obliged to add that the worthy chaplain's
digestion has at length proved unequal to the double burthen
imposed upon it; but the Court of Aldermen, considering him a
martyr to their cause, have very properly agreed to grant him an
adequate pension for his services."

Dinners for three sessions, a total of 19 days, in 1807-8 are
said to have cost the sheriffs £35 a day. The total cost, including
the price of 145 dozen bottles of wine consumed, was £1,115—
no small sum even now, and worth very much more at that
period. The cost of the modest luncheon served nowadays is
shared between the Lord Mayor and the two sheriffs in a proportion of one-third each.

A 19th century practitioner at the Old Bailey, Serjeant
Ballantine, wrote disapprovingly in his memoirs (published in
1882) of the bygone dinners: "There was much general
hospitality extended towards the Bar, and the junior members
were given frequent opportunities of meeting the judges and
other people of position, but one cannot but look back with a
feeling of disgust to the mode in which eating and drinking,
transporting and hanging were shuffled together. The City judges
rushing from table to take their seats upon the Bench; the leading
counsel scurrying after them, the jokes of the table scarcely out
of their lips, and the amount of wine drunk not rendered less
apparent from having been drunk generously."

Between May 1 and September 30 the ledges of the docks and
the floor of the benches in the Old Bailey courts are strewn with
herbs, and the judges are provided with posies. The herb strewn
is rue, a variety of which (Ruta graveolens) is cultivated in this
country. The plant, a woody perennial, is a native of Southern
Europe. It possesses a strong scent and has medicinal uses. The
posies—a total of about 16 are distributed each day to the various
Commissioners and others—consist of various garden flowers.
On one occasion they were made up of mignonette, Virginia
stock and lavender; on another, of yellow tulips and red rose-
buds clustered round wallflowers. The recipients carry their
posies into court, then place them on the desk before them.

These customs, like the similar ones observed in some assize
towns (see Chapter 7), may have arisen from a belief that the
scent of aromatic herbs and flowers would serve to ward off jail

fever; and certainly they were an antidote to the noisome smells. It is during the summer months, when smells and jail fever (typhus) must have been most prevalent, that the customs are observed.

As early as 1414, according to Stow, the jailer and 64 of the prisoners in Newgate died of the fever. Outbreaks of disease were frequent in the old, insanitary prison, and infection was a constant danger in the adjacent Old Bailey. In May, 1750, one of these outbreaks caused the death of a judge of the Common Pleas (Sir Thomas Abney), a Baron of the Exchequer (Baron Clark), the Lord Mayor (Sir Samuel Pennant) and a number of barristers and jurymen. This disaster was probably the immediate cause of the Old Bailey herb-strewing and posy-carrying customs. Nevertheless there was another severe infection in 1772, in which several people lost their lives.

11. The Circuit Mess

NOWADAYS barristers briefed in a case at assizes can often travel to the circuit town in the morning, conduct their case there, and travel back to London the same evening. In days when travelling was more difficult, the barristers who customarily practised on a particular assize circuit journeyed from one town to another round the whole circuit, as the judge and court officials may do still. The entire circuit personnel, from judge to junior counsel, formed a sort of unwieldy caravan. Before the age of railways, stage-coach or horseback was the means of transport, with perhaps a separate vehicle—or saddle-bags—for baggage and books. It is only 60 years since the Western Circuit barristers sold (to a travelling menagerie!) the pantechnicon which they had used to trundle their books from town to town, under the care of one of their number termed the baggage-master.

When the courts rose at Westminster at the end of a term in the old days, everyone would move off on circuit. This arrangement naturally brought the barristers on each circuit into particularly close contact. After the close of the day's work in a provincial assize court, the circuit Bar would all foregather and dine together. They brought with them much of the communal life of the Inns of Court, and observed at dinner many of the dining customs to which they were used, with local variations growing up in course of time. Apart from the social side, these circuit Bars maintained (as they still do to some extent) professional discipline among their members, and saw that their interests were protected against "outsiders" who did not normally practise on the circuit.

The system still exists and flourishes today, in spite of inroads made upon it by the opportunities for circuit members to return to London from many assize towns. Most barristers join one or other of the circuits soon after they are called. Their membership of the circuit Bar—an arrangement which has no legal sanction but is rigidly enforced by etiquette—enables them to practise at all assizes and quarter sessions on that circuit. If they wish to take a case at any time upon another circuit, they must require and receive an additional "special" fee, and even then they must be accompanied by a junior from the circuit where they are appearing. Membership of a circuit also confers the right to dine at the Bar mess which is established during the assizes in each town.

Each circuit bar has its own officers, chosen from among members. The chief of these officers is the Leader, the senior Queen's Counsel on the circuit, who is ex officio Treasurer of the mess. (It will be remembered that Treasurer is the title of the chief officer of each of the Inns of Court). The secretary or officer responsible for conducting the day to day affairs of the circuit Bar is on most circuits known as the Junior. Usually a barrister fairly recently called, he holds office for six months or a year, and during this period he is expected to travel the entire circuit. His duties include the summoning of circuit meetings, taking a leading part at mess dinners, and adjudicating on matters in dispute. He may name his own successor after consulting senior Q.C.s on the circuit, or else the circuit "wine committee" chooses the new Junior. The Junior of the Northern Circuit is required to swear "that you do always uphold the rights and privileges of the stuffs and do ever watch and guard against the vile aspirations of the silks."

Each circuit has a Recorder (nothing to do with the judicial officer who bears that title) whose office on most circuits is separate from that of the Junior, and who keeps records of the circuit Bar. The oldest records now existing are those of the Northern, beginning in 1763, those of the Midland commencing ten years later. There is also a Junior Treasurer, who sees to the mess accounts; the true Treasurer, who is also the Leader, is a busy senior barrister and naturally can have little time for circuit business.

The Old Bailey has had its own Bar mess, like those of the circuits, since 1891. It is administered by a committee which includes the three senior Treasury counsel ex officio. Each year the mess entertains the Lord Mayor and sheriffs at dinner.

At circuit mess dinners the chair is taken by the Leader, or in his absence the senior member present. He is always referred to as "Mr. Leader," and not by name. At the bottom of the table sits "Mr. Junior" or "Mr. Recorder." Other members sit in order of seniority of call, from the Leader down to the Junior.

On the Midland circuit something like the Inner Temple formula for permission to smoke is adopted. Mr. Recorder tells the Leader "Twenty minutes have elapsed since Grace," and whatever the actual time this is taken as permission for members to light up.

A Grand Night is held at each assizes, and the judges are entertained to dinner. "Grand Night" on circuit is not the solemn affair which it has become at the Inns of Court. Its chief feature is the "Grand Court" held after dinner, at which members are fined for real or (more usually) fictional breaches of circuit rules. Circuit business is normally done on these nights, and new members are elected, proposed and seconded by existing members. Membership continues for as long as the barrister remains in practice; it is possible to change one's circuit for strong reasons, but such changes are rare and there is seldom cause.

Even admission may be clothed with the half-mocking, half-serious ceremonial of the Grand Court. The late Lord Justice MacKinnon, dining with the Welsh circuit Bar in 1932, watched the admission of three new members. "The senior man present delivered an allocution to the novices," he says in his book "On Circuit" (1940), "and added to the affected solemnity of it by adorning his head with a table-napkin in the manner of the black cap. This appears to be an ancient circuit jest. Lord Campbell, in a letter of 1807, describes his admission to the Home Circuit (now extinct). 'I was tried for some mock offences, and being found Guilty, the judge, putting a doyley on his head for a black cap, sent me to be carried back to the place from whence I came.'" The reference is, of course, to the ancient wording of the death sentence.

When the Grand Court is summoned, it is the Leader who presides but the Junior who is judge. One of the senior members acts as Attorney-General of the circuit, to conduct the "prosecutions."

Members may be found "guilty" in jest, of some good fortune which has befallen them and which their colleagues regard as a good reason why they should contribute by way of fine to the mess funds. The taking of silk or judicial appointment as a

Recorder are both events of this character. And barristers have been "convicted" of having twins—in one case the member's father, also a barrister, was charged with being "an accessory before the fact." Old circuit records show such out-dated crimes as wearing hair-powder. Dancing with the daughter or other feminine relative of an attorney incurred penalties. Once a newly-elected member was convicted of "puffing" (advertising) because an inn signboard displayed a landlord's name which was unfortunately the same as his own!

The prosecution puts its case, and the victim is then asked if he has anything to say "in aggravation" or in mitigation. Then the Junior asks the court if they desire to congratulate or condole with, the prisoner. If they decide upon "congratulation," the matter ends. If the answer is "condoled with," it means a "conviction" and a fine. The Junior asks "In how many?" meaning bottles of wine to be contributed to the mess cellar. This is the procedure on the Northern Circuit, described by Mr. J. B. Sandbach in his book "This Old Wig," and may be taken as typical.

Sometimes such an imaginary case may be a hint directed against a member who has actually offended against Bar etiquette in some way. If he is wise he will take the hint. However, a serious instance of professional misbehaviour would not, of course, be dealt with in such a light-hearted way. A special meeting of the circuit Bar would be called and, if necessary, the matter reported to the benchers of the offending member's Inn of Court.

12. The Greater Judges

IF the office of Lord Chancellor did not exist it is doubtful if even a Chesterton or a Gilbert could invent it. Its combination of diverse duties accumulated over the centuries is fantastic. And as long ago as 1918 a Select Committee was told that "Successive holders of this office have testified that it is beyond the strength of any one man to perform the work that ought to be done."

The Lord Chancellor today is keeper of the Great Seal, speaker of the House of Lords and a member of the Cabinet. He takes precedence after the Archbishop of Canterbury, who himself comes first after the royal family. It is treason to kill the Lord Chancellor in the performance of his duties. He is "keeper of the sovereign's conscience" and has extensive Church patronage. He is head of a Government department of his own, whose responsibilities cover the appointment of High Court judges and —except in the County Palatine of Lancaster—County Court judges and Justices of the Peace.

He is head of the judiciary, and as a judge often presides over the House of Lords as final court of appeal, and sometimes sits in the Judicial Committee of the Privy Council. Although he is also ex officio a judge of the Court of Appeal, and President of the Chancery Division of the High Court (in an historical sense his own Division) he does not normally sit in these courts. Lord Halsbury did sit frequently in the Court of Appeal, and Lord Birkenhead tried some divorce cases at a time when there was particular pressure on the divorce courts. At the opening of the Law Courts at the beginning of each legal year, the Lord Chancellor and all the puisne judges of the Chancery Division sit as a Divisional Court to hear applications. But this is only a formality and no applications (rather disappointingly) are ever forthcoming.

Among other duties of a more or less ceremonial nature, the

Lord Chancellor must be present when newly-appointed judges of the Court of Appeal and High Court take the oaths (see Chapter 7). At the beginning of each legal year he customarily gives a "breakfast" reception to the judges and leaders of the profession (see Chapter 14). Up to 1871 the Lord Chancellor presided at the annual Trial of the Pyx (see Chapter 14). His ceremonial duties connected with Parliament fall outside our scope in this book.

The name "chancellor" is of Roman origin, and at first denoted the office of usher who sat at the "cancelli" or lattice-work screens of a law-court (Enc. Britt.). In the later Eastern Roman Empire the "cancellarii" became notaries, and the early medieval Western kingdoms knew chancellors as royal secretaries. In England the office is said to date at least from the time of Edward the Confessor, the first King of England to adopt the Norman practice of sealing documents.

As custodians of the Seal, without which no State document was valid, and as close advisers of the King, the Chancellors grew in power and influence during the Middle Ages. When the office of Justiciar—a sort of deputy to the King and Chief Justice combined—was abolished in the reign of Henry II (1154-89) the Chancellor was left as first officer in the realm. Cardinal Wolsey was the last of a long succession of eminent ecclesiastics who held the Chancellorship in medieval times, and Sir Thomas More who succeeded him is regarded as the first of the modern lawyer-Chancellors.

The judicial duties and status of the Lord Chancellors grew up very gradually. Anyone who wished to seek justice in the royal courts had first to obtain a writ: a command in the King's name that the alleged wrongdoer should appear before the court. Writs had to bear the Seal of the kingdom, so the Chancellors were—as they still are—responsible for the issue of all writs in the King's name. The Chancellor had a certain discretion as to the circumstances in which he would issue writs. But it was probably in another way that the Lord Chancellors came to hold the highest judicial position in the realm.

"In the rough days of the thirteenth century," a modern authority (Snell, "The Principles of Equity," ed. 1939) puts it, "a plaintiff was often unable to obtain a remedy in the Common Law Courts, even when they should have had one for him, owing to the strength of the defendant, who would defy the Court or intimidate the jury. Either deficiency of remedy or failure to administer it was a ground for petition to the King in Council to exercise his extraordinary judicial powers. A custom developed of referring certain classes of these petitions to the Chancellor, and this custom was confirmed by an order of Edward III in 1349. The Chancellor acted at first in the name of the King in Council, but in 1474 a decree was made on his own authority, and this practice continued, so that there came to be a Court of Chancery as an institution independent of the King and his Council." The court gradually developed principles of its own, which today form the part of the law which we call Equity, still administered mainly by the Chancery Division of the High Court.

The office of Lord Keeper of the Great Seal, though now merged in that of Lord Chancellor as it was originally, has at various periods been separate. In early times the Chancellors frequently had to travel on business—perhaps, in the case of the ecclesiastics, on the affairs of their own diocese—and on these occasions the Great Seal was left in the charge of a Lord Keeper. The Lord Keeper also functioned during any vacancy in the Chancellorship, and by an Act of 1562 he was declared to have the same powers as the Chancellor, and in fact at this period he usually succeeded to the Chancellorship. The only difference between the two offices then was that the Lord Keeper was appointed only by delivery of the seal, whereas the Lord Chancellor occasionally also had letters patent. The last Lord Keeper was Sir Robert Henley, who held the position from 1757 to 1761, from which date until 1766 he was Lord Chancellor, having become a peer.

When the Lord Chancellor signs official documents he does so with his name (being a peer, his title), followed by the letter "C." In fact the prefixes "Lord" and "High" were originally no part of his title. Nor were the early Chancellors peers. They attended the House of Lords as officials, when the House was still the King's Council, and continued to do so as its "speaker" when other royal officials had ceased to attend. Even today the Woolsack is technically outside the precincts of the House, and it is not necessary—though obviously convenient—for the Lord Chancellor to be a peer. In Henry VIII's reign an Act was passed forbidding any Chancellor not a peer to vote in the upper house. Since the Chancellorship of Lord Cowper (1705, made a Baron 1706) every Chancellor not already a peer has had a peerage conferred on him on taking office.

Well before this period the Chancellors were addressed as "Lord" by courtesy, as in the case of the Lord Chief Justices (see below in this chapter). The Oxford English Dictionary gives a quotation "My Lord Schanchler . . ." as early as 1485. The same dictionary gives 1589 as the earliest date for "Lord High Chancellor." The "High" was a title of distinction from other, lesser, chancellors such as those of Church dioceses or the Chancellor of the Exchequer.

The Lord Chancellor is appointed by the Crown on the nomination of the Prime Minister and, as a member of the Cabinet, must resign when the Government leaves office. Unlike almost all other judicial appointments, there is no statutory qualification for the holder of the Chancellorship. In practice those appointed are nearly always either judges or past or present Law Officers of the Crown. It is generally accepted that only Protestants are eligible, on account of the guardianship of the royal conscience and the ecclesiastical patronage. Lord Chancellors are made Privy Councillors, if not already so, on taking office.

The Lord Chancellor receives his position by delivery of the Seal of office. As Lord Campbell said ("Lives of the Lord Chancellors," vol. 1, 1845-7): "The appointment to the office of Lord Chancellor in very remote times was by patent or writ of Privy Seal or by suspending the Great Seal by a chain round his neck." Not a very pleasant proceeding, one would think—it is of silver and weighs 17 pounds Troy: "But for many ages the Sovereign has conferred the office by simply delivering the Great Seal to the person who is to hold it, verbally addressing him by the title which he is to bear. He then instantly takes the oaths, and is clothed with all the authority of the office, although usually, before entering upon the public exercise of it, he has been installed in it with great pomp and solemnity."

Today the Lord Chancellor is installed in the Court of Appeal. Though less magnificent than of old, the ceremony is by no means devoid of pageantry. All, or as many as possible, of the judges assemble in the court for the occasion. The greater judges wear their full dress robes, but others who have come from sitting in their respective courts attend in ordinary bench costume.

The Lord Chief Justice, in full-bottomed wig, scarlet and ermine, takes his place on the bench on the left of the Master of the Rolls, who wears his black and gold State robe. The President of the Probate, Divorce and Admiralty Division and the Lords Justices are all there in their full dress. Behind them stand the High Court judges.

Then the Lord Chancellor himself enters, in his black and gold robe of State, with its train, and preceded by his mace-bearer and purse-bearer. He takes his place at the right hand of the Master of the Rolls, with his attendants stationed behind him. The Master hands him a New Testament, and the Clerk of the Crown (who is also Permanent Secretary to the Lord Chancellor) administers the oath of allegiance and the judicial oath (see Chapter 7).

The oaths taken, the Lord Chancellor kisses the Testament, and the Attorney-General formally moves that the proceedings be recorded. (At the swearing-in of Lord Simonds in 1951 this was moved by the former Solicitor-General, Sir Lynn Ungoed-Thomas, K.C.). The Lord Chancellor replies "Be it so, Mr. Attorney." It is the duty of the Queen's Remembrancer to carry out the recording.

In the days when the Chancery court sat in Westminster Hall the ceremony took place there. Dugdale ("Origines Juridiciales," 1666, etc.), drawing from the work of the antiquary Camden, tells us of the swearing in of Sir Francis Bacon, when he received the Great Seal as Lord Keeper, in March, 1617, being then Attorney-General.

The ceremony took place on the first day of Easter term, and those taking part entered Westminster Hall in procession thus: "First the Clerks and inferior Officers of the Chancery, Secondly, young Students of the Law, Thirdly, the Gentlemen of his own Family, Fourthly, the Serjeant at Arms, and the bearer of the Seal (all on foot).

"Then the Lord Keeper himself on Horseback, in a Gown of Purple-Satin, betwixt the Lord Treasurer, and the Lord Privy Seal; divers Earls, Barons and Privy-Councillors, as also the Judges and many Gentlemen of note following after.

"Being come into the Court, the Lord Treasurer, and Lord Privy-Seal received his Oath, the Clerk of the Crown reading it."

The ancient oath of the Lord Chancellor, used until the Promissory Oaths Act, 1868, is given in Coke's "Institutes," 1628 (4 Inst. 88) as follows:

"That well and truly he shall serve our Sovereign Lord the King and his people in the office of Chancellor. That he shall do right to all manner of people poor and rich and after the laws and usages of the realm. That he shall truly counsel the King and his counsel he shall layne (conceal) and keep. That he shall in no way suffer the hurt or disinheriting of the King or that the rights of the Crown be decreased by any means as far as he may let it. If he may not let it he shall make it clearly and expressly to be known to the King with his true advice and counsel. And that he shall do and purchase the King's profit and in all that he reasonably may, as God him help."

The oath for the Lord Keeper given in the anonymous "Book of Oaths" (1649) is basically the same.

As the Lord Chancellor's judicial functions arose from his position as a great officer of State, it is natural to find that his official costume follows the traditions of statesmen rather than of lawyers. It bears little resemblance to that of the Common Law judges, but is the prototype of the costume now worn by a number of other high judicial officers.

On State occasions the Lord Chancellor wears a rich robe of flowered black damask ornamented with bars of gold lace, with a train; a black velvet court suit, lace stock and cuffs (no bands); white gloves; full-bottomed wig. He carries a three-cornered beaver hat.

When presiding over the House of Lords, whether for political or judicial business, he wears a black silk gown with train; a black cloth court suit; lawn bands; and a full-bottomed (never a bench) wig. How long has this "everyday" costume been customary? In "Bleak House" (1852-53) Dickens writes—in Chapter 3—of "his lordship," just returned to his room after sitting judicially in Lincoln's Inn Hall "whose robe, trimmed with beautiful gold lace, was thrown upon another chair." The Chancellor, disrobed, was "plainly dressed in black."

The Lord Chancellor also has a peer's robes appropriate to his degree. When, as in November, 1951, he executes a Royal Commission to open Parliament in the absence of the Sovereign, he wears his peer's robe with full-bottomed wig and three-cornered hat. At Coronations he wears his black and gold State robe with full-bottomed wig and—with odd effect—his coronet surmounting it.

An illumination, now in the Inner Temple Library (see Chapter 7), showing the Chancery Court in the time of Henry VI (1422-61) depicts the Lord Chancellor wearing scarlet judicial robes like those of the Common Law Judges. Apart from this instance there is nothing to indicate that such robes were worn by the Chancellors; perhaps their use was dropped with the disappearance of the limited Common Law jurisdiction exercised by the early Chancellors in addition to their own budding system of Equity. By the Apparel Act, 1532-3, repealed under James I, the Lord Chancellor was declared entitled "to wear in his apparel velvet satin and other silks of any colours except purple, and any manner of furs except *cloke genettes.*" Apart from these cases, presumably the clerical Chancellors who held office up to the time of Sir Thomas More wore their appropriate ecclesiastical dress.

Sir Thomas More himself is depicted with a furred black robe, and a black biretta-type cap. Nicholas Bacon, Lord Keeper, is shown in a portrait of 1577 with a similar cap and robe, and with ruffs at neck and sleeves. Francis Bacon, when he rode from Gray's Inn to Westminster on being made Lord Keeper in 1617, wore a suit of purple satin. "A handsome velvet gown" is the rather vague description (quoted by Inderwick, "The King's Peace," 1895) of another garment worn by Lords Keeper at about this time.

The black and gold State robe of the Lords Chancellors dates from the later 16th century. The fashion of decorating gowns, particularly those of official personages, with "guards" or bands of material began about 1500. Just as benchers of the Inns of Court and others (see Chapter 2) wore black gowns with velvet guards, so towards the middle of the century did more eminent and wealthy officers use guards of gold lace. A portrait of Sir Robert Broke, Speaker of the House of Commons in 1554, shows a black and gold robe of much the same type as is now worn by the Lord Chancellors (as well as the Speakers). Neither Nicholas Bacon, Lord Keeper (1558-79), nor Bromley, Lord Chancellor

JUDICIAL COSTUME II. Sir Edmund Anderson, Chief Justice of the Common Pleas 1582-1605. The full robe opens only down to the waist; the girdle is narrow; the mantle is still fastened at the right shoulder. The ruff is worn, following contemporary fashion. The black cornered cap is worn over the white coif. (From a painting by an unknown artist in the National Portrait Gallery.)

JUDICIAL COSTUME III. Sir John Holt, Chief Justice of the King's Bench, 1689-1709. The robe is less full, the cuffs are deeper, the girdle is broader. Wide bands are now worn at the neck. The mantle is now fastened at the throat, and turned back to show the lining. The full black wig is of the style worn by gentlemen of the time. The coif has gone, but the cornered cap is still important enough to be held in the hand. (From a painting by R. Van Bleeck in the National Portrait Gallery.)

JUDICIAL COSTUME IV.
Sir Charles Abbott (afterwards Lord Tenterden), Chief Justice of the King's Bench 1818-32. The bands are longer, and have lost any resemblance to the square collar from which they derived. The wig is grey, but still full and has not yet acquired the formalised "doormat" effect of today. (From a painting by J. Hollins after W. Owen in the National Portrait Gallery.)

JUDICIAL COSTUME V.
Lord Goddard, Lord Chief Justice of England 1946-. The robe opens down its whole length, with a wide trimming of fur. The black scarf is now invariably worn; the mantle is now abbreviated. The wig is formalised with rows of tight curls. The Lord Chief Justice today wears a lace stock with State dress.

1579-87, are shown with robes of this type. It seems to appear among the Lord Chancellors first with Bromley's successor, Sir Christopher Hatton, Lord Chancellor 1587-91, who is shown with such a robe in a portrait attributed to the year 1587 (and which in 1947 was in the possession of Mr. Justice Pearce). Hatton was a wealthy courtier without legal training. His tastes were flamboyant, and it is entirely in keeping with his character that he should be the first holder of his office to adopt the gold-ornamented robe.

Henceforth this style of robe was worn by each successive Chancellor, and was retained after the fashion disappeared from wider use about the time of Charles I. In its early days it was worn by many men of dignity, such as ambassadors. Privy Councillors retained it, as did the Chancellors, but for them the robe has now been replaced by a uniform. The Privy Council use of the black and gold robe has led to a suggestion that the modern use of the robe by certain high judges is because they are "Privy Councillors acting judicially." The robe (with variations in detail) is worn among judges by the Master of the Rolls, the President of the Probate, Divorce and Admiralty Division, and by the Lords Justices of Appeal. Although all these judges are in fact Privy Councillors and may on occasion sit in the Judicial Committee of the Privy Council, their robes surely derive more directly from that of the Lord Chancellor, which in turn is a survival of a general fashion not at first specifically connected with the Privy Council. Outside the law, similar robes are worn by the Speaker of the House of Commons, the Chancellor of the Exchequer, the Lord Mayor of London and some other civic heads, and by University dignitaries.

The illumination of the Court of Chancery in the reign of Henry VI, referred to above, shows two judges taken to be the Lord Chancellor and the Master of the Rolls. One is bare-headed and tonsured, and the other has a brown cap. Cohen ("A History of the English Bar," 1929) suggests that the latter may be untonsured, and perhaps the only lay Chancellor of the period, Neville, Earl of Salisbury, 1454. In the 16th century Chancellors are depicted with the square biretta-like black cap. During the later years of this century and the earlier part of the 17th century the Chancellors customarily wore a round, conical hat. About the reign of Queen Anne they adopted the three-cornered hat, in

L

common with the other judges, and this is their official headgear today.

The hat is not now worn on any occasion when the Lord Chancellor is sitting judicially. But Lord Campbell ("Lives of the Lord Chancellors," 1845-57) tells us that the Lord Chancellor used to be covered and returned no answer, when the Lord Mayor came into the Chancery Court to invite him to the Lord Mayor's Day banquet. This resembles the custom at present observed by the judges of the High Court and Court of Appeal (see Chapter 14), and the reason is doubtless the same, namely to assert the dignity of the Crown in the face of the pretensions of the first citizen of London. But, as Lord Campbell also says, the Lord Chancellor is covered when he addresses others than the members of the Upper House. And when he goes before a Commons committee he dons his hat "to assert the dignity of the Upper House, and then, having uncovered, gives his evidence."

Once the Lord Chancellors were accustomed to carry sweet-smelling nosegays, like those used at assizes and the Old Bailey (see Chapters 9 and 10). Foss ("Lives of the Judges," 1848-64) says that the custom "which has only lately been discontinued" existed in the reign of James I. Bacon, he says, wrote in a letter to the King "It is my Lord Chancellor's fashion, especially towards the summer, to carry a posy of wormwood." The Common Wormwood (Artemisia Absinthium), used medicinally as a vermifuge and in absinthe for its bitter taste, is presumably the herb meant. There are two references to the Lord Chancellor's nosegay in Dickens' "Bleak House" (1852-53). In Chapter 5, Miss Flite, the little mad woman who frequents the court of the Chancellor in Lincoln's Inn Hall, speaks of "when . . . there are no more flowers in bloom to make up into nosegays for the Lord Chancellor's court." And in Chapter 24: ". . . the Lord Chancellor . . . sitting in great state and gravity, on the bench; with the mace and seals on a red table below him, and an immense flat nosegay, like a little garden, which scented the whole Court."

The Lord Chancellor is everywhere preceded by his mace-bearer and—except in two instances—by his purse-bearer. Both these officials wear court dress.

The mace is of silver-gilt; there are in fact two, one for normal use and the other in reserve. The Chancellor's use of the mace, says Foss, "may probably" be traced to Cardinal Wolsey's love of splendour, though in his case the mace may have attached rather to his office as Legate and Cardinal. On an historic occasion in 1677 a notorious burglar named Thomas Sadler broke into the house of the Lord Chancellor, Lord Finch, and stole the mace. This theft is no doubt the reason for the unusual arrangement of having a "reserve" mace available.

Following the mace-bearer, and immediately preceding the Chancellor when he walks in formal procession, comes the bearer of the purse which in theory holds the Great Seal of the realm. The purse is a flat pouch of red velvet, some 18 inches square, embroidered with the royal arms in colour, and with big tassels. The seal itself—which weighs 17 pounds Troy—is no longer carried in the pouch. When the Lord Chancellor appears in his official capacity before the Sovereign or receives messengers of the Commons at the Bar of the Lords, he carries the purse himself : at the opening of Parliament he carries in it the Sovereign's speech. When he is on the woolsack, it is placed behind him.

The first reference to a purse for the Great Seal is in 1307-8, and the colour is already "rubea" (red). In 1351, the first year of Edward III's reign, the seal is described as being in a linen bag; and in the following year a purse is again mentioned, perhaps as outer protection, with the bag as inner covering. The purse is referred to a little later as being of white leather. In 1516-17 Cardinal Wolsey became Lord Chancellor, receiving the seal in its white leather bag or purse. But when he gave up office in 1529 we are told that the bag was contained in another one of crimson velvet, bearing the royal arms : in essentials the purse as we know it today. The purse of the 16th century is well illustrated in a portrait of Lord Keeper Nicholas Bacon in the National Portrait Gallery, painted in 1579; at this date it was of red velvet, embroidered with the royal arms and cipher E R, gathered at the top (contrary to present practice) with gold cord handles, and tassels hanging from the bottom. James I is said (Inderwick, "The King's Peace," 1895) to have devised some additions of gold embroidery. The history of the purse is to be found in Foss ("Lives of the Judges," Vol. V) and Maxwell-Lyte ("The Great Seal," 1926). An early 18th century purse is in the London Museum.

From the early years of the 16th century it was the custom to renew the purse yearly—doubtless necessary when 17 pounds of seal were carried in it. The old purses were (and are) perquisites of the Chancellors. Lord Hardwicke, Lord Chancellor for 20 years, 1736-56, acquired quite a collection of them, and his wife is said to have used a number to decorate the velvet drapery in a state bedroom at their Cambridgeshire mansion, Wimpole Hall. Other purses are said to have adorned chairs and a fire-screen. In 1872, when the price of a new purse was £65, the Treasury and the Lord Chancellor agreed that the yearly renewals should be stopped—but not until the death of an old lady who made the purses! She died the following year in fact, and the purses were afterwards renewed only every three years.

The present (1954) Great Seal is of silver, and the impression is six inches in diameter. The Seal proper weighs 135 oz., some 3 ounces more than the counter-Seal. On the Seal (obverse) is the Queen on horseback, with the crowned cipher below, the whole surrounded by the royal title in Latin. On the counter-seal (reverse) is the Queen throned and robed, with shields of the royal arms on either side, and the motto "Dieu et mon droit" below; the main legend is as on the obverse. The story of the Seal and its design is outside the scope of this book.

We have already seen that the delivery of the Great Seal is the means by which the office of Lord Chancellor is conferred. When a new seal is needed, either on a new reign or because of some change in the royal titles or arms, the old one is officially "damasked" or "broken" by the Sovereign defacing it with a hammer. The old seal is a traditional perquisite of the Lord Chancellor, who gives one of the two silver discs (Seal and Counter-Seal) of which it is composed to his predecessor. The gift of the old seal to the Chancellor is first heard of as early as 1327. In 1260 the fragments had been given to the Chancellor for the benefit of the poor, and this may have been the original idea.

Like the mace, the Great Seal was once stolen—in 1784, from the house of the Lord Chancellor, Lord Thurlow, in Great Ormond Street. This seal was never found, and a replacement had to be made.

The Lord Chancellor is one of the officers who receive from the Corporation of London at each year's end a traditional 4½ yards of "livery cloth." (See Chapter 5).

THE LORDS OF APPEAL IN ORDINARY

The King's Great Council was the original dispenser of royal justice, and the law courts of today almost all sprang from the Council at one time or another during the Middle Ages. We have seen earlier how, one after another, the three great Common Law courts split from the Council, or Curia Regis, in the 13th and 14th centuries. Until this period the King's Bench Court, while still a department of the Curia, was the highest court of appeal for civil actions. About the reign of Edward I, with the King's Bench now a separate court, the jurisdiction seems to have passed back to the Council itself. Out of that Council grew the House of Lords.

The House of Lords today is the highest court of appeal in both civil and criminal cases in the United Kingdom. Its civil appellate jurisdiction is, as we have seen, of great antiquity. Its similar function as regards criminal cases was gained only by the Criminal Appeal Act, 1907—which recognised for the first time a true right of appeal in criminal matters. The fiat of the Attorney-General is needed before criminal appeals may go to the Lords, and this is given only when the case involves a point of law of exceptional public importance.

Theoretically the peers as a whole are the judges when the House of Lords sits as appeal court. As law became more technical it was found necessary to restrict the duty in practice to those peers who were also judges of high rank. The last time a lay peer claimed the right to attend and vote on an appeal was in 1882, though even today it is only convention which prevents the exercise of the right. In 1876 the Appellate Jurisdiction Act provided for the appointment of Lords of Appeal in Ordinary— the number provided in the Act was two, since increased to eight —as life peers who would be salaried judges both of the House of Lords and also of the Judicial Committee of the Privy Council. In addition to the Lords of Appeal, the Lord Chancellor and any peers who hold or have held high judicial office may sit as judges of the House of Lords. High Court judges and the Attorney-General and Solicitor-General, all of whom receive summonses to "assist" at the opening of each Parliament, may be called in to advise.

Until 1948 it was customary for the House of Lords to sit for judicial business each day until about 4 p.m., and for Parliamentary business from 4.15 p.m. onwards. Thus the Lord Chancellor was often able to take part in both the judicial and the political work of the House on the same day. In 1948, by a curiously trivial circumstance, there came a change which some consider may have far-reaching constitutional results. Pile-driving for a new boiler-house made such a noise outside the Lords chamber during the daytime that judicial work there became impossible. So the Law Lords moved to a quiet room in another part of the building. But as they were not now sitting in the official chamber, they had to become an Appellate Committee, later reporting to the House itself for judgment. The noise has gone, but the arrangement has been found convenient; it enables the House to meet at 2.30 p.m. instead of 4.15 p.m. if it so wishes, to cope with the pressure of Parliamentary business. Judicial work goes on simultaneously with the Parliamentary debates; during the Parliamentary vacation the court sits in the chamber as of old. (The criticism levelled at this system is based on the fact that the Lord Chancellor must now choose whether he will be on the Woolsack or in the Appellate Committee—and it is feared that Lord Chancellors may be forced to plump for the Woolsack, and become pure politicians with evil consequences for their responsibilities in the legal field).

The Lords of Appeal in Ordinary are appointed by Letters Patent, on the nomination of the Prime Minister. They must have held certain high judicial positions for two years or more or else must have practised at the Bar for 15 years or more. Like the other judges of High Court rank and above, they hold office "during good behaviour," and in practice can be removed only by an address to the Sovereign from both Houses of Parliament. They rank as Barons for life, and may sit and vote in the House of Lords for Parliamentary as well as judicial business. Their peerages are not hereditary, but their wives become "Lady," and their children "The Honourable." Lords of Appeal like other peers of their rank are entitled "The Right Honourable Baron So-and-So."

The Law Lords possess peers' robes appropriate to their degree. When sitting judicially they wear lay dress (ordinary lounge suits) as do all peers for day-to-day Parliamentary business. The Lord Chancellor, when presiding, is robed, however, and counsel pleading before the House of Lords are wigged and gowned. Queen's Counsel wear full-bottomed wigs.

THE JUDICIAL COMMITTEE OF THE PRIVY COUNCIL

From many parts of the Commonwealth overseas, and originally from all, the ultimate appeal court is "The Queen in Council." The Privy Council is also the final arbiter in a variety of branches of the law including Admiralty prize matters and Church of England ecclesiastical concerns.

The Privy Council shares with the House of Lords descent from the King's Great Council of the Middle Ages. Appeals are heard today by a Judicial Committee of the Council, set up by an Act of 1833. Its membership comprises the Lord President, the Lord Keeper or first Lord Commissioner of the Great Seal (in practice the Lord Chancellor), and such Privy Councillors as hold or have held high judicial office. Lawyers qualified for this kind of work —for instance eminent judges of some Commonwealth countries —are appointed to the Privy Council specifically for the purpose of sitting on the Judicial Committee when necessary. Judgments are given in the form of a "report" from the Committee, recommending that the Sovereign should take this or that course in the matter concerned.

Like the Law Lords, who themselves are also members of the Privy Council, the Committee sits without ceremony and in lay dress. Counsel appearing before the committee, however, are wigged and gowned.

THE LORD CHIEF JUSTICE OF ENGLAND

When the holder of this great judicial office signs his name officially, he writes after it by way of title the two letters "C.J." for Chief Justice. He is not alone in this simplicity, for as has been seen the Lord Chancellor himself uses the simple suffix "C." But in the case of the Lord Chief Justice of England the unassuming signature is in a way symbolic of the history of his office. There were once no less than three "chiefs"—one for each of the old Common Law courts.

The Lord Chief Justice today is President of the Queen's Bench Division of the High Court, and both the senior permanent judge (excluding the Law Lords) and the senior Common Law judge.

It has been claimed that the ancient Justiciars of the realm, those magnates of the King's Council who were as much politicians or deputy-monarchs as judges, were the forerunners of the Lord Chief Justices of today. Certainly it is clear that the immediate line of ancestry of the office is in the Chief Justices of the King's Bench, the first of whom was appointed in 1268. In 1272 came the first Chief Justice of the Common Pleas. And not until 1312 was there a Chief Baron of the Exchequer to preside over the other Barons.

It is hard to say when any of the Chief Justices was first addressed as "Lord." In the dramatis personae of King Henry IV (Part 2) Shakespeare refers to "Lord Chief Justice of the King's Bench," presumably Gascoigne, who was Chief Justice of that court, 1400-. No peerage went with the office, and the "Lord" was purely a title of respect as in the case of the Lord Chancellor; it may well have come into use at about the same time, namely the end of the 15th century. Certainly it was accepted by the early 17th century.

During the battle between the Common Law courts to wrest power from each other some of the Chief Justices of the King's Bench thought they could score a nice point of precedence over their opposite numbers by calling themselves "Lord Chief Justice *of England*." Probably the first to adopt this title was Sir Edward Coke, the great champion of the Common Law, who was Chief Justice of the King's Bench from 1613-16. According to Lord Campbell (author of "Lives of the Chief Justices," 1849-57) Coke "took particular delight" in doing so. It brought him no good, for it is thought to have been one of the charges which finally caused his downfall. When the Lord Treasurer, the Earl of Suffolk, dismissed him, he is reported to have said: "Amongst other things, the King is not well pleased with the title of the book wherein you entitle yourself 'Lord Chief Justice of England,' whereas by law you can challenge no more than Lord Chief Justice of the King's Bench." Nevertheless, an Act of 1543 had referred, accidentally or otherwise, to "the King's Chief Justice of England and other the Justices of the King's Bench."

By statute, the title dates only from November 1, 1875, when the Judicature Act, 1873, which created it came into force. When the High Court was first formed by that statute, it included divisions corresponding to the three Common Law Courts. Sir Alexander Cockburn, Chief Justice of the Queen's Bench Division, died in 1880. Coleridge, Chief Justice of the Common Pleas Division, succeeded him as the first—official—Lord Chief Justice of England, and an Order in Council abolished the Common Pleas and Exchequer Divisions entirely in 1881.

The Common Pleas had scored one point at the last. The Judicature Act itself speaks of the "*Lord* Chief Justice of the Common Pleas," though no good ground is provided for doing so. The Chief Barons of the Exchequer (who, of course, in spite of their title were lawyers and not peers) were at least in recent times dignified with the prefix "Lord."

Nowadays the Lord Chief Justice is customarily given a peerage, if he does not already hold one, so that he is doubly entitled to be styled "Lord," and also to the prefix "Right Honourable," for he is always made a member of the Privy Council. His peerage, of course, enables him to sit, vote, and speak in the House of Lords—for Parliamentary or appeal business. Frequently the office is given to an Attorney-General or former Attorney-General. The official qualification for the office is 15 years practice at the Bar, unless the candidate is a High Court judge or a Lord Justice of Appeal.

The Lord Chief Justice is appointed by the Crown on the nomination of the Prime Minister. He is sworn in at the Lord Chief Justice's Court at the Law Courts, in the presence of the Lord Chancellor, with the customary two oaths—the oath of allegiance and the judicial oath.

The duties of the Lord Chief Justice are multifarious. He may sit as an ordinary Queen's Bench Division judge at the Law Courts, on circuit or at the Old Bailey. He sits from time to time in the Queen's Bench Divisional Court, the Court of Criminal Appeal and the Courts Martial Appeal Court; less often in the Court of Appeal, the House of Lords and the Judicial Committee of the Privy Council. In the Lords and Judicial Committee he sits in seniority as a peer, but in the other courts he presides. His public functions are numerous, and include serving as a trustee of "The Times". His ceremonial duties include administering the oaths to new Queen's Bench judges and to the Lord Mayor of London.

His robes and costume are similar to those worn by other

judges of the Queen's Bench Division with the following exceptions :

All his robes have trains, borne by a clerk when he walks.

He wears lace stock and cuffs instead of bands with full dress. The Judges' Rules on Dress made in 1635 (see Chapter 7) indicated velvet or satin tippet (scarf) and facings for the robes of the Chief Justices, in distinction to the taffeta of their puisne brethren. This distinction is no longer made.

The distinctive badge of office of the Lord Chief Justice is a golden collar of SS, worn on all occasions when State dress is worn. (The occasions for its wear given in the 1635 Rules are : the swearing of the Lord Mayor of London; Gunpowder Day (Nov. 5); in church on "any grand days" such as Ascension Day, Midsummer Day, All Saints Day and Candlemas Day.)

The collar of SS is a golden chain or necklace, formed of 28 capital Ss interspersed with 27 "Garter" knots (those which form part of the badge of the Order of the Garter), with a rose flanked by two portcullis at the base which rests on the breast. It is said to contain no less than four pounds weight of gold. Similar collars are worn by the Lord Mayor of London, the Officers of the College of Arms, and by the Serjeants-at-arms of the royal household. The collar of the Lord Mayor contains 28 Ss, 14 roses, 13 Garter knots and one portcullis, from which hangs a badge bearing the coat-of-arms of the City. This collar weighs 40 oz. Av. The age and origin of the chain is unknown, but it was owned by Sir John Allen, Lord Mayor in 1535, who left it to his successors in office. The present badge is thought to have replaced a gold and jewelled cross given in 1558.

Authorities agree that the original significance of the collar of SS was as a livery badge of the royal House of Lancaster. So much having been said, no one really has the faintest idea of what the SS represent—if anything more than a purely ornamental design. The 17th century antiquaries Camden and Dugdale held the unlikely theory that the SS derived from the name of St. Simplicius, "a Christian judge" martyred under the Emperor Diocletian. Other suggestions are "Suveniras," "Soverayne," "Seneschallus," and even the liturgical "Sanctus."

Certainly the chain of SS was a badge of John of Gaunt, head of the House of Lancaster (1340-99); a collar of this type was shown encircling his coat-of-arms in a window opposite his tomb in old St. Paul's Cathedral. The portcullis, added by Henry VII, was the badge of the Beaufort family; the Garter knots have been held to refer to the linking of the Houses of York and Lancaster in that of Tudor, whose symbol was the rose. Similar chains of roses and suns were used by the Yorkists.

The effigy of the poet Gower (d. 1408) in Southwark Cathedral shows him wearing a collar of SS, and this is perhaps the earliest known instance apart from that of Gaunt himself. Though at first the collar may have been awarded as a personal decoration to royal favourites and courtiers, it later became attached to the holders of specific offices, such as the Lord Mayors and the Chief Justices of the three Common Law courts.

Authorities differ on when the collar of SS was first worn by a judge. An effigy in Yatton parish church, believed to be that of Sir Richard Newton, Chief Justice of the Common Pleas (d. 1449) may provide the earliest known example. There is a tradition that the collar of SS was awarded to a successor of Newton, one Brian, who held the office during the reign of Henry VII. Sir Thomas More is shown wearing the collar of SS in a Holbein painting of 1527, but he was never a Common Law judge, was not yet Lord Chancellor, and held several non-legal offices by virtue of which the collar might have been awarded to him.

Sir Richard Lyster, Chief Baron of the Exchequer, 1529, and Chief Justice of the King's Bench, 1545 (d. 1554) is shown wearing the collar in the effigy on his tomb in St. Michael's Church, Southampton. If the Newton monument is not correctly attributed or adorned, this is the first known instance of the collar being worn by a Chief Justice. According to Inderwick ("The King's Peace," 1895) the Chief Justices from this time onwards are invariably shown with the collar. Richard Harper, an Elizabethan judge of the Common Pleas, is shown wearing the collar in his effigy at Swarkestone, Derbyshire; Foss ("Lives of the Judges," 1848-64) doubts that the collar is correctly attributed to Harper, and if it is, this is probably an isolated instance of it being awarded to a puisne judge and it would be interesting to know what service he performed to merit it.

The details of the collar have varied considerably during its history. In early times, according to Inderwick, it was made of leather with gold SS sewn upon it, but in Henry VII's time it had come to be made entirely of silver or gold links. All collars made before the Commonwealth had a jewelled rose, and those thereafter have had a plain gold rose. Some other differences in early judicial collars include : no Garter knots, rose suspended from an S between two portcullis (Dyer, C.J. of Common Pleas 1559-1582); SS interspersed with knots, but only about 15 of each and rose between portcullis forming part of chain instead of pendant (Wray, C.J. of Queen's Bench, 1574-82) and Bell (Chief Baron, 1577); similar, but with number of knots and SS nearer to present figure (Coke, C.J. of Common Pleas, 1606, of King's Bench, 1613-16); similar, but with SS reversed on right side facing wearer (Crewe, C.J. of King's Bench, 1625-26).

The Common Pleas collar, at least in later times, was State property, but those of the King's Bench and Exchequer were bought by the Chief Justices themselves. Surprisingly little is known about the fate of the many collars which must have existed, even though often they would be sold by one holder of an office to the next. The following is a summary of the known facts as hitherto published :

Common Pleas : There is a long-standing tradition that the collar said to have been given by Henry VII to Chief Justice Brian passed to Sir Edward Coke, and eventually to Lord Coleridge, the last Chief Justice of the Common Pleas. Mr. B. A. Riches, the learned librarian of the Bar Library at the Royal Courts of Justice, believes the tradition is not substantiated. When the Common Pleas Division was abolished in 1881, and Lord Coleridge became Lord Chief Justice of England, he succeeded to the Queen's Bench collar. But the collar held in respect of his former office became an heirloom in his family, and in 1943 it was still in the possession of his grandson, the 3rd Baron Coleridge, at Ottery St. Mary, Devonshire. Apparently no Government claim was put forward to the effect that the collar might be State property. Mr. Riches says (Law Quarterly Review, 59.120) that 1714 seems to be the earliest date to which the Coleridge collar can be positively traced. The portrait of Lyttelton, Chief Justice of the Common Pleas (1640), by Van Dyk, has a jewelled rose in the centre of the chain, and—Riches adds—the collars made before the Commonwealth were all jewelled. But the Coleridge collar has a rose of plain gold. Nor, says Mr. Riches, is there any record of any jewelled collar made before 1640 being still in existence.

Exchequer : The collar worn by Sir Richard Richards (Chief

Baron, 1817-24), and said by Foss ("Lives of the Judges," 1848-64) to be traceable for more than 150 years earlier, was recently in the possession of his great-grandson, Major Richards, of Dolgelly. Richards' successor, Alexander, passed on his collar to his successor, Lord Abinger (Chief Baron, 1834-44) and this was bought by the Inner Temple a few years ago. After Abinger came Sir Frederick Pollock (1844-66), who on his retirement had his collar broken up and the links distributed among his family.

King's Bench: The collar which belonged to Sir Matthew Hale, the great Chief Justice of the King's Bench (1671-76) was sold from one holder of the office to another until it came to Lord Ellenborough. Unfortunately when the noble lord retired in 1818 he broke the continuity by keeping his collar, by then of some historical and sentimental importance. The next Chief Justice of the King's Bench, Sir Charles Abbott (1818-32) thus had to buy a new collar of SS for himself. On his retirement he sold this to his successor, Lord Denman. When Denman retired in his turn in 1850 he offered to sell it to Lord Campbell, the new Chief Justice, but Campbell would not buy. So Denman sold it to the Corporation of Derby, whose mayor wears it as his chain of office. The Corporation paid £100, the price at which the collar had been offered to Campbell. Campbell bought his own, and so did his successor, Sir Alexander Cockburn (1859-80), the last Chief Justice of the Queen's Bench. On Cockburn's death in 1880 he left his collar of SS for the use of his successors in perpetuity, and this is the collar now worn by the Lord Chief Justices of England.

A minor privilege of the Lord Chief Justices is that, in common with certain other high officers, they receive each year $4\frac{1}{2}$ yards of "livery cloth" from the City of London Corporation. (See Chapter 5).

THE MASTER OF THE ROLLS

From medieval times the Chancery had twelve clerks, who became known as Masters in Chancery. At first they were concerned with the preparation of writs and examination of witnesses; later the Lord Chancellor delegated to them cases in which they were allowed to conduct hearings themselves, afterwards reporting so that the Lord Chancellor could give judgment.

The chief of the Masters, entrusted with the records, was called the Master of the Rolls: the title goes back as far as 1286. As the Chancery jurisdiction rapidly widened in the 15th and 16th centuries he became an assistant judge. By the early 17th century he was a deputy of the Lord Chancellor, to whom, however, an appeal could always be made from his decisions. Until the reign of George II he was allowed to sit judicially only when the Chancellor was not sitting.

Today the Master of the Rolls sits most frequently in, and presides over, one of the several divisions of the Court of Appeal. In 1851, by which time there were other Chancery judges as well as the Lord Chancellor himself and the Master, a Court of Appeal in Chancery was set up in which the Master of the Rolls might sit if asked to do so by the Lord Chancellor. When that court's jurisdiction passed to the Court of Appeal in 1873, the Master of the Rolls was named one of the judges of the new tribunal. It is usually unnecessary for him to sit as a Chancery judge of first instance because today there is a number of puisne judges of the Chancery Division to perform this work.

Until the Judicature Act, 1873, the Master of the Rolls was able to sit in the House of Commons, a right which the other judges had not enjoyed for centuries. The last Master to do so was Sir John Romilly (1851-73), who was M.P. for Devonport until 1852.

The Master of the Rolls is always a Privy Councillor, and therefore styled Right Honourable, and frequently if not always receives a peerage on his retirement. A link with the ancient origin of his office is his responsibility for the Public Record Office, and his chairmanship of the Historical Manuscripts Commission. It was in a former chapel on the site of the modern Public Record Office in Chancery Lane that the Masters of the Rolls held their court until the Judicature Act. The Master of the Rolls, also by historical survival, had supervisory control of the solicitors' branch of the profession (see Chapter 6).

His ceremonial duties include taking part in the swearing in of a new Lord Chancellor at the Court of Appeal (see under Lord Chancellor, earlier in this chapter).

The qualification for the office of Master of the Rolls is 15 years' practice at the Bar, unless the candidate is a High Court judge or a Lord Justice of Appeal. The appointment is made by the Crown by Letters Patent, on the nomination of the Prime Minister. The new Master must take the customary oaths (of allegiance and the judicial oath) in the presence of the Lord Chancellor.

The ancient oath taken by the Masters of the Rolls is given in the anonymous Book of Oaths (1649). It reads in part: "That well and lawfully ye shall serve the King our Sovereign Lord and his people, in the office of Clerk or Master of the Rolls, to the which ye be called; ye shall not assent, ne procure the disinheritance, ne perpetual damage to the King, to your power; ne fraud shall ye do, nor cause to be made wrongfully, to any of his people, ne in any thing that toucheth the Seal; . . . and the counsel that ye shall give touching him ye shall not disclose; and if ye know anything to the disinheritance or damage of the King or fraud be made upon any thing that toucheth the keeping of the Seal, ye shall put your lawful power that to redress and amend; and if that ye cannot, ye shall advise the Chancellor or other which may that amend to your power. So God you help, and His saints."

On State and full-dress occasions, the Master of the Rolls wears a robe and other costume similar to those of the Lord Chancellor, except that the gold lace trimmings on the robe differ slightly. He has a train on this and all his robes.

For royal Court occasions, his dress follows that of other judges (see Chapter 7).

When sitting as judge he wears a black silk gown like the Chancellor's, but with a bench wig instead of the Chancellor's full-bottomed one.

Even in the illumination depicting the Chancery Court in the time of Henry VI, referred to earlier in this chapter, the costume of the Master of the Rolls is clearly differentiated from that of the other masters in Chancery. The Master of the Rolls is shown on the bench wearing a scarlet robe trimmed with white fur, like those of the Common Law judges and also identical with that of the Lord Chancellor shown sitting with him. He is tonsured. The other masters have robes of saffron colour.

It should be added that the office of Master in Chancery has long been abolished, and the modern Masters attached to the Chancery Division of the High Court are not their direct successors.

The Master of the Rolls, in common with the Lord Chancellor

and other high officers, receives 4½ yards of "livery cloth" each year from the Corporation of London. (See Chapter 5).

THE PRESIDENT OF THE PROBATE, DIVORCE AND ADMIRALTY DIVISION

This office dates only from the establishment of the High Court, of which the Probate, Divorce and Admiralty Division forms part, by the Judicature Act of 1873. Before that time (see Chapter 7) there were separate courts for marriage, probate and Admiralty matters.

The qualification for the office is 15 years practice at the Bar, a High Court judgeship, or the position of Lord Justice of Appeal. The appointment is made by the Crown by Letters Patent on the nomination of the Prime Minister. The President is required to take the oath of allegiance and the judicial oath in the presence of the Lord Chancellor.

His dress for State occasions is similar to that of the Lord Chancellor (q.v.). For royal Courts his dress follows that of other judges (see Chapter 7). When sitting in court his costume follows that of the Master of the Rolls (q.v.).

THE LORDS JUSTICES OF APPEAL

The title of Lord Justice of Appeal dates only from 1876, and perhaps owes something to the feeling for pageantry of Mr. Disraeli. His Act of 1876 substituted "Lord Justice of Appeal" with membership of the Privy Council for the "Judge of Appeal" in Mr. Gladstone's monumental Judicature Act of three years earlier. The Judicature Act, 1873, which transformed our court system, created a Court of Appeal to be staffed by five special appeal judges and certain high judicial officers ex officio. The title of Lord Justice had previously been used for the judges of a Court of Appeal in Chancery, set up in 1851 and merged by the Act of 1873 into the present Appeal court.

The Court of Appeal today hears appeals in practically every kind of case from all three divisions of the High Court and from the County Courts. From it a further appeal lies to the House of Lords. Its judges are eight Lords Justices of Appeal, and ex officio, the Lord Chancellor, Lord Chief Justice, Master of the

Rolls, President of the Probate, Divorce and Admiralty Division, the Lords of Appeal, and any ex-Lord Chancellor whom the Lord Chancellor may invite to sit. In practice, because of the volume of business, the Court of Appeal sits today in two or three sections. In one the Master of the Rolls presides over two Lords Justices, and the others are staffed by three Lords Justices each.

Lords Justices of Appeal must have practised for 15 years at the Bar, or hold a High Court judgeship. They are appointed by the Crown by Letters Patent on the nomination of the Prime Minister, and are made Privy Councillors. They must take the oath of allegiance and the judicial oath in the presence of the Lord Chancellor.

On State occasions the Lords Justices wear a costume similar to that of the Lord Chancellor (q.v.), and at royal court functions their dress follows that of other judges (see Chapter 7). When sitting on the bench they wear a costume similar to that of the Master of the Rolls (q.v.).

Their black and gold State robe "descended" to them from the Lord Chancellors, by way of the former Vice-Chancellors and the Lords Justices of the old Court of Appeal in Chancery. Robes of this type were once worn also by Privy Councillors, so the Lords Justices of Appeal have some claim to it in this respect also.

The Lords Justices wear their three-cornered hats on one occasion only—when receiving the Lord Mayor of London when on November 9 he comes to the Court of Appeal to ask them to his banquet. (Cf. the similar practice of the Lord Chief Justice and puisne judges, who wear their black caps on the corresponding occasion. See Chapters 7 and 14).

M

13. The Lesser Judges

COUNTY COURT JUDGES

FOR centuries the time and expense involved in an action brought in the superior courts have made it often not worth a poor man's while to seek justice there : except, of course, where in quite modern times he has been able to get State legal aid. And while a complicated legal process may be justified when a large sum or an important issue is involved, no one wants to incur over a small case costs totalling more than the amount at stake.

During the Middle Ages there grew up a committee of the Privy Council to provide relief for the poor and for royal employees. In the reign of Henry VIII this became a separate Court of Requests. It soon found itself at loggerheads with the Common Law judges, because it followed the rules of Equity rather than those of the Common Law; and it came to an end in 1642. For the next two centuries the only courts open to the poor litigant were a few ancient local civil courts and, from the 18th century, new local Courts of Requests established in many towns.

In Middlesex at about the same period there were created courts known as County Courts, empowered to try civil cases concerning amounts up to forty shillings. This plan was taken as the model when, in 1846, Lord Brougham's County Courts Act provided a network of similar courts for the whole country. These modern County Courts, it should be made plain, have no connection whatever with the ancient and extinct County Courts over which the sheriffs presided, and which had some criminal jurisdiction.

The monetary limit of the County Court's jurisdiction has been progressively extended to keep pace with the changing value of money. These courts now provide a quick and simple remedy in cases involving sums or values up to several hundred pounds. Their powers have been added to under a succession of statutes, until they can now deal with a variety of subjects from guardianship of infants to agricultural holdings. The courts are not, despite their name, organised on a county basis, but in small circuits or districts of which there are 59, each with one or more judges of its own.

County Court judges are appointed by the Lord Chancellor, except those whose circuits lie in the Duchy of Lancaster, in respect of which appointments are made by the Chancellor of the Duchy. The judges, who must be barristers of at least seven years' standing, hold office during good behaviour, but unlike the superior judges they can be dismissed by the Lord Chancellor or the Chancellor of the Duchy, and must retire at 72. They are not required to take the oath of allegiance and the judicial oath. Their full title is "His Honour Judge So-and-So." This was granted by an Order in Council made in 1884, and a royal warrant in 1919 allowed the judges to retain the prefix "His Honour" even after retirement. In court they are addressed as "Your Honour."

For the first 70 years after the County Court system was established the judges had no robes peculiar to their office, but sat in black gowns. Just before the first World War it was decided that they should have a distinctive robe of black with violet facings (in this case continued round the neck like a collar), cuffs, and casting-hood. A black girdle, but no scarf, is worn. A black hood, trimmed with violet, is substituted for the casting-hood on ceremonial occasions. The war supervened, and the new robe was not in fact worn until 1919. C. P. Hawkes ("Chambers in the Temple," 1930) thought the robes "may be presumed to be vestiges of the violet gowns of the 17th century serjeants and justices." Certainly violet was the colour worn by the judges at Nisi Prius (civil actions in the superior Common Law courts) at that period; and black and ermine is now worn on such occasions. So a combination of black robe with violet, instead of ermine, cuffs is perhaps a happy recalling of tradition. At royal Court occasions the judges wear the same dress as the Solicitor-General (see Chapter 5).

THE RECORDER

The office of Recorder is typical of the historical compromises of which our legal system is full. For the 100-odd Recorders of

England and Wales are part-time judges—practising barristers who act as judges in criminal cases in a single borough for perhaps a fortnight during the year. Their position may be regarded very roughly as half-way between that of the lay, unpaid magistrate and that of the full-time judge. A nominal salary is paid, but recordships are valued both as an honour and because they afford an opportunity to gain judicial experience which may be the stepping-stone to a judgeship later on.

The Recorder (with a very few anomalous exceptions) is judge of the Quarter Sessions court (see p. 188 below) of the borough to which he is appointed. Far back into medieval times the right to hold a local court was one of the valued privileges of England's ancient boroughs, frequently conferred by royal charter. The original judges were the mayor and aldermen, but in time legal procedure became so complicated that the clerk of the court, whose duty at first had been to record its proceedings, gradually took over on the Bench because of his superior knowledge. The Recorder became a judge. By the 18th century or before these local courts had been superseded by the justices of the peace. The mayor and aldermen were usually themselves justices, and so where a borough had its own Quarter Sessions (i.e., quarterly justices' court), the old local criminal jurisdiction came to be exercised by the Quarter Sessions court. The Municipal Corporations Act, 1835, completed the transformation and tidied up the position by abolishing the criminal jurisdictions of boroughs without separate Quarter Sessions courts.

In early times the Recorder was (in London at least) an alderman. Until 1835 it was not necessary for him to be a lawyer, though he had to be *"vir idoneus et jure peritus"*—"a man fitted for the position, and learned in the law." The position before 1835 varied haphazardly from borough to borough. Up to that date the Recorder, although as a judge he came under the authority of the Crown, was appointed by the corporation of the borough concerned. (A few corporations still enjoy the right to name their own Recorders). "During the 'Judicial War' which marked the reign of James II," says W. Barnard Faraday ("The English and Welsh Boroughs," 1950), "the Crown endeavoured to dismiss Recorders unfavourable to the prevailing court prejudice. This was stubbornly resisted and with success by the boroughs except in those cases where they had been compelled to surrender their charters." From this time the appointment of Recorders was gradually brought under Crown control by being made subject to approval.

Faraday says the criminal courts of the old boroughs took definite shape only after the Quarter Sessions Act (presumably that of 1842). Before that date in some cases the mayor, and sometimes also another justice, sat with the Recorder as judges. At Bristol early in the 19th century the Recorder tried prisoners at the City assizes as a Commissioner, but did not attend the quarter sessions, where the judges were theoretically the mayor and aldermen, but in practice the town clerk! At Bradninch, Devonshire, at the same period, an attorney presided over the borough sessions.

The history of the Recordership of London is better documented than most, although—like other City of London institutions—it is in a number of ways exceptional. The first known Recorder of London (at this period also an alderman) was Jeffrey de Norton, in 1298, or John de Wengrave, 1303-4. In 1304 the Recorder was sworn "to well and faithfully render all the judgments of the Hustings . . . and also all other judgments touching the City of London; to do justice to rich and poor, and to oversee orders . . ." (For further references to the Recorder's oath, see below p. 183). The first example of the title "Recorder" in the Oxford English Dictionary refers to London: *"Solone le record des Recordours de la Gilhale"* (Riley, Munim. Gildh. Londoniensis (Rolls) II 1.151), and a further mention appears in the Rolls of Parliament for 1347. Many other recorderships undoubtedly date to this period.

From some time in the 14th century it became the invariable practice to choose a lawyer as Recorder of London. Probably quite early in that century it was laid down (in 1 Lib. Alb., Pt. 1 (Rolls) 42, translation (1861) 38, quoted by Cohen "A History of the English Bar," 1929): The Recorder of the City of London should be and of usage has been (solebat) one of the most skilful and upright (virtuosissimis) apprenticii of the law in the whole kingdom." Cohen adds "by 1304-5 the City had, it seems, got into the habit of looking for this official in the second and not in the first row of practitioners; a junior, so to say, was all they wanted." Indeed, up to the late 19th century, the Recorder of London was not invariably a Queen's Counsel or a serjeant.

Until the Justices of the Peace Act, 1949, 124 boroughs had their own Quarter Sessions courts, and therefore their own Recorders. That Act provided for the abolition of Quarter Sessions in boroughs with a population of under 20,000, on the ground that these courts, however historic, had little business. Twenty-four boroughs fell in this category and lost their courts in 1951. These boroughs may probably still appoint Recorders, although there are no courts of which they can be judges; such appointments would not be mere sinecures because the Recorder's office is still closely linked with local dignity and he often takes a considerable part in the municipal life of his borough.

Recorders today are in nearly all cases appointed by the Crown, on the recommendation of the Lord Chancellor. In London and some other cases, including Preston, appointment still lies with the court of aldermen (London) or corporation, subject to Crown approval of the candidate chosen. In 1935 at Preston an awkward situation arose when Whitehall forgot the town's privilege. The council and the Home Office named "rival" candidates for the Recordership. The situation was eventually resolved by an apology from the Home Office.

The qualification for Recordership is five years standing at the Bar, except in the case of London, where no qualification is laid down. The salary (again with the notable exception of London, where the Recorder receives a salary of £2,500 for his full-time services) is usually nominal. Durham, Hartlepool, Kingston, Preston, and Wycombe, still appoint Recorders though they now have no Quarter Sessions. At Kingston when the Recordership has fallen vacant in recent years it has been customary to offer the position to the Attorney-General of the day who, if he accepts, retains it even after ceasing to hold office as Attorney. Under a charter of James I the Recorder of Kingston is entitled to a "fee" of 18 sugar loaves each year, in addition to a monetary salary. Up to the second World War a token payment of two sugar loaves was maintained, although the salary had lapsed. Another curious edible "fee" is presented to Recorders of Wells when they take office. They are presented with a cheese. The custom dates from 1687; once the cheeses were local Cheddar, but on the most recent occasion, in 1953, the new Recorder was given a Dutch cheese—on account of post-war restrictions on manufacture—but adorned with the arms of the city painted upon it. At Bristol, the Recorder used to receive as part fee a hogshead of port or sherry annually; and at Southampton, New Year's gifts of sugar, spices, wine or olives. The borough of Haverfordwest, which lost its right to Quarter Sessions under the 1949 Act, held the anomalous position of appointing no Recorder.

The Recorder holds office during good behaviour. Within his borough he ranks second only the mayor. In some boroughs his civic duties are considerable, and he takes part in all borough ceremonies such as Mayor's Sunday. If an address is to be presented to royalty, it is the Recorder who does it. In 1951 the then Recorder of Walsall resigned because he was not given the precedence due to his office when Princess Margaret was received in the borough.

In London, the greatest of all Recorderships, the duties of the office—in this case a full-time one—are heavy and varied. The Recorder is the Corporation's principal officer, and Senior Law Officer. When questions concerning City customs arise in court, the Recorder attends to certify the usage, and the court will not look beyond his statement. He is at least nominally legal adviser to the Lord Mayor and aldermen, and normally sits as a judge at the Old Bailey. He is High Steward of the Corporation's manor of Southwark. He attends the ceremonial election of the Lord Mayor, and subsequently presents the new Lord Mayor to the Lord Chancellor for the royal approval, and to the judges at the Law Courts on Lord Mayor's Day. (See Chapter 14). He declares the election of Sheriffs at Midsummer, and sits at the first court of aldermen in each mayoralty. He attends the Lord Mayor on the presentation of addresses to the Sovereign, and on all big public occasions. Perhaps in reward, he receives (in common with the Lord Chancellor, Lord Chief Justice, Master of the Rolls, Law Officers of the Crown, the Common Serjeant and certain non-legal personages) a gift of $4\frac{1}{2}$ yards of "livery cloth" from the Corporation of London each December. (See Chapter 5). He is also entitled to a buck and a doe each year from the royal deer forests.

Recorders must take the oath of allegiance and the judicial oath, and must also make the following declaration before the mayor or two other members of the borough council: "I

————. hereby declare that I will faithfully and impartially execute the office of Recorder for the borough of ———— according to the best of my judgment and ability." The swearing-in may conveniently take place at the Recorder's first quarter sessions although (except in London) the Recorder is sole judge of the court and therefore there is no need for the mayor or aldermen to attend. In London the Lord Mayor, Recorder and aldermen are all (in theory) judges of the sessions at the Central Criminal Court (see Chapter 10).

The earliest known example of the oath taken by the Recorder of London has been mentioned earlier in this chapter. A later (medieval?) oath is quoted by Cohen ("A History of the English Bar," 1929) from the City's Liber Albus (1.308): "You shall swear that you shall be good and true unto Richard King of England and unto his heirs, kings and unto the City of London, in the office of Recorder; and the franchises and usages of the same City . . . according to your power you shall maintain and the counsel of the same city you shall not discover; and that well and continually you shall keep and rule the King's Courts, in the Chamber, and the Hustings according to the custom of the City. And that you shall not omit for gift or for favour or for promise or for hate, that equal law and right you shall do unto all manner of people as well to poor as rich, to denizens as to strangers who before you shall plead . . . And readily you shall come at the warnings of the Mayor and Sheriffs or of their officers for good and wholesome counsel unto them to give; and at all times when need shall be with them you shall go and ride, to keep and maintain the state of the City . . . and no fees or robes shall you take from any one, except only from the Chamber of London, during your office. . . ."

The date of this oath, said to be of the reign of Richard II (1377-99), is considered by Cohen to be "very suspicious." However the wording is given almost exactly in the Book of Oaths (1689).

The form of oath for the Recorder of Southampton in 1461 has been preserved (Speed MSS, Southampton Corporation, p. 72; History of Southampton, J. S. Davies, 1883, p. 185).

Recorders are styled "The Worshipful Recorder," and are addressed in court as "Your Worship." The Recorder of London is, by exception, styled "The Right Worshipful," or—as a Commissioner of the Central Criminal Court—"My lord" or "His Lordship."

The official dress of the Recorder, with two exceptions, is the black silk gown of Queen's Counsel—even if he is not a member of the inner Bar—and counsel's bob-wig, with full-bottomed wig and white gloves for State occasions, including civic ceremonies such as the reading of an address or presentation of the freedom of the borough. Beneath the gown he wears court dress, of cloth or velvet according to the occasion. At royal Court functions his dress is the same as that worn by the Solicitor-General (see Chapter 5).

The Recorder of London wears on various occasions gowns of scarlet, violet and black. The scarlet gown is of the same colour as that of a Queen's Bench Division judge, but of different cut and with black velvet facings. It is worn on State occasions, including the election of a Lord Mayor; the presentation of a Lord Mayor-elect to the Lord Chancellor; the Lord Mayor's Show and the swearing-in of the Lord Mayor at the Law Courts; when reading addresses to the Sovereign; when sitting at the Old Bailey on Red Letter Days. The violet gown is worn at the Old Bailey, except on Red Letter Days. The black gown is worn at Southwark Sessions, of which the Recorder is judge, but at which proceedings are now purely formal.

On State occasions he wears velvet court dress beneath his gown, and at other times a cloth court suit.

The other exception to the general rule is the Recorder of Exeter, who wears a gown of plain dark blue material, edged with black velvet along front edges and quarter sleeves. The Town Clerk tells me he has no information on the origin and history of this robe, and MacKinnon ("on Circuit," 1940) was unable to discover it.

The Recorders were among the senior counsel who wore the tufted black robe with "guards," until the introduction of the silk gown at the end of the 17th century. (See Chapter 2). Many, if not all, would be entitled to the tufted gown as past or present Readers of their Inns. The old type of gown is illustrated in a standing effigy of Clement Spelman, Recorder of Nottingham (died 1679) in Narborough Church, near King's Lynn, Norfolk.

THE COMMON SERJEANT OF THE CITY OF LONDON

The Common Serjeant, the second of the City's Law Officers and judges, holds an office as ancient as that of the Recorder. Its name is misleading. He was not necessarily (or at all?) a member of the Order of the Coif. He held, in fact, the same relation towards the City as the King's Serjeants did to the Crown. Pulling ("Order of the Coif," 1884) gives this explanation, and adds that the office may have been "in accordance with and to some extent in imitation of" the older royal institution. "In many of the ancient free cities of Europe there seems to have been an old officer called the Defensor, whose duty was to protect the general interests of the community and to prosecute all those who offended; and it is not improbable that the office of Common Serjeant was based on this old institution." There were formerly similar officers in some other cities, including Norwich, Leicester, Oxford and Lincoln.

The first known Common Serjeant appears to be Thomas Juvenal, elected in 1291. A charter of Edward II in 1307 provides that "the Chamberlain, the Common (Town) Clerk, and the Common Serjeant be chosen by the commonalty" and that no serjeant should "take a fee, or do execution on the citizens, except he be elected by the commonalty." The Common Serjeant is also mentioned in the City constitutions of 1319.

Today the duties of the Common Serjeant are mainly judicial. He is one of the commissioners of the Central Criminal Court, and sits in one of the courts there or presides in the Lord Mayor's and City of London (Sheriffs') civil court. He is deputy to the Recorder as a Law Officer of the Corporation, and also has certain civic duties, in which he also deputises for the Recorder. He attends the Lord Mayor on public occasions, and at the election of a new Lord Mayor has a part of his own as "mouthpiece" of the Sheriffs. He is, at least in theory, the legal adviser of the Common Council of the City, as the Recorder is of the Court of Aldermen.

In former times his position and duties were much more akin to those of an Attorney-General than of a judge. He was "advocate or representative of the whole civic community" (Pulling) and in Westminster Hall he took precedence after the serjeants of the Order of the Coif, but before ordinary barristers.

Until the Local Government Act, 1888, the Common Serjeant was elected by the Common Council, but that Act transferred the right of appointment to the Crown, although the Corporation retains the right of fixing the salary and duties of the office. By the same statute the Common Serjeant is required to be "a duly qualified barrister."

The oath formerly taken by the Common Serjeant was lengthy. He had (from at least the 15th century and in some similar form doubtless from the beginning of the office) to swear to "keep and defend" the "laws, usages and franchises of the City." And "good and lawful counsel you shall give in all things touching the common profit of the same city . . . And attendant you shall be on the Mayor and Aldermen and Commons, for the causes and needs of the City, at all times when you shall be thereunto required and charged and the same in all places where need shall be you shall lawfully show and declare and shall attentively prosecute and speed for the common profit of the City. . . ." This text is quoted by Cohen ("A History of the English Bar," 1929) from the City's Liber Albus 1.310. The Book of Oaths, edn. 1689, retains practically the same wording, but with an addition.

The official dress of the Common Serjeant is a black tufted and "guarded" gown (see Chapter 2), with barrister's wig and bands; and on State occasions a full-bottomed wig. Under his gown he wears court dress, of cloth or velvet according to the occasion.

The Common Serjeant is one of the officers entitled to receive a gift of $4\frac{1}{2}$ yards of "livery cloth" from the Corporation each year (see Chapter 5), and a buck and a doe from the royal deer forests.

JUSTICES OF THE PEACE

For more than 600 years our system of criminal justice has rested on a broad basis of lay judges—Justices of the Peace—entrusted with keeping order in their own county or borough.

A statute of 1327 gave the Crown power to appoint such "good and lawful" men in every county. Before the century was out they had come to be known as justices of the peace. A statute of 1344 gave them the power to hear and determine felonies and trespasses against the peace, and in 1346 separate commissions were provided for each county. Those authorised by each such commission were to include a peer, three or four commoners, and some learned in the law, who would commonly be one of the judges of assize (according to Potter, "Historical Introduction to English Law," 1935).

Since 1388 justices of the peace in each county, and in those boroughs so privileged, have held a court four times a year known as Quarter Sessions. The number of justices who may be appointed is now unlimited (at present there are about 15,000), and in the centuries since the office was created their powers have been altered and added to many times.

In addition to Quarter Sessions, J.P.s now also sit at more frequent intervals in a court of Petty Sessions to try minor cases. This jurisdiction grew up gradually when various statutes conferred power on justices to deal with certain matters outside Quarter Sessions. The name Petty Sessions itself dates only from the first half of the 19th century, however.

In boroughs which have the right to their own Quarter Sessions a Recorder must be appointed as sole judge. In London and some other great towns a salaried full-time magistrate is appointed, and his court takes the place of the normal Petty Sessions.

The justice of the peace has a variety of duties and powers besides those attaching to his position as a judge of certain types of case. In cases which, by reason of their serious nature, the J.P.s are forbidden to try in Petty Sessions, they must nevertheless hear evidence to determine whether the accused person should be committed to a higher court for trial. All warrants of arrest and search warrants must be signed by a justice.

Justices of the peace act under a Commission of the Peace addressed to the justices of the county or borough concerned. Certain high officials, such as the High Court judges, are always named in every Commission though they seldom sit as local justices. The Commission, whose wording is now laid down by an Order in Council of 1878, reads in part:

"Greeting Know ye that we have assigned you jointly and severally and every one of you Our justices to keep Our peace in the county of ——— and to keep and cause to be kept all the ordinances and statutes for the good of Our peace and for the preservation of the same and for the quiet rule and government of Our people. . . . And to chastise and punish all persons that offend against the form of those ordinances etc. . . . We have also assigned you and every two or more of you Our justices to inquire the truth more fully by the oath of good and lawful men of the aforesaid county by whom the truth of the matter shall be the better known of all and all manner of crimes trespasses and all and singular other offences of which the justices of Our peace may or ought lawfully to inquire by whomsoever and after what manner soever in the said county done or perpetrated or which shall happen to be there done or attempted. . . ."

The "two or more of you" refers to the fact that two is the minimum number of J.P.s who can act judicially in Quarter or Petty Sessions. The Commission is formally read at the opening of each Quarter Sessions.

The form of Commission issued to borough justices is addressed only to the justices themselves, and omits the latter part of the wording, inapplicable since borough J.P.s now do not sit as judges of Quarter Sessions.

The general wording and form of the Commission was finally settled by the judges in 1590. Until the Municipal Corporations Act, 1835, mayors and other borough justices held office under the charter or grant which created the borough. The City of London is now an exception in retaining this practice.

Justices of the peace are appointed by the Crown, on the recommendation of the Lord Chancellor or, in the Duchy of Lancaster, by the Chancellor of the Duchy. Anyone under seventy-five and not personally disqualified may be a J.P. In counties the Lord Lieutenant and an advisory committee submit names to the Lord Chancellor, and in boroughs the Lord Chancellor may take notice of a nomination by the borough council. Until 1835 the mayor and aldermen of boroughs were, by charter or grant, justices for their towns, and this still holds in the City of London. Elsewhere only the mayor is now a justice ex officio, and then only during his year of office. The chairmen of county and district councils are similarly J.P.s for their year of office. All justices must take the oath of allegiance and the judicial oath, and this is usually done in Quarter Sessions for the county for which they are appointed, or in the case of borough justices before local J.P.s or councillors.

The ancient oath for justices of the peace, given in the "Book of Oaths" (1649) and used until 1868 ran in part: "That as Justice of Peace in the County of ——— in all Articles in the King's Commission to you directed, ye shall do equal right, to the poor as to the rich, after your cunning, wit and power, and after the

Laws and Customs of this Realm, and Statutes thereof made; These things all ye shall truly keep, as God you help, you and his Saints."

Justices hold office until the age of 75, but may be removed by the Lord Chancellor for due cause.

Stipendiary magistrates are appointed by the Crown on the recommendation of the Home Secretary. They must be barristers of seven years' standing in the case of boroughs, or five years in the case of urban districts.

Both J.P.s and stipendiaries wear lay clothes when sitting in their respective courts, and there is curiously little pageantry about the office of justice of the peace, ancient as it is.

It can hardly be termed pageantry, but it is perhaps worth mentioning as a curiosity that MacKinnon ("On Circuit," 1940) records hearing "that it has always been the practice for the chairman of (Dorset) Quarter Sessions to wear a top hat when presiding. I have since heard that this Dorchester custom also survives in part at Warwick. It is there the custom for the chairman to enter the court and take his seat wearing his hat, but he takes it off when the business begins, and sits uncovered."

Pageantry apart, the office of the justice of the peace is so important in the English legal system that no account of our judges would be complete without some reference to it.

14. *The Legal Year*

LIKE the universities, so many of whose traditions it shares, the legal world in England divides its year into terms. Again like the universities, its whole progamme of work and vacation is based on the Calendar of the Church with its feasts and fasts.

The legal year has four terms: Michaelmas, Hilary (so named from the feast of St. Hilary, January 13, at its commencement), Easter and Trinity. These divisions are of great antiquity. The system seems to have arisen in a negative way, in the sense that certain periods of the year were set aside for religious observance, and during those periods State business including court sittings might not take place. The 17th century antiquary Spelman places the origin of the terms in the reign of Edward the Elder (901-924), long before our modern legal system existed even in embryo. Edward the Confessor (1041-66) provided for three periods of the year to be appropriated to the Church, and the statute which made this provision was confirmed by William I. In fact, the early legal writer Glanville says (in his "De Legibus Angliae," written about 1188) that the terms were instituted from Norman usage.

William I held a court three times a year, at Christmas, Easter and Pentecost. The Curia Regis or Great Council—which was then the only royal law court—sat after each of these festivals when the barons were assembled to keep the feasts. This practice would account for three terms. There remains the problem of the Michaelmas term, and of why this is the commencement of the legal year. Under the system of Edward the Confessor the whole period from the octave of Pentecost to the beginning of Advent was free from the calls of the Church and available for official business. Foss ("Lives of the Judges," 1848-64) suggests with some reason that this long "term" became divided because of the need for a vacation at harvest-time. The division must have been made at a very early date, for Glanville in the late 12th century says the long vacation was suited to the time of the vintages in France.

Why was Michaelmas chosen as the beginning of the year? Doubtless because it preceded Advent, the beginning of the Church's year. Throughout the Middle Ages Michaelmas was also the beginning of the financial year and the most important accounting date, when sheriffs were required to render their accounts in the Exchequer. Moreover, it was a natural choice for practical reasons as marking approximately the end of the harvest period.

The "dining terms" kept at the Inns of Court today still correspond roughly with the terms observed in former times by the whole legal world, so we shall use them for comparison. From 1875, when the Judicature Act, 1873, came into force, the dates between which the courts sit are no longer those observed by the Inns. Pressure of work made it necessary for the "sittings" (as they are now called officially) to be extended more and more until they bear today a mere token resemblance to the old terms. The "dining terms" of the Inns of Court are now observed for one purpose only—to regulate "keeping term," i.e., dining the requisite number of times within this restricted period as a qualification for call to the Bar or, in the case of benchers, for some particular office. The Inns also recognize "educational terms," which are nowadays rather longer than the dining terms.

The following are the main changes in the terms since their institution:

Michaelmas Term. The third term provided in Edward the Confessor's statute lasted from the Octave of Pentecost to the beginning of Advent, but it seems that the division of this period into the Trinity and Michaelmas terms, separated by the long vacation, was already observed by the time Glanville wrote in 1188. From some time in the Middle Ages, Michaelmas term commenced on October 9—ten days after the actual feast of St. Michael, September 29. An Act of 1640 provided for the term to begin on October 23. One of the Acts made necessary by the calendar change of 1752 (24 Geo. II c. 48) provided for the full term thenceforward to begin on the fourth day after the morrow of All Souls, i.e., November 6. In 1830 the beginning of the term was altered to November 2, All Souls' Day, at which it remained until 1951, when it was fixed at the first Wednesday in November.

The end of Michaelmas term must originally have been

AN ASSIZE PRO-
CESSION OF THE
MID-19th CEN-
TURY. The scene is
Lincoln. Sheriff's
trumpeters, moun-
ted, are followed
by some thirty
"javelin-men" also
on horseback. The
"javelins" in this
instance seem al-
ready to have be-
come mere staves.
A coach, probably
that of the assize
judge, can be seen
through the arch-
way.

ASSIZE PAGEANTRY OF TODAY. At Monmouth: in 1938, the last occasion when an assize was held in that town. The sheriff's trumpeters are still in livery, with armorial banners; but the mounted escort of the past is represented by a handful of embarrassed policemen bearing staves, preceding a limousine.

immediately before the beginning of Advent, and later fixed at
November 28. The date provided in the 1830 statute was
November 25, at which it remained until 1951, when it was fixed
at 23 days after the commencement.

These are the changes in Michaelmas term referred to above
(with moveable dates given as for 1954):

Period	Begins	Ends	Length
Early Middle Ages ..	Oct. 9	Nov. 28	51 days
1640 onwards ..	Oct. 23	Nov. 28	35 days
1752 onwards ..	Nov. 6	Nov. 28	22 days
1830 onwards ..	Nov. 2	Nov. 25	23 days
1951 onwards ..	1st Wed. in Nov. (Nov. 3)	23 days ltr (Nov. 26)	23 days

The corresponding Michaelmas sitting of the courts is now
October 1 to December 21.

Hilary Term. By the statute of Edward the Confessor this term
began on January 13, the feast of St. Hilary, and the Octave of
the Epiphany. This date was retained up to the time of Henry II
(1154-89), according to Dugdale, who adds that it is "nine days
before our term beginneth," so that in his time (the late 17th
century) Hilary term must have begun on January 22. The Act of
1830 fixed the beginning at January 11, and the 1951 alteration
changed this to the third Wednesday in January. Up to Henry II
the term ended on the Saturday before Septuagesima; from 1830
on January 31; and from 1951, 23 days after the commencement.

These are the changes in summary form:

Period	Begins	Ends	Length
Up to Henry II ..	Jan. 13	Sat. before Septuagesima. (Feb. 13)	Variable
Late 17th century ..	Jan. 22	Presumably as last	Variable
1830 onwards ..	Jan. 11	Jan. 31	20 days
1951 onwards ..	3rd Wed. in Jan. (Jan. 20)	23 days ltr (Feb. 11)	23 days

The Hilary court sittings are now January 11 to the Wednesday before Easter.

Easter Term. This term began, under the Confessor's statute, on the Octave of Easter; a charter of Henry I changed this to 15 days after Easter. In Dugdale's time it commenced "two days after Quindena Paschae," i.e., the 17th day after Easter. The Act of 1830 fixed the beginning at April 15, and this was later altered to the second Tuesday, i.e., 9 days after Easter, and in 1951 to the first Wednesday after Low Sunday. The term originally ended on the day before the Vigil of Ascension; by Dugdale's time the date was "six or seven" days later. The end of term was fixed by the 1830 Act at May 8, and later altered to two days before the Vigil of Ascension; in 1951 this was fixed at 23 days after the commencement.

These changes, in summary form, are as follows:

Period	Begins	Ends	Length
Edward Confessor to Henry I	Oct. of Easter (April 26)	Day before Vigil of Ascesn. (May 25)	30 days
Henry I onwards ..	15 days after Easter (May 3)	Presumably as last	23 days
Late 17th century ..	17 days after Easter (May 5)	"6 or 7" days later than in Confessor's time (May 31 or July 1)	26 or 27 days
1830 onwards ..	April 15	May 8	23 days
Some later date up to 1951	2nd Tuesday after Easter (April 27)	2 days before Vigil of Ascension (May 24)	28 days
1951 onwards ..	1st Wednesday after Low Sunday (April 28)	23 days later	23 days

The Easter court sittings last from the second Tuesday after Easter to the Friday before Whitsun.

Trinity Term. The statute of Edward the Confessor provided

for Trinity term—or rather the long term now divided into
Trinity and Michaelmas, separated by the long vacation—to
begin at the Octave of Pentecost, that is the day after Trinity
Sunday. A statute of 1266-7 altered this to the Octave of Trinity.
In 1540 the beginning of the term was moved back three days to
the Friday after Corpus Christi. The Act of 1830 laid down the
fixed date of May 22; this was later altered to the second Tuesday
after Pentecost, and in 1951 to the first Wednesday after Trinity.
The statute of 1266-7 fixed the end of term at "two or three days
after Quindena S. John Baptist," i.e., about July 30 or 31. The
Act of 1540 provided that the term should last 19 days. In 1830
the end was fixed at June 12, afterwards changed to 20 days from
the second Tuesday after Pentecost. In 1951 the term was
lengthened to the standard 23 days, calculated from the first
Wednesday after Trinity.

Period	Begins	Ends	Length
Edward Confessor to 1266-7	October of Pentecost (June 14)	—	—
1266-7 onwards ..	October of Trinity (June 21)	" 2 or 3 " days after Quindena S. John Baptist (July 30 or 31)	Variable
1540 onwards ..	Friday after Corpus Christi (June 18)	19 days thereafter (July 7)	Variable
1830 onwards ..	May 22	June 12	22 days
Some later date up to 1951	2nd Tuesday after Pentecost (June 15)	20 days thereafter	20 days
1951 to present day	First Wednesday after Trinity (June 16)	23 days later (July 9)	23 days

Trinity sittings of the courts last from the second Tuesday
after Whitsun until July 31. If the fixed date for beginning any
of the sittings falls upon a Sunday, the following day is
observed.

It will be noticed that the old law terms were extremely short

—a total of perhaps 12 weeks in a year. However, until well into the 19th century all the assizes took place outside term. Full "term" was in fact only the period in which the superior courts sat at Westminster. Today circuit work goes on simultaneously with the London sittings, and even during vacations a judge is on hand to deal with urgent business and the Court of Criminal Appeal sits on one or more occasions.

Hours of business at the courts have varied through the centuries. Nowadays at the Law Courts the judges normally sit from 10.30 to 4.30, with a break for lunch of about an hour, usually around 1 p.m. At the Old Bailey and on circuit the hour of beginning is usually the same but judges sometimes sit quite late into the evening if it is more convenient to do so, for example to save a jury or counsel the necessity of returning the following day. Fortescue tells us that in the 15th century the courts customarily sat from 8 a.m. to 11 a.m., and that the judges spent the rest of the day in studying the law and preparing for the next day's work. It is said that Cardinal Wolsey, when Lord Chancellor, sat in his Chancery Court until 11 a.m., then moving to the Court of Star Chamber. Christian ("A Short History of Solicitors," 1896) says, apparently of the 18th century, that the Chancery Court sat in the evening, and the Common Law judges also sat in chambers in the evening after dinner. Sometimes at this period the criminal courts would sit for many hours at a stretch, continuing until nearly midnight if the judge felt so inclined. At the New Sessions House of the Old Bailey, built in 1774, the courts sat from 9 a.m. to 9 p.m., with relays of judges, until at least the middle of the 19th century.

Now we may look at some of the chief annual ceremonies of the legal year, under the dates when they occur:

October 1, or if that day be a Sunday, October 2, is the first day of Michaelmas term and the opening of the legal year. The reopening of the courts and the reassembly of the judges after the long vacation, during which in bygone days many would have been on circuit, have long been marked with some solemnity. By the tradition observed today judges and counsel attend special services then those invited attend a "breakfast" reception given by the Lord Chancellor, and finally walk in procession through the great hall of the Law Courts.

The Lord Chancellor, judges and other members of the profession (except those who are Roman Catholics) assemble at Westminster Abbey for a service held at 11.30 or 11.45 a.m. Those attending are robed, the judges and Queen's Counsel in full dress.

After the hymn before the Blessing the Dean says a prayer "for Her Majesty's Judges and all concerned in the administration of justice." This reads: "O God, the just and merciful Judge of all mankind: Look down from heaven, we beseech thee, on these thy servants, who are set by thy appointment to minister justice between man and man, to clear the innocent, and to convict and punish the guilty: Grant unto them they Holy Spirit, the Spirit of unrightness, the Spirit of discernment and the Spirit of love: that they may boldly, discreetly and mercifully fulfil their sacred duties, to the good of thy people and the glory of thy Name; through Jesus Christ our Lord. Amen."

Dean Robinson (1902-11) was on one occasion unable to stop the inclusion of a psalm including the verse "How long will ye continue to give wrong judgments?"!

Meanwhile at Westminster Cathedral the Roman Catholic judges, barristers and solicitors have been attending a "Red Mass." This is a votive Mass (i.e., one unconnected with a particular feast) of the Holy Ghost, and so called from the red vestments worn in symbolism of the tongues of fire which descended on the Apostles. The collect of this Mass is as follows: *"Deus, qui corda fidelium Sancti Spiritus illustratione docuisti: da nobis in eodem Spiritu recta sapere; et de ejus semper consolatione gaudere. Per Dominum nostrum Jesum Christum filium tuum, qui tecum vivis et regnas in unitate ejusdem Spiritus Sancti."* "O God, who hast taught the hearts of thy faithful by the light of the Holy Spirit; grant that by the same Spirit we may be always truly wise; and ever rejoice in His consolation. Through Our Lord Jesus Christ Thy Son, who livest and reignest with Thee in unity with the same Holy Spirit."

After the services, the judges, attended by their clerks and others who have been invited, go in procession to the Royal Gallery of the House of Lords. The Royal Gallery is now used for the "breakfast," which formerly took place in the Lord Chancellors own house. Only in quite recent times has the Lord Chancellor resided within the Palace of Westminster itself. In the Great Gallery, over 100 feet long and with gilded pillars, are buffet tables. The menu for the 700 or 800 guests used to include champagne and *paté de foie gras*. Now beer and sandwiches are the order of the day (and sometimes in recent years the whole function has been cancelled on grounds of economy). The Lord Chancellor, with the train of his black-and-gold State robe borne behind him, moves among his guests exchanging a word here and there. The reception is an opportunity for judges and lawyers to meet executive officials and legal staffs on a social basis.

Afterwards the Lord Chancellor, judges and counsel drive by car to the Law Courts, and re-form their procession in the Great Hall there (designed after the plan of Westminster Hall). In order of precedence the judges in their gorgeous robes of state move slowly the length of the hall. Leading the procession is a tipstaff, who carries a staff bearing a silver-gilt crown; the staff was given by Lord Chancellor Selborne when the Law Courts were opened in 1883. Next come the Lord Chancellor's macebearer, and the bearer of his Purse of State. Then the Lord Chancellor himself, the Lord Chief Justice, and the Master of the Rolls. The Marshal of the Admiralty Court, with a small black wooden staff, and another official bearing the silver Admiralty oar (see Chapter 7) precede the President of the Probate, Divorce and Admiralty Division. And so on to the Lords Justices, the puisne judges, the Queen's Counsel and junior barristers.

The procession takes its stately way to the Lord Chief Justice's Court. There any new judges are welcomed and finally judges and counsel disperse to the business of the new term. The Lord Chancellor and the puisne judges of the Chancery Division first sit formally to hear applications; it is the only occasion nowadays when the Lord Chancellor sits in the court which is properly his, but unfortunately no one today ever has the temerity to provide him with any business there!

The general principle of the ceremonies attending the opening of the legal year is many centuries old, though there are naturally variations in detail. "At the opening of the Courts at Westminster Hall," says Pulling in "The Order of the Coif" (1884), "the Judges and Serjeants had been long accustomed to attend in regular procession. The Judges up to the middle of the sixteenth century seem, on these occasions, usually to have gone on mules, like the old bishops and abbots."

Cardinal Wolsey, when Lord Chancellor, is said to have ridden on a mule from his home at Old York House (afterwards the Palace of Whitehall) to Westminster Hall. His Eminence's beast was decked for the occasion with saddle-housings of crimson velvet and with gilt stirrups. Dugdale tells us that Mr. Justice Whiddon, who became a judge of the Common Pleas in 1553, was the first to make the journey—presumably from Serjeants' Inn—on horseback instead of muleback.

Pulling continues: "the cavalcade, we are told, was sometimes very imposing, the Lord Chancellor or Lord Keeper and great officers of State, with the Judges and leaders of the Bar and many of the nobility on horseback in full state." The processions were apparently not confined to Michaelmas Term. We have seen earlier (Chapter 12) the pomp which attended Sir Francis Bacon when he went to Westminster Hall on the first day of Easter Term in 1617 to receive the Great Seal as Lord Keeper; he was accompanied by Prince Charles, the Lord Treasurer, the Lord Privy Seal and over 200 horsemen. Although this was a special occasion, the installation of a new Lord Keeper, still it does not seem to have been entirely unique. In 1660 Pepys noted in his diary: "In my way thither I met the Lord Chancellor with the Judges riding on horseback, it being the first day of the term."

On the death of Lord Chancellor Hyde in 1665, the cavalcade was changed to a carriage procession. (This had previously been tried, particularly during the Commonwealth). But seven years later there occurred a procession worth recalling for its amusing side. Pulling quotes the account of it given by Roger North. The Earl of Shaftesbury, Anthony Ashley Cooper, was the last Lord Chancellor untrained in the law, and perhaps the most unsuited for the office. He was in office for only one year, from November 17, 1672, to November 9, 1673. Whatever his faults, he was minded to restore some of the ancient glories of the judicial cavalcade.

"And accordingly the Judges were spoken to to get horses, as they and all the rest did by borrowing or hiring, and so equipped themselves with black footcloths in the best manner they could; and divers of the nobility, as usual in compliment and honour to a new Lord Chancellor, attended also in their equipments. Upon notice in town of this cavalcade, all the show company

took their places at windows and balconies, with the foot
guard in the streets, to partake of the fine sight, and being
once settled for the march, it moved, as the design was, statelily
along. But when they came to straights and interruptions, for
want of gravity in the beasts, or too much in the riders,
there happened some curvetting which made no little
disorder.

"Judge Twisden, to his great affright, and the consternations
of his grave brethren, was laid along in the dirt, but all at length
arrived safe, without loss of life or limb in the service. This
accident was enough to divert the like frolic for the future,
and the very next term after they fell to their coaches as
before."

At about this time we find the first mention of the Lord Chancellor's "breakfast" or reception. Although the religious services
at present held before the reception are of quite recent origin, it
may well be that in pre-Reformation times the judges and
serjeants were accustomed to hear Mass in the chapels of their
Inns before proceeding to Westminster. If they had received
Holy Communion they would be fasting and the "breakfast"
provided by the Lord Chancellor at his house would be a natural
corollary, to fortify the company before going to the courts to
begin the day's business.

Pulling quotes an account of a reception very like that of
today, from "a paper undated of the time of Charles II and found
among the muniments of a noble family numbering a Lord
Chancellor in the ancestral roll, and therefore supposed to be
authentic." It reads as follows:

"His Lordship the first day of every terme, about eight of the
clock in the morning is attended at his own house by the Lord
Chief Justice, the Master of the Rolls, the Chief Justice of the
Common Pleas, and the Chief Baron of the Exchequer, together
with all the Judges, the Attorney, and Solicitor General, and the
rest of the King's and Queen's Counsel, and the Serjeants at Law
with all the Officers belonging to the High Court of Chancery,
where they are treated with biscuit wafers, round cakes, and
macaroons, and with brewed and burnt wine, served after this
manner—Thirdly the brewed wine in a fair, great cup, containing
a gallon, brought in by the Usher of the great Chamber, and
presented to the Lord Chancellor, who drinks to the Master of the
Rolls, and Lord Chief Justice of the Common Pleas, and so goes
about to the Judges and the rest of the Officers in that room."

The reception came to be known as a levée, the Lord Chancellor and the Speaker of the House of Commons being the only subjects privileged to hold levées. Doubtless the Chancellor's reception was once an occasion for presentation of gifts to him (as was certainly done at New Year) in exchange for the exercise of his wide patronage.

After the reception the Lord Chancellor set out for Westminster Hall. If he went by coach, the remaining judges followed in their coaches in order of precedence. At the doors of the Hall —to continue with the Charles II manuscript—"his Lordship takes leave of the Chief Justice and the rest, and so passing by the Court of Common Pleas, there finds the Serjeants at Law placed before the Bar of that Court, presenting themselves to his Lordship. According to their seniority, his Lordship shaking them by the hand as he passes along; which ceremony ended, his Lordship goes up to the Chancery Court." If, however, the Chancellor went on horseback, there was also a procession, but "before all go the Tipstaves of the Court and the Constables, who clear the way for his Lordship's passage through the streets to Westminster Hall door. . . ."

The present procession through the great hall of the Law Courts is surely a remnant of this longer journey.

Whether or not the judges and serjeants attended Mass on these occasions in pre-Reformation times, and surprising as it may seem in view of the proximity of the Abbey to Westminster Hall, the addition of the service to earlier ceremonial dates only from 1897. At the Jubilee service at St. Paul's Cathedral in that year the Bar had been represented as a body, and this was probably felt to be an opportunity to approach the Abbey authorities to institute a service for the opening of the legal year. The Roman Catholic members of the profession had had a Mass on this occasion in earlier years, since 1895 at least. Solicitors were not invited to the first Abbey service, at Michaelmas term, 1897, but the omission was soon remedied.

The Red Mass, which is organised by the Society of Our Lady of Good Counsel (whose primary object is provision of free legal advice for the poor) has been held at Westminster only since the Cathedral was opened in 1903. From 1895 until that date it was held at what is now the Church of St. Anselm and St. Cecilia in Kingsway. That church, since rebuilt, was then still known as the

Sardinian Chapel from its connection with the former Sardinian Embassy. It was a noted Mass-centre in penal days. The custom of celebrating a Red Mass for the legal profession is of long standing in some Catholic countries. The Archbishop of Paris offers—or used until comparatively recent times to offer—a Red Mass at the Sainte Chapelle, adjoining the Palais de Justice in Paris.

At the *end of October* the sheriffs of the City of London for the year just ended are called to account and the ancient "quit-rents" are rendered to the Crown for certain lands held by the City Corporation. Both ceremonies take place, one following the other, before the Queen's Remembrancer at the Law Courts. The Remembrancer's court acts in place of the now extinct Court of Exchequer. Although a day at the end of October is now usually chosen, the Queen's Remembrancer Act, 1859, provides that the quit-rents may be rendered on the morrow of St. Michael, i.e., on September 30, or between that day and the morrow of St. Martin, i.e., November 12.

The sheriffs of the City of London are elected at Midsummer, and royal approval of their election is handed by the Queen's Remembrancer to the City Secondary (see Chapter 8) on a date before September 30. On September 30 it was formerly customary for the Recorder to "present" the new sheriffs for swearing before the Court of Exchequer; this ceremony, abolished in 1859, closely resembled that of Lord Mayor's Day, with a procession to Westminster and a banquet afterwards. The presentation was followed by the rendering of the quit-rents.

The first of the two ceremonies as now observed begins with the Secondary of the City reading a warrant calling on the outgoing sheriffs to appear to render their account for the year's office. He then reads a second warrant, by which they have appointed an attorney (nowadays the Chief Clerk of the Queen's Remembrancer) to account on their behalf, and prays that the two warrants may be recorded. The Queen's Remembrancer orders that this be done. The only "account" now rendered is the quit-rents paid to the Crown which are the subject of the second ceremony.

This is opened by a proclamation by the Chief Clerk: "Oyez, Oyez, Oyez—Tenants and occupiers of a piece of waste ground called the 'Moors' in the county of Salop, come forth and do your service." The City Solicitor then takes a hatchet and tests its edge by using it to chop a faggot, one of two placed ready on a table in the court. He then takes a billhook, and cuts the second faggot. "Good service," the Queen's Remembrancer declares. The two implements are handed over to him, and nowadays he keeps them as a **perquisite**.

The lands known as "The Moors" in Shropshire—no one knows for certain their identity—were held of Henry III by a certain Nicholas de Mora. The first mention of the tenure is in 1211, and it is recorded that in Michaelmas term, 1245, Nicholas paid his "rent" at the Exchequer with two knives "one good and the other very bad." The quality of the knives thus described was intentional, for an entry in 1254 refers to them as "one to cut hazel rod, the other to bend in green cheese." In 1521 we are told that the rent is "2 knives of which one must be of such strength that a Knight, if one be present, or someone else if he is not, holds a hazel stick of one year's age and of one cubit's length and striking the said stick with the weak knife, the weak knife makes little or no mark on the stick, and a good knife at the first stroke on the stick ought to cut it in half." At some date unknown the hatchet and the billhook were substituted for the knives : or it may be that "knives" was merely the ancient description of these instruments. By the reign of Henry VIII the land had come into the possession of the Corporation of London.

The second quit-rent payment is prefaced by another proclamation : "Oyez, Oyez, Oyez—Tenants and occupiers of a certain tenement called the Forge in the Parish of St. Clement Danes, in the county of Middlesex, come forth and do your service." This time the City Solicitor counts, aloud, six horseshoes and sixty-one nails. The Queen's Remembrancer declares them "Good number."

The forge is one granted in the reign of Henry II to a certain Walter le Brun, a farrier in the Strand (then probably meaning merely "the river-bank")—the exact site is now unknown. Le Brun is thought to have repaired the armour and fitted shoes to the horses of the Knights Templar. His rent of six horse-shoes is recorded in the reign of Henry III, and the land at some later date passed to the Corporation of London. The horseshoes used today have been used every year for the past five centuries, so it is said. They are a considerable size, such as would be suitable for a war-horse.

Until comparatively recent times the two quit-rents were rendered by the senior City alderman below the chair, instead of by the City Solicitor as is now the practice.

On *November* 9 (or if that date happen to fall upon a Sunday, then on the following day) the new Lord Mayor of London comes to the Law Courts to be "presented" and sworn. This visit is the object and raison d'être of the great procession from Guildhall known as the Lord Mayor's Show.

(The Lord Mayor of London is elected by the Livery and Aldermen of the Corporation on Michaelmas Day. As soon as convenient afterwards the Lord Mayor-elect goes in state to the House of Lords to receive from the Lord Chancellor the consent of the Sovereign to his election. He is accompanied by the aldermen, in robes of office, with the beadles of the City wards bearing their ward maces. The Lord Mayor-elect is introduced to the Lord Chancellor by the City Remembrancer. Silver loving-cups, decorated with white ribbons and lily-of-the-valley and filled with hot punch, are exchanged by the Lord Mayor-elect and the Lord Chancellor. The white posies are then, by tradition, presented to their wives).

On November 9—Lord Mayor's Day—the great civic pageant sets forth in procession to the Law Courts in the Strand, where it arrives about 1 p.m.

The Lord Mayor goes to the Lord Chief Justice's court. The Lord Chief Justice and the Queen's Bench judges assembled there for the occasion wear their scarlet and ermine robes and full State dress (except their ermine mantles) and—for the only occasion in the year—their black caps. (See Chapter 7). The Queen's Remembrancer, also present, wears during part of the proceedings a three-cornered hat on top of his full-bottomed wig. The reason for this unusual assumption of headgear in court is a desire to assert the right of Her Majesty's judges and Remembrancer to remain covered in the presence of the Lord Mayor, to "keep him in his place," in fact. Lord Goddard, in his evidence on the black cap to the Royal Commission on Capital Punishment, 1949-53, said that as the Lord Mayor was the one subject with the right to come into court covered, so the judges also cover. For the occasion the Lord Mayor himself wears his scarlet robe and collar of SS (as, of course, does the Lord Chief Justice), with a feathered hat. The central position facing the bench is taken by the Recorder of London, in court dress, scarlet gown, and full-bottomed wig. The Lord Mayor stands to his right, and the former Lord Mayor, in the court dress, scarlet gown and chain of a City alderman, to his left. The City Swordbearer, in his picturesque fur-hatted costume, and Serjeant-at-arms, in wig and gown, are in attendance, with the sword pointing downward and the mace reversed, as is the rule in the presence of the Sovereign or her representative.

A declaration and warrant have been prepared by the Queen's Remembrancer. The Lord Mayor bows three times to the court, and is then presented by the Recorder. The Lord Chief Justice addresses him, customarily with a short laudatory speech, during which the Lord Mayor stands bare-headed, afterwards resuming his hat. Next the Lord Mayor repeats the words of the declaration, promising to perform the duties of his office faithfully, phrase by phrase after the Queen's Remembrancer, and then signs it. The Recorder then reads a warrant from the Mayor, Commonalty and Citizens of London appointing the Chief Clerk in the office of the Queen's Remembrancer their attorney (see under quit-rents earlier in this chapter) to "sue, prosecute, defend and lay claim to all their liberties," etc., in the Queen's Bench Division. The Recorder asks that the warrant be recorded, and the Lord Chief Justice instructs the Queen's Remembrancer to do this.

The proceedings end with an invitation from the Recorder, on behalf of the Lord Mayor, to the judges to attend the Lord Mayor's banquet that evening at Guildhall. The City procession then goes to the Court of Appeal to extend a similar invitation to the Lords Justices, who wear their three-cornered hats to receive the Lord Mayor on this occasion.

The ceremony of "presenting" the Lord Mayor of London is of great antiquity. The citizens of London obtained from King John in 1215 a charter giving them the right to elect their mayor, provided that the King's consent were obtained to the chosen candidate. The new mayor was to be presented to the Sovereign "or our justices if we be not present, and shall swear fealty to us." In 1253 a charter of Henry III provided that in the King's absence the presentation be made to the Barons of the Exchequer.

When the Exchequer Court, and its successor the Exchequer Division of the High Court, had in turn disappeared, the Queen's Bench Division was substituted by an Act of 1883, and it is as successors of the Court of Exchequer that the Lord Chief Justice and other Queen's Bench judges receive the presentation today.

Originally there must have been a dual ceremony, in which the new Lord Mayor received royal approval of his election and also made his declaration of fealty. This ceremony took place at Westminster, where the judges sat within the precincts of the palace. At some time the two parts of the proceedings became separated. The presentation of the Lord Mayor to the Lord Chancellor, who conveys royal approval, dates back to at least the 15th century, though apparently there is still no statutory provision for this as there is for the declaration.

From the 13th century until the calendar change of 1752 the Lord Mayor took office on October 28, the feast of St. Simon and St. Jude. When the Gregorian Calendar was adopted, omitting 11 days from the year 1752, Lord Mayor's Day was changed to November 9, equivalent to the former October 28. It has been suggested that the old style day was retained so that the Lord Mayor at the changeover period should not lose 11 days of his mayoralty. However, the change was made by an Act of 1750, which also altered the date of the nomination of sheriffs, a function which then took place, as did the presentation of the Lord Mayor, in the Court of Exchequer. The date of the beginning of Michaelmas Term was altered, therefore (as the Act expressly states in the case of the sheriffs) the dates of the functions had also to be changed so that they fell in term-time.

The Mayor of Oxford was similarly presented to the Court of Exchequer until 1839.

On *November* 12 (or if that day is a Sunday then on the next day) there takes place at the Law Courts the nomination of high sheriffs of the English and Welsh counties (except Lancashire and Cornwall) for the following year. (City of London sheriffs are chosen at Midsummer, and those of other towns and cities which possess the office generally on November 9. See Chapter 8).

On a date in *February or March*, at a meeting of the Privy

Council, the Sovereign "pricks" the names of those chosen as county sheriffs for the ensuing year. (See Chapter 8).

Early in March each year the Trial of the Pyx is opened at Goldsmiths' Hall, in the City of London. The "pyx" is a box in which are placed samples of coinage produced by the Royal Mint during the preceding year. (The word derives from the Greek πύξις, a box; its use in English is almost confined to the present instance, and in ecclesiastical terminology). Its "trial," of very ancient origin, is carried out by a jury of independent experts who assay the samples to see that they are correct in weight and fineness. Unfortunately even the opening procedure takes place in private.

The trial is held nowadays by the authority of the Coinage Act. 1870, and Orders in Council made under that statute. Two Lords Commissioners of the Treasury sign each year warrants which name the day and summon the jurors for the trial. On the appointed date there assemble at Goldsmiths' Hall the Queen's Remembrancer, the Deputy Master or other officials of the Mint, officials of the Board of Trade and a jury of 15 freemen of the Worshipful Company of Goldsmiths.

The Queen's Remembrancer, in his ceremonial dress—black silk gown, lace stock, full-bottomed wig and velvet court suit, presides. He swears the jurors in the following form (printed in Sir George Bonner's "The Office of the King's Remembrancer," 1930):

"I, ———, swear by Almighty God that I shall well and truly, after my knowledge and discretion, make the assays of these moneys of gold and silver, and truly report if the said moneys be in weight and fineness according to the standard weights for weighing and testing the coins of the realm, and the standard trial plates of gold and silver used for determining the justness of the gold and silver coinage of the realm in the custody of the Board of Trade, and be in conformity with the first schedules of the Coinage Acts, 1870 and 1891, and the Coinage Act, 1920. So help me God."

The Deputy Master of the Mint (in practice the head of the Mint, for the Mastership is held by the Chancellor of the Exchequer ex officio) and his officials have brought with them the pyx, or rather several pyxes. In these boxes are the samples to be assayed. Each day's production at the Mint is divided into batches of a specific number or weight, known as "journeys" because in early times—until some time after the 15th century —they were actually the entire day's output. For gold coins each journey comprises 2,000 coins, and for silver 60 lbs. Troy. The modern cupro-nickel is treated as silver, and bronze is not assayed. Out of each journey one coin is put aside at the Mint to await the annual trial (another is assayed on the spot). Coinages produced by the Royal Mint for Southern Rhodesia and New Zealand are dealt with in the same way as those for Britain.

Officials of the Board of Trade standards department produce standard trial pieces of gold and silver, scales, balances and weights, by which the return of the jury is made each year, to ensure that the criteria are always the same. The scales are accurate to the 800,000th part of a grain.

The pyxes and the trial pieces and standards handed over, proceedings are adjourned. The jury of goldsmiths carry out their duties over the following six or eight weeks, and the court then reassembles at Goldsmiths' Hall.

The jury return their verdict to the Queen's Remembrancer, reporting whether they have found the number, weight and fineness of the coins to be as required. A slight—very slight— margin is allowed, and it is seldom indeed that any inaccuracy is reported. The verdict, signed by all the jurors, is presented in writing, and read aloud by the Clerk to the Goldsmiths' Company. Then it is handed to the Queen's Remembrancer for recording and filing, and it is published in the London Gazette that all who are interested may see it.

The precise antiquity of the Trial of the Pyx is uncertain. There is evidence indicating a trial in 1140, in the reign of Stephen. The earliest extant record of a formal trial is dated 1248, in Henry III's reign. In that year a jury of "twelve discreet and lawful citizens of London with twelve skilful Goldsmiths of the same place" officiated at a trial before the Barons of the Exchequer. A writ formally directing a Trial of the Pyx is found for the first time in 1281, under Edward I. The standard and trial plates were long kept in the Chapel of the Pyx at Westminster Abbey, which may still be seen, and until 1842 the trial and assay were held at Westminster. At one time it took place in the inner chamber adjoining the Star Chamber in the old Palace of Westminster,

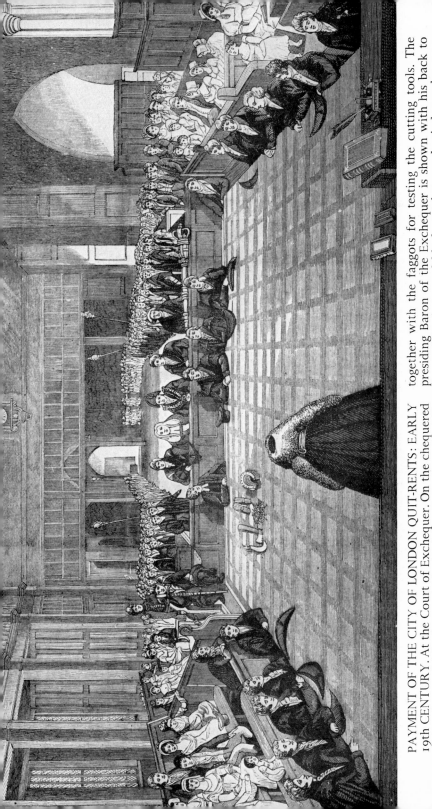

PAYMENT OF THE CITY OF LONDON QUIT-RENTS: EARLY 19th CENTURY. At the Court of Exchequer. On the chequered table—from which the court derived its name—are the bill-hook, hatchet, nails and horseshoes which form the "rents", together with the faggots for testing the cutting tools. The presiding Baron of the Exchequer is shown with his back to the reader; the round black patch worn by judges who were also serjeants is clearly seen. At the bar of the court are the Lord Mayor, the Recorder and the two Sheriffs.

PAYMENT OF THE CITY QUIT-RENTS TODAY.   In the
"court" of the Queen's Remembrancer. The City Solicitor
is seen counting the nails; close by are the horse-shoes
used each year for five centuries past, and the faggots.

now superseded by our modern Houses of Parliament. From 1844 the assay has been carried out at Goldsmiths' Hall, and from 1870 the whole proceedings have taken place there.

The Lord Chancellor, the Lord Treasurer or Chancellor of the Exchequer and other members of the King's Council, or the Barons of the Exchequer, presided over the trial in former days. The Privy Council was still summoned to the trial well after the accession of Charles II in 1660. Occasionally—notably in 1611 (James I) and 1669 (Charles II)—the Sovereign himself attended. Normally the Lord Chancellor or the Chancellor of the Exchequer presided. As late as 1866 the Lord Chancellor was presiding, though as a senior official of the Exchequer the King's Remembrancer must have attended from early times, and it was his duty to record the verdict. The Coinage Act, 1870, provided that from thenceforth the Remembrancer should preside over the trial each year, and the Lord Chancellor and Chancellor of the Exchequer do not now attend.

Since the reign of Elizabeth I or earlier the jury has consisted entirely of members of the Goldsmiths' Company. The Wardens of the Company are summoned by precept to form the jury, which always includes their assay master. An account of the procedure during the early 19th century given in Herbert's "City Companies" says: "This jury are sworn, receive a charge from the Lord Chancellor; then retire into the Courtroom of the Duchy of Lancaster, where the pix . . . is delivered to them by the officials of the Mint. The indenture or authority under which the Mint Master (a separate office until 1870) has acted being received, the pix is opened, and the coins to be assayed being taken out, are enclosed in paper parcels, each under the seals of the Wardens, Master and Comptrollers." Later the parcels were opened for the assay, and if the number, weight and fineness were accurate a certificate was given to the Master of the Mint.

In the second half of the 14th century the trials were held every three months, and coins had a "privy mark" to show in which such period they were minted. Edward VI increased the interval to a year, but under Elizabeth I it was brought back to three months. Later the period again varied, and sometimes the trial was held only when the pyx was full. When Dean Stanley wrote his "Memorials of Westminster Abbey" in 1868 the

o

interval was five years. The present annual period was fixed by the Coinage Act, 1870.

From at least the late 17th century there was held a Pyx Dinner or Feast, at which the Goldsmiths' Company entertained everyone concerned in the trial, together with other guests. A Pyx Luncheon is still held.

A complete set of the verdicts at the trials since 1603 is in the Public Record Office, where they may be inspected.

On the *first Sunday of Trinity Term* the judges of the Supreme Court drive (or used so to do, for the custom was allowed to lapse during the second world war and has not—1954—been revived) in procession from the Law Courts to the Mansion House to lunch with the Lord Mayor, afterwards attending a service at St. Paul's Cathedral. St. Paul's is reputed to have been associated from time immemorial with the serjeants and judges. During the Middle Ages, it is said, the serjeants met their clients there, each serjeant having his allotted pillar as rendezvous. The pillars are said to have been ceremonially allotted at each call of serjeants, until old St. Paul's perished in the Great Fire of 1666. Cohen ("A History of the English Bar," 1929) seems—p. 489 note—to cast some doubt on the location of the pillar custom, apparently holding that the serjeants stationed themselves in Westminster Hall.

The Lord Mayor, sheriffs, aldermen, Recorder and other officials of the City of London accompany the judges in processions to the cathedral. The Recorder, like the judges, wears his full State dress. At the service the judges carry posies, a custom said in this case to date from the Great Plague of 1665.

The origin and antiquity of this annual service is obscure. An account of the function in the Law Times for April 29, 1865—it apparently took place earlier in the year in those days—shows some variation in detail. "On the first Sunday in Easter term," says this account, there took place the "ceremony well known in civic language as churching the judges." The judges assembled at 3 p.m. in the hall of Serjeants' Inn, Chancery Lane, and "were conducted to St. Paul's in three carriages by the City Marshal on horseback." They were received in the nave of the cathedral by the Lord Mayor and other City officials.

Early in July the Lord Mayor of London entertains Her Majesty's judges and other leaders of the profession, including

Commonwealth visitors, at a Mansion House banquet. Until the second world war the judges attending wore State dress, as they do at the Lord Mayor's Day banquet. Nowadays ordinary evening dress is worn. Neither the Guildhall Library nor the secretary of the Lord Mayor were able to give me any information on the history of this customary banquet.

APPENDIX

The assize circuits in the time of Edward I were as follows, according to Dugdale:

1. Lincoln, Leicester, Warwick, Stafford, Salop, Northampton, Rutland, Gloucester, Hereford, Worcester.

2. York, Northumberland, Westmorland, Cumberland, Lancaster, Nottingham, Derby.

3. Cornwall, Devon, Somerset, Dorset, Wiltshire, Hampshire, Oxford, Berkshire, Sussex, Surrey.

4. Kent, Essex, Hertford, Norfolk, Suffolk, Cambridge, Huntingdon, Bedford and Bucks.

It would be tedious to recount all the changes made during succeeding centuries, but as an example the following are the assize circuits as they were in 1682, according to "The Office of the Clerk of Assize":

1. Hertfordshire, Essex, Kent, Sussex, Surrey.

2. Hampshire, Wiltshire, Dorset, Devon, Cornwall, Somerset.

3. Oxfordshire, Worcestershire, Staffordshire, Shropshire, Herefordshire, Monmouth, Gloucestershire, Berkshire.

4. Norfolk, Suffolk, Cambridgeshire, Huntingdonshire, Bedfordshire, Buckinghamshire.

5. Warwickshire, Leicestershire, Derbyshire, Nottinghamshire, Lincolnshire, Rutland, Northamptonshire.

6. In Trinity term, Yorkshire, Durham, Northumberland, Cumberland, Westmorland, Lancashire. In Hilary term (i.e., the winter assize) Yorkshire and Lancashire only.

The circuits and assize towns as they are to-day (1954):

South Eastern: Huntingdonshire (Huntingdon); Hertfordshire (Hertford); Cambridgeshire and Isle of Ely (Cambridge); Suffolk (Ipswich or Bury St. Edmunds); Norfolk (Norwich city and county); Essex (Chelmsford); Surrey (Kingston); Kent (Maidstone); Sussex (Lewes).

Midland: Buckinghamshire (Aylesbury); Bedfordshire (Bedford); Northamptonshire (Northampton); Leicestershire (Leicester city and county); Rutland (Oakham); Lincolnshire (Lincoln city and county); Derbyshire (Derby); Nottinghamshire (Nottingham city and county); Warwickshire (Warwick); Birmingham.

Northern: Westmorland (Appleby); Cumberland (Carlisle); Lancashire (Lancaster); Liverpool; Manchester.

North-Eastern: Northumberland (Newcastle city and county); Durham (Durham); Yorkshire (York); Leeds.

Oxford: Berkshire (Reading); Oxfordshire (Oxford); Worcestershire (Worcester city and county); Gloucestershire (Gloucester city

213

and county); Monmouth (Newport); Herefordshire (Hereford); Shropshire (Shrewsbury); Staffordshire (Stafford).

Western: Wiltshire (Devizes or Salisbury); Dorset (Dorchester); Somerset (Taunton or Wells); Cornwall (Bodmin); Devon (Exeter city and county); Bristol; Hampshire (Winchester).

Wales and Chester: Montgomery (Welshpool or Newtown); Merionethshire (Dolgelly); Caernarvonshire (Caernarvon); Anglesey (Beaumaris); Denbighshire (Ruthin); Flintshire (Mold); Cheshire (Chester); Radnorshire (Presteign); Brecknockshire (Brecon); Cardiganshire (Lampeter); Pembrokeshire (Haverfordwest); Carmarthenshire (Carmarthen); Glamorganshire (Cardiff or Swansea).

ADDENDA

p. 26. Reader's Feast. For a description of a modern Reader's Feast at the Middle Temple see Law Times 218 (Nov. 19, 1954) p. 266.

p. 41. Green Bag. Perhaps the true reason for the "unpopularity" of the green bag lies in the "Green Bag Riots" of 1817-18. A green bag full of allegedly seditious documents was laid before Parliament by Lord Sidmouth.

p. 100. Black gown worn by judges of the Probate, Divorce and Admiralty Division. The doctors who sat as judges in the ecclesiastical courts at Doctors' Commons (except in the Court of Arches) wore black gowns. ("Doctors' Commons," London Topographical Record XV, 1931).

p. 100 and p. 159. Lord Chancellor's black gown. A painting of "The Court of Chancery during the reign of George I" (B. Ferrers) in the National Portrait Gallery shows the Lord Chancellor (Lord Macclesfield) in a black gown, however.

p. 101. Court of Admiralty. A gilt fouled anchor on a blue ground, emblem of the Lord High Admiral, hangs over the bench in the modern court as in its predecessor. A further touch of colour is provided by the blue uniforms and gold braid of the Elder Brethren of Trinity House who sometimes sit with the judge as assessors.

p. 171. Collar of SS worn by puisne judges. An account of Charles II's Coronation procession in 1661 (in Guillim's "Heraldry," 5th edn.) lists "Justices of the King's Bench and Common Pleas, 6, in Robes, Caps, and Collars."

INDEX

ADMINISTRATION of Justice Act, 1938, 140
Admiralty, Court of, 101, 198, 215
Admiralty Oar, 100, 198
Aldermen, City of London, 68, 144, 146, 210
Ancients, 24, 41, 49
Appeal, Court of, 79, 154, 157, 174, 176, 205
Appeal, Lords of, 165, 166
Appellate Jurisdiction Act, 1876, 165
Articled clerk, 73-74
Assize circuits, 121-123, 213-214
Assize, Clerk of, 123, 124, 135, 136
Assize, Commission of, 133, 134, 136
Assize, Commissioners of, 134
Assize customs (see under Assize towns and Judges of assize)
Assize, judges of (see Judges of assize)
Assize, Maiden, 139
Assize of Clarendon (1166), 13
Assize, opening of, 132-137
Assize service, 95, 130-132
Assize towns:
  Appleby, 119, 121-122, 127
  Aylesbury, 118, 120
  Bedford, 120, 127
  Bristol, 122, 127, 181
  Caernarvon, 118
  Cambridge, 115, 126, 130-131, 137
  Cardiff, 127
  Carlisle, 138
  Carmarthen, 140
  Chelmsford, 128
  Chester, 118, 127
  Derby, 127, 130
  Exeter, 122, 127, 130
  Haverfordwest, 140
  Hereford, 127
  Lancaster, 118
  Leeds, 122
  Lincoln, 120, 122, 130, 140
  Liverpool, 120, 122, 130
  Manchester, 120, 122
  Newcastle, 113, 114, 122, 127, 137
  Norwich, 122, 127
  Nottingham, 122
  Oxford, 115, 119, 125, 126, 130, 131, 137

Assize towns—contd.
  Ruthin, 132
  Sheffield, 122
  Shrewsbury, 132
  Swansea, 118
  Taunton, 130
  Warwick, 114
  York, 122, 125, 129, 130, 132
Assizes, 115-118, 121-141
Assizes, possessory, 134
Attorney-General, 65-68:
  appointment, 67
  chosen from Double Readers, 23
  costume, 67
  duties, 65-66, 158, 165
  elected bencher, 43
  first, 67
  gift of livery cloth, 68
  head of Bar, made, 67
  history of office, 66-67
  Lord Chancellor's Breakfast, 200
  precedence in court, 14
  qualifications, 67
  Recorder of Kingston, 182
  Swearing-in of Lord Chancellor, 158
Attorneys:
  admission, 75
  bag used by, 76
  costume, 76
  duties, 70-72
  Inns of Court, members of, 73
  oaths, 75-76
  origin, 70-71
  qualifications, 74
  roll, 75
  solicitors, become known as, 72
  striking off, 77

BAGS, brief—or book—attorneys, 76
  barristers, 39, 40, 41, 215
  judges, 100
  Queen's Counsel, 59
  solicitors, 76
Bands, 36, 37, 89
Bar, the, 14, 27
Barons of the Exchequer, 79, 85

Barristers, 31-41 :
  circuit, on, 150-153
  clergy may not be, 13-14
  costume, 34-39, 167
  duties, 12-13
  first woman, 34
  junior, 34
  number, 13
  oaths, 33
  opening of legal year, at, 198, 199
  qualifications, 19-20
  title, origin of, 14-15
Bench, The judicial, 79
Benchers, 41-46 :
  Attorney-Generals as, 43
  call to Bar, 21, 32, 33
  costume, 22, 23, 46
  dining customs, 50, 53
  duties, 12, 15, 42
  elect Ancients, 41
  election and call of, 42, 43, 44, 45
  honorary, 43
  keeping terms, 46
  meetings of, 45
  numbers, 44
  offices held by, 45, 46
  pleaded within Bar, 60
  Queen's Counsel as, 43, 58
  Readership qualifications for, 22,
    45
  royal, 43
  Solicitor-General as, 43
  title, origin of, 42
Black Cap, 91-93
Bouquet, judge's (see Posy)
Brasses, monumental, 97
Breakfast, Lord Chancellor's, 94, 155,
  196-8, 200, 201

CALL to the Bar, 28, 31-33
  qualifications for, 19
Call Day, 31, 46
Caps, 20, 48-49
Captain of mess, 49-50, 52, 53
Casting-hood, 87, 98, 179
Central Criminal Court (see Old
  Bailey)
Chancellor, Lord (see Lord Chan-
  cellor)
Chancellor of the Exchequer :
  costume, 107, 161
  nomination of sheriffs, at, 106
  Pyx trial, formerly at, 209

Chancery, Court of, 38, 80, 161, 175,
  196, 201
Chancery Division, 79, 80, 96, 154,
  198
Chaplain (Inns of Court), 46, 49
Chaplain, sheriff's :
  assize procession, in, 124
  assize sermon, 131-132
  assize service, drives to, 127
  Cambridge, at, 131
  costume, 115, 131
  duties, 115, 124, 127, 131-132,
    137
  Old Bailey, at, 147-148
  opening of assize, at, 133
Cheshire Regiment, 127
Chief Baron of the Exchequer, 168,
  200
Circuit mess, 150-153 :
  Junior, 151
  Junior Treasurer, 151
  Leader, 151
  Recorder, 151
  Treasurer, 151
Circuits, assize, 121-123, 213-214
Clerk, judge's, 133, 136
Clerk of Assize, 123, 124, 135, 136
Clerk of the Crown, 158
Coaches, state, 127
Coif, Order of the, 23, 85
Coinage Act, 1870, 207, 209, 210
Collar of SS, 170-173, 205, 215
College of Arms, Officers of, 170
Commission Day, 125
Commission :
  Assize, 133, 134, 136
  Jail Delivery, 134, 137, 144, 145
  Oyer and Terminer, 134, 137, 143,
    144, 145
  Peace, 134, 188
Commissioners of Assize, 134
Commissioners of Central Criminal
  Court, 144
Common Cryer, 137
Common Cryer (London : Serjeant-
  at-arms), 146, 170, 205
Common Pleas, Chief Justice of the,
  200
Common Pleas, Court of, 27, 57, 60,
  79, 80, 98, 169, 201
Common Serjeant, 144, 186-187
Costume :
  Attorney-General, 67
  Barristers, 34-39

Costume—*contd.*
Benchers, 22, 23, 46
Chancellor of the Exchequer, 107, 161
Common Serjeant, 187
Judges (County Court), 179
Judges (High Court), 37, 85-101, 127, 129, 132, 135, 136, 210, 211
Judges of assize, 127, 132
Lord Chancellor, 158-162, 166, 198
Lord Chief Justice, 169, 170-173, 204
Lord Mayor of London, 161, 204
Lords Justices of Appeal, 161, 177, 205
Lords of Appeal, 166
Macebearer, Lord Chancellor's, 162
Master of the Rolls, 161, 175
Mourning, 37, 64, 65, 96
Porters (Inns of Court), 50
President of P.D.A. Division, 161, 176
Privy Councillors, 161
Pursebearer, Lord Chancellor's, 162
Queen's Counsel, 37, 61, 64, 65, 167
Queen's Remembrancer, 207
Readers, 22, 23, 26
Recorders, 22, 184, 185, 205, 210
Secondary (London), 114
Serjeant-at-arms (London), 205
Serjeants-at-law, 22, 85, 97
Sheriffs, 112
Solicitors, 76
Solicitor-General, 69
Speaker of House of Commons, 161
Students (Inns of Court), 20, 31
Swordbearer (London), 205
Under-sheriff, 114
when dining at Inns of Court, 48-49
Council (Lincoln's Inn), 45
Council of Legal Education, 20, 26, 30
County Courts, 178-179
County Courts Act, 1846, 178
Courts-Martial Appeal Court, 169
Criminal Appeal Act, 1907, 165
Criminal Appeal, Court of, 169
Cupboard (Middle Temple), 17, 26

DEAN of the Arches, 144
Dean of the Chapel, 45
Declarations:
Lord Mayor of London, 205
Queen's Counsel, 61
Recorder, 183
Dining customs at Inns of Court, 44, 48-56
Dinners, eating of, 19, 20, 29-32

EDUCATION, legal, 19-30, 34
Examinations, Bar, 19, 29, 30
Exchequer, Barons of the, 79, 85, 208, 209
Exchequer, Chancellor of the (*see* Chancellor of the Exchequer)
Exchequer, Chief Baron of the, 168, 200
Exchequer, Court of, 79, 98, 202, 205
Exchequer Division, 205

GARTER, Order of the, 170
Girdle, judge's, 88
Gloves:
Barristers, 38
Judges, 94
Presentation of, 125-126, 139-142
Queen's Counsel, 64
White, at Maiden Assize, 139-142
Gowns (*see* also Costume)
Barristers, 34-36
Benchers (formerly), 22
Queen's Counsel, 65
Recorders, 22, 185
Solicitors, 76
Students (Inns of Court), 20
Grace prayers, 50-52
Grand Days (Nights), 25, 54, 55, 56, 152
Grand Juries, 124, 136, 137
Gray's Inn, 18
Ancients, 41
armorial bearings, 18
Benchers, 33-34, 42-43, 44, 50
Butler, 50
call to Bar, 31, 33
costume, 39, 48, 49
dining customs, 48-56
grace prayers, 51
Grand Day, 55, 56
Hall, 18, 55
loving-cup, 56

Gray's Inn—*contd.*
  mace or staff, 50
  Master of the Moots, 46
  Master of the Common Room, 46
  moots, 28
  origin and history, 18, 19
  Pension, 45
  Porter, 50, 55
  Preacher, 46, 49
  readings, 26, 33
  students, 49, 53
  toasts, 52, 56
  Treasurer, 56
Great Seal, the, 134, 154, 155, 163, 164

HATS, tricorne, 93-94, 132-133, 135, 161-162, 205
Herbs, 130, 162
High Court of Justice, the, 79-81
Historical Manuscripts Commission, 174
Hood, judge's, 88, 98
Hours of business at courts, 196
House of Lords, 165-166
Inner Temple, 16-17
  Ancients, 41, 52
  Armorial bearings, 17
  Benchers, 32, 42, 43, 44, 46, 53
  call to Bar, 32
  call to Bench, 44
  costume, 39
  dining customs, 48-56
  first woman barrister, 34
  grace prayers, 50-51
  Hall, 17
  mace or staff, 50
  Master of the Garden, 46
  Master of the House, 46
  Master of the Moots, 46
  Master of the Temple, 46-47, 59
  origin, 16
  Panniers, 48
  Parliament, 32, 45
  Porter, 50
  Reader, 26, 49
  Reader's Feast, 25
  toasts, 32, 52, 53, 55
  Treasurer, 32, 53, 56

INNS of Court (*see under* titles)

JAIL Delivery, Commission of, 134, 137, 143, 144, 145
Javelin-men, 118, 127, 129
Judges, County Court:
  appointment, 179
  costume, 179
  duration of office, 179
  qualifications, 179
  title, 179
Judges, High Court, 78-101
  appointment of, 81
  costume, 85-101, 127, 129, 132, 135, 136, 210, 211, 215
  duration of office, 81
  knighthood, 83-84
  number, 84
  oaths, 81-83
  powers and duties, 81
  privileges, 78
  qualifications, 81
  summoned to Parliament, 84
  swearing-in, 81-83
  title, 84
Judges of assize, 121-142:
  allow troops out of barracks (Exeter, Chester), 127
  arrival of, 124-125
  assize procession, in, 127, 129
  assize service, at, 130-132
  circuits, allocation of, 123
  costume, 127, 132
  entertaining, 137
  gift of bouquet (York, Exeter), 130
  gift of coins (Newcastle), 137
  gift of gloves (Oxford), 125, 126
  gift of herbs (York), 130
  gift of white gloves, 139-142
  in commission, 123
  Lord Mayor's Breakfast, at (York), 125, 129
  number of, 122
  opening of assize, at, 132-137
  staff, 123
  travel, method of, 124
  visits to, 126
  who are, 123
Judicature Act, 1873, 72, 79, 95, 168, 174, 176, 192
Judicial Committee (*see* Privy Council)
Junior of circuit mess, 151
Justices of the Peace, 187-190
  appointment, 154, 189

Justices of the Peace—*contd.*
  duration of office, 190
  duties, 187, 188
  history of office, 180, 187, 188
  oaths, 189-190
  qualifications, 189
Justices of the Peace Act, 1949, 182

Keeper of the Black Book
  (Lincoln's Inn), 45
King's Bench, Court of, 80, 165
King's Bench Division (*see* Queen's
  Bench Division)
King's Counsel (*see* Queen's Counsel)
King's Serjeants, 59, 60
Knights of St. John, 16
Knights Templar, 16, 203

Law Society, The, 73, 75
  Law Society Disciplinary Com-
    mittee, 77
Leader of circuit Bar, 151
Legal Year, opening of, 196-202
Lincoln's Inn, 15-16:
  Ancients, 41, 52
  Armorial bearings, 16
  Benchers, 32, 42, 44, 46, 55
  Butler, 50
  call to Bar, 32
  call to bench, 44
  Captain of mess, 53
  Chancery connections, 19
  Chaplain, 46, 49, 52
  costume, 48
  Council, 45
  Dean of the Chapel, 45
  dining customs, 32, 48-56
  dinners, 29
  grace prayers, 51
  Grand Days, 55
  Hall, 16
  Keeper of the Black Book, 45
  mace or staff, 50
  Master of the Library, 45
  Master of the Walks, 46
  moots, 28
  origin, 15
  Porter, 50
  readings, 26
  toasts, 32, 52, 53, 55
  Treasurer, 32, 55
Livery cloth, 68, 69, 164, 173, 176
Liverymen, sheriff's, 115, 116

London :
  Aldermen, 68, 144, 146, 210
  City Marshal, 146, 211
  City Remembrancer, 204
  City Solicitor, 203
  Lord Mayor, 96-98, 143, 144, 146,
    161, 162, 170, 204, 205-206
  Quit-rents, 202-204
  Recorder, 181, 182, 183, 202, 205,
    210.
  Secondary, 114, 202
  Serjeant-at-Arms (Common Cryer),
    146, 170, 205
  Sheriffs, 111, 202, 210
  Swordbearer, 205
Lord Chancellor, 154-164 :
  appointment of, 157
  Breakfast, 94, 155, 196-198, 200,
    201
  Commissioner of Central Criminal
    Court, 144
  Commissioner of Old Bailey, 144
  costume, 61, 158-162, 166, 198, 215
  duties, 154-155, 156
  gift of livery cloth, 164
  gift of old Seal, 164
  history of office, 155-156
  judge, as, 80, 154, 155, 156
  Levee, 201
  mace-bearer, 198
  oaths, 158, 159
  peerage, 157
  powers, 154-155, 156
  privileges, 154
  purse-bearer, 198
  qualifications, 157
  swearing-in, 158
  swearing-in of judges, at, 82, 83
  title, origin of, 155-157
Lord Chief Justice, 167-173
  appointment, 169
  costume, 169-173, 204
  duties, 169
  gift of livery cloth, 173
  history of office, 168-169
  legal year, opening of, 201
  Lord Chancellor's Breakfast, 200
  nomination of sheriffs, 107
  oaths, 169
  peerage, 169
  presentation of Lord Mayor,
    204-205
  qualifications, 169
  swearing-in, 169

Lord Chief Justice—*contd.*
  swearing-in of judges, 82
  swearing-in of Lord Chancellor,
    158
  title, history of, 167-169
Lord Keeper of the Great Seal, 156,
  160, 167, 199
Lord Mayor :
  Bristol, 127
  London (*see under* London)
  York, 125, 129-130
Lord President of the Council,
  107, 167
Lord Privy Seal, 158, 199
Lord Treasurer, 82, 168, 199, 209
Lords Justices of Appeal, 176-177
  appointment, 177
  costume, 161, 177
  duties, 176
  legal year, opening of, 198
  Lord Mayor's banquet, 205
  oaths, 177
  qualifications, 177
  swearing-in, 177
  title, 176

Mace, civic, 133
  Mace, Lord Chancellor's, 162,
  163
Mace-bearer, Lord Chancellor's, 158,
  162, 198
Magistrates, stipendiary, 188, 190
Maiden Assize, 139
Mantle, judge's, 89
Marshal, judge's, 123, 124, 127, 130
Marshal of the Admiralty, 198
Master in Chancery, 173, 175
Master of the Bench (*see* Benchers)
Master of the Common Room, 46
Master of the Crown Office, 82
Master of the Garden, 46
Master of the House, 46
Master of the Kitchen, 46
Master of the Library, 45
Master of the Moots, 46
Master of the Rolls, 173-177 :
  appointment, 174, 175
  costume, 161, 175
  duties, 174
  gift of livery cloth, 175-176
  history of office, 173-174
  legal year, opening of, 198
  Lord Chancellor's Breakfast, 200

Master of the Rolls—*contd.*
  M.P., 174
  oaths, 175
  qualifications, 174
  solicitors, admits, 74
  solicitors, discipline of, 77
  swearing-in of judges, 83
  swearing-in of Lord Chancellor, 158
Master of the Temple, 47, 49
Master of the Walks, 46
Mayor :
  assize judge, arrival of, 124
  assize judge, visit to (Oxford), 125
  assize, opening of, 133
  assize service, 131
  precedence (Appleby), 127
  presented to Court of Exchequer
    (Oxford), 206
Middle Temple, 16, 17 :
  Ancients, 41
  armorial bearings, 18
  barristers, 27
  Benchers, 24, 27, 32, 33, 44, 46, 50
  call to Bar, 31, 32, 33
  call to bench, 44, 45
  Captain of mess, 52
  costume, 39
  Cupboard, 17, 24, 32, 33, 41
  dining customs, 48-56
  grace prayers, 50-51
  Grand Days, 55
  Hall, 17, 48, 54
  loving-cup, 55
  mace or staff, 50
  Master of the Garden, 46
  Master of the House, 46
  Master of the Kitchen, 46
  Master of the Moots, 46
  Master of the Temple, 46, 47, 49
  moots, 26, 27
  origin, 17
  Pannier, 48
  Parliament, 33, 45
  Porter, 48, 50
  Reader's Feast, 25, 26, 215
  Readers, 24, 26, 27, 32, 33, 45
  readings, 24
  students, 27
  toasts, 33, 52
  Treasurer, 32, 33, 45, 56
Moots, 15, 21, 26 :
  Master of the, 46
Municipal Corporations Act, 1835,
  180, 189

NEWGATE Prison, 143
    Nosegay, judges (see Posy)

OAR, the Admiralty, 100, 198
    Oaths :
    Attorneys, 75-76
    Barristers, 33
    Common Serjeant, 187
    Judges, County Court, 179
    Judges, High Court, 81-83
    Justices of the Peace, 189
    Lord Chancellor, 158, 159
    Lord Chief Justice, 169
    Lords Justices of Appeal, 176
    Master of the Rolls, 175
    President of P.D.A. Division, 176
    Pyx jury, 207
    Readers, 24
    Recorders, 181, 183, 184
    Solicitors, 75
Old Bailey, 143-149 :
    Bar mess, 151
    Central Criminal Court, as, 121
    commissions at, 143, 144, 145
    dinners and luncheons, 147, 148
    herbs strewn at, 148, 149
    history, 143
    hours of sittings, 196
    jail fever, 148-149
    judges of, 143, 144, 147
    jurisdiction of, 143
    opening of session, 146
    posy carried at, 147, 148, 149
    Red Judge, 146
    sessions of, 146
Our Lady of Good Counsel, Society
    of, 201
Outer Temple, 16
Oyer and Terminer, Commission of,
    134, 137, 143, 144, 145

PANNIERS, 48
    Parliament (Temple), 45
Parliament, Opening of, 84, 94
Peace, Commission of the, 134, 188
Pension (Gray's Inn), 45
Petty Sessions, 188
Porters (Inns of Court), 48, 50, 55
Posy, judge's, 130, 147, 148, 162, 210
Preacher (Gray's Inn), 46
Precept, sheriff's, 135
Privy Council, 178, 209 :
    Judicial Committee, 154, 165, 167

Privy Councillors, 161, 167
Probate, Divorce and Admiralty
    Division, 79, 81, 96, 100
Probate, Divorce and Admiralty
    Division, President of, 176
    appeal judge, 177
    appointment, 176
    costume, 161, 176
    creation of office, 176
    legal year, opening of, 178
    oaths, 176
    qualifications, 176
    swearing-in of Lord Chancellor,
        158
Promissory Oaths Act, 1868, 76
Protonotary, 75
Public Record Office, 174
Purse of Great Seal, 163, 164
Purse-bearer, Lord Chancellor's, 158,
    162, 198
Pyx, Chapel of the, 208
Pyx luncheon and dinner, 210
Pyx, Trial of the, 155, 207-210

QUARTER Sessions, 144, 180, 182,
    188, 189, 190
Quarter Sessions Act, 1842, 181
Queen's Bench, Court of (see King's
    Bench)
Queen's Bench Division :
    judges, 83, 84, 95, 146, 169, 204,
        206
    Lord Chief Justice is President of,
        167
    scope, 79, 205
    title, 80
Queen's (King's) Counsel, 57-65 :
    appointment, 61
    Benchers, as, 43
    bowing-in, 62-64
    Commissioner of Assize, as, 134
    costume, 61-64, 65, 167
    Crown, may appear against, 59
    declaration, 61
    first, 57
    first women, 59, 64
    history of office, 57-59
    legal year, opening of, 198
    Lord Chancellor's Breakfast, 200
    numbers, 58-59
    precedence at Bar, 14
    privileges, 60-61
    red bags, 59
    salary, former, 59

Queen's Remembrancer:
  costume, 107, 204, 207
  nomination of sheriffs, 107
  presentation of Lord Mayor, 204, 205
  Pyx, Trial of the, 207, 208
  Quit-rents, City of London, 202, 203
  swearing-in of Lord Chancellor, 158
Queen's Remembrancer Act, 1859, 202
Quit-rents, London, 202-204

READERS, 21-28:
  call to Bar, 21, 22, 32, 33
  costume, 22, 23, 26
  duties, 21, 24
  Double Readers, 23
  Gray's Inn, 26
  Inner Temple, 25, 26
  Lincoln's Inn, 21, 26
  Middle Temple, 24-25, 26, 32
  modern, 26
  moots, at, 26-27
  oaths, 24
  origin of office, 21
  precedence, 49
  qualifications, 22, 41, 46
  qualified for benchership, 23, 42, 45
Recorders, 179-185:
  appointment, 182
  Bristol, 183
  costume, 22, 184, 185, 205, 210
  declaration, 183
  duration of office, 183
  Durham, 182
  duties, 179-180, 183, 188
  Exeter, 185
  Hartlepool, 182
  history of office, 180, 181
  Kingston-on-Thames, 182
  London, 144, 146, 181, 182, 183, 202, 205, 210
  oaths, 181, 183, 184
  Preston, 182
  qualifications, 180, 182
  salary, 182
  Southampton, 183
  title, 184, 185
  Walsall, 183
  Wells, 182
  Wycombe, 182

Recorder of the circuit mess, 151
Red Judge, 146
Red Letter Days, 95
Red Mass, 197
Requests, Court of, 178
Revels, 54, 55
Robes (see also Costume and Gowns):
  Judges, County Court, 179
  Judges, High Court, 85-86
  Lord Chancellor, 159
  Lord Chief Justice, 169-170
  Lords Justices of Appeal, 177
  Master of the Rolls, 175
  President of the P.D.A. Division, 176

ST. PAUL'S Cathedral, 210
  Sash, judge's, 88
Scarf, judge's, 86
Seal, the Great, 134, 154, 155, 163, 164
Secondary (London), 114, 202
Serjeant-at-arms (London), 146, 170, 205
Serjeants-at-law:
  costume, 22, 85, 97
  Crown, could appear against, 59
  duties, 14
  Inns, Serjeants', 18
  last, 14
  legal year, opening of, 201
  Lord Chancellor's Breakfast, 200
  origin of, 14
  pillars at St. Paul's, 210
  privileges, 14, 57, 60
  title, 14,
Serjeants' Inns, 18
Services:
  assize, 95, 130-132
  Judges' (St. Paul's), 210
  legal year, opening of, 197, 201, 202
Sheriff, 102-120
  appointment, 104, 110, 111
  assize, 131
  assize court, 137
  assize, opening of, 133
  assize procession, 127, 129, 130
  borough, 103, 104
  called to account (London), 202
  costume, 112
  declaration, 109

Sheriff—*contd.*
  duties, 102, 103, 105
  history of office, 102
  judge's service (London), 210
  meets assize judges, 124
  nomination, 105-108, 111, 206
  oaths, 110, 111
  Old Bailey, 146, 147
  posse, 103
  posts, 113
  precept, 135, 136
  presentation of (London), 202
  pricking, 108, 109
  qualifications, 104
  royal approval (London), 112
  swearing-in (London), 111
  title, 102, 104
  visits assize judges, 126
  wand, 112, 129
Sheriffs Act, 1887, 105, 109
Sheriff's Court, 102, 144
Sittings, court, 192, 196
Society of Our Lady of Good
  Counsel, 201
Solicitors, 70-77
  admission, 74, 75
  articled clerk, 74
  costume, 76
  discipline, 77
  duties, 13, 70, 72, 77
  excluded from Inns, 73
  history of, 70, 71
  legal year, opening of, 200
  Master of the Rolls and, 74
  number, 13, 70
  qualifications, 73
  title, 71, 73, 77
Solicitor-General, 68-69 :
  appointment, 69
  Bencher, as, 43
  chosen from Double Readers, 23
  costume, 49, 69
  duties, 57, 66, 69
  first, 68
  gift of livery cloth, 69
  knighthood, 69
  Lord Chancellor's Breakfast, 200
  privileges, 14

Solicitor-General—*contd.*
  qualifications, 69
  summoned to Parliament, 165
Speaker of the House of Commons,
  161
Students of Inns of Court, 25 :
  costume, 20, 31
Sword of Justice (Old Bailey), 147
Swordbearer (London), 146

Temple Church, 17
  Terms, dining, 192
Terms, Law, 191-195
Tippet, judge's (*see* Scarf)
Tipstaff, 198, 201
Treasurer (Inns of Court), 15, 32, 33,
  44, 45, 53, 55, 56
Trial of the Pyx, 155, 207-210
Troops at assize time, 127-129
Trumpeters, sheriff's, 115, 119, 125,
  127

Under-sheriff :
  appointment, 114
  assize, opening of, 133, 135, 136
  assize procession, 127, 129
  costume, 114
  declaration, 114
  duties, 113, 114
  London, 114, 146
  meets assize judges, 124
  wand, 114
Under-Treasurer (Inns of Court), 19,
  32, 33

Weepers, 64, 65, 96
  Westminster Abbey, 197, 201,
  208
Westminster Cathedral, 201
Wigs (*see also* Costume) :
  bob-wig, 37
  full-bottomed, 90-91
  tye-wig, 90
Willow-wand, 142
Woolsack, the, 156